HOGGIN' THE PAGE

Groundhogs:
The Classic Years

Martyn Hanson

First published in 2005 by
NORTHDOWN PUBLISHING LIMITED
PO Box 49, Bordon
Hants GU35 0AF

www.northdown.demon.co.uk

British Library Cataloguing-in-Publication Data
A catalogue for this book is available from the British Library

ISBN 1900711 16 8

Designed by Simon Joslin
Printed by Ashford Colour Press

Contents:

When you
are one of life's
weary foot soldiers,
very few shining
beacons appear
on the horizon.
Our granddaughter,
Ellie-Anne, is certainly
one of them.
With the ebb and flow
of life ever rolling relentlessly on,
it was during the final stages
of preparing this book
that our mum left us forever.
I dedicate this book
to both of them.

Foreword
by Captain
Sensible

Tony McPhee was the British Hendrix. He could do soaring feedback solos, and really took the whole guitar-playing thing as far as he could. And what he doesn't know about the blues isn't worth knowing. I mean, Clapton? Don't get me on that tosspot – he had one solo and bored us to death for 30 years with it. He's a turgid git. McPhee's the real thing. Every night he plays a song, he plays it differently. And that's a wonderful thing, not to repeat yourself.

'Thank Christ For The Bomb' is the most amazing album I've ever heard. I got it when it first came out in 1970, and must've worn out about three vinyl copies over the years. I used to play it all the time. When I got into songwriting myself – I wouldn't say I nicked from it, but I was grateful to be influenced by that stuff. I though of it as psychedelic punk – the Hogs, Soft Machine and Syd Barrett.

The problem with the expression 'prog rock' is that it's been sullied by the likes of Yes and Genesis and ELP. So if you say you're into prog rock, everybody thinks you're into that (booming voice) 'Oh I saw a wizard walking through the woods the other day. The pixies were running around...' Dum dum dum dum – 20 minute guitar solo... 'And then the wizard said...' I mean, fuckin' ell, what's that shit about?

But it's like classical music. There's great classical music. Rachmaninov – he's brilliant. Sibelius – fucking genius. And then there's crap like Mozart and Beethoven. Same with prog rock. There was some wonderful stuff, like all the Krautrock stuff with Neu! and Kraftwerk, and then there was the bombastic nonsense that Yes produced. The Groundhogs were probably the finest example of prog rock you can possibly get – a mixture of blues and psychedelia and pop that's never been bettered, before or since.

'Thank Christ... is a perfect album. There's not a filler track on it and the sequence is brilliant. Plus, McPhee produced it all himself. One minute it's a full-on power trio playing this manic, almost punk rock – angrier, anti-establishment, anti-war stuff – and the next minute it drops right down into this extremely quiet and subtle finger-picking stuff.

Tony McPhee is an absolute genius, I used to stand and watch him at the Croydon Greyhound. I'd stand right at the front and work out which chords he was playing. But he made most of them up himself. Read this book and try to work out some of his secrets.

With thanks to Scott Rowley, *Classic Rock*

Acknowledgements

After having written two books on completely different bands, I thought it would be interesting to do something on a band that came from the blues. It's clear that ELP and the Nice inspirations came from European classical music, so it was a breath of fresh air to write from another perspective. I interviewed a lot of people involved in the story. There were a few people that couldn't be traced, but despite a lot of effort they had to be filed as 'the ones that got away'.

First and foremost I would like to thank Tony for the in-depth series of interviews. I got used to travelling to his house and journeyed there many times. Apart from that there was the usual torrent of phone calls. I would also like to thank Tony's partner, Joanna Deacon. It was thanks to her that Tony's voluminous archive was catalogued and this made my job much easier. Joanna also compiled the gig list and put a huge amount of other work in behind the scenes.

A million thanks to Michael Heatley of Northdown Publishing for having faith in me and publishing this book.

I would also like to thank the following for their co-operation: Pete Cruickshank, Ken Pustelnik, Dave 'Jim' Wetton delved into his diaries with gusto and compiled an accurate order of events from Tony's early musical life, John 'Cakey' Weeks, John 'Oscar' Wild, John Cruickshank, Roy Fisher, Bob Hall, Terry Goldberg, Terry Slade, Clive Brooks, Wilf Pine, Simon Prager, Andrew Lauder, Mike Vernon, Dave Kelly, Mike Batt, Mick Hubbert, Jerry Gilbert, Chris Welch, Bob Glass, Denis Knowles, Len Tempan, Alan Fish and Mick Kirton.

The fans came to my aid too, but I give special thanks to Tony Sherratt and Mick Stones because they provided me with a lot of material; their valuable insights were also very helpful. I would also like to thank Steve Thompson. All three contributed 'I was there' reports. Garry Bodenham provided the Weeley photo and Paul Brears came up trumps with pictures of Tony's 'Two Sides' tour. Paul Freestone also kindly supplied pictures. Nick Moss deserves a mention in dispatches for ploughing through the first draft and making useful comments. My old friend David Flavell has proved to be a good sounding board for my projects over the years too. Graham Vosper also deserves a mention. Jenny Seager and Linda Hardy did all the work in acquiring and setting up the computer I used to write the book.

Now here's the back-up team. My wife, Carole, has put up with my different projects over the years and deserves a medal. Dale and Leanne still provide me with plenty of inspiration. All had to put up with my gripes when things were not going well; I can tell you that in the course of a book they are many indeed!

chapter **1**
Scratching
the surface

'Don't you know you are wasting your time with that guitar?'
Teacher to Tony McPhee

'Mac was the electrical whizz-kid so we just did what he advised.'
Seneschals bassist Dave Wetton

A nthony Charles McPhee was born on 23rd March 1944, at two
o'clock on a snowy Thursday afternoon, to Eileen and Charles,
just outside the small Lincolnshire town of Humberston on the
east coast of England. His astrological sign is Aries, but it is
not something that influences him in any way: 'I am definitely not hot-
tempered or have any of the fiery attributes of the typical Aries male! But
I consider the astrology myths, along with religious ones, as being good
stories, make nice epic films, but are
basically legends and half–truths which
I don't need to live a moral life.'

The Second World War was
coming to its conclusion. Every
family was affected by it and the
McPhee family was no exception.
Tony's father was in the Navy and
worked as a wireless operator at nearby
New Waltham.

The house where he was born has
long since been knocked down, but the
McPhee family didn't stay at 'Redlands'
for long after Tony's birth. Hostilities
had ended and, in just over a year,
they moved to a two-up, two-down
in Okeburn Road, Tooting,
South London.

On the face of it, this corner of the
world was no different to most.
Rationing affected everyone: shared
baths, hand-me-downs and austerity.
But fate had provided more than a
helping hand: 'Moving to London was
probably the luckiest thing that
happened to me, because when the
blues came to England this was where
bands like the Stones, the Yardbirds
and Jeff Beck, who was in a band called
the Tridents, first played.' Clubs like
the Marquee, the Jazz Club (now the
100 Club) and the Crawdaddy were in
easy reach via public transport.

**Tony's dad Charlie,
mum Eileen, sister
Olive and brother
Sam in 1943, before
the move to London.**
TS Personal Collection

The young McPhee attended the local Ensham Infants School. This was still the time of rationing, slates and chalk instead of paper and pencil the order of the day. One of Tony's earliest memories at school was the visit of the school photographer. He hated having his picture taken: 'I have an inordinately large head which was on top of a fairly puny body and when I foolishly showed the picture to Jo Ann Kelly about twenty years later she exclaimed 'Good God, The Mekon!' (The Mekon was an alien featured in the *Eagle* comic and the arch–enemy of hero spaceman, Dan Dare).

In the 1950s the radio was still the main source of entertainment and Tony's family would gather around it to hear shows like *The Goons* and *Journey Into Space*. The former moulded his sense of humour and the latter his interest in science–fiction and fantasy. Tony's dad made certain there was never a dull moment, even when the radio was switched off, imparting his general knowledge to his children in the form of quiz nights. He taught Tony and Olive Morse code and they would decode messages he had sent them. The young McPhee was a very inquisitive boy and the stimulus he received from his father was an important factor in developing this.

The McPhee family was a tight unit. His parents hardly ever went out, save for a couple of occasions, until Tony was in his teens. His father was not a strict disciplinarian, but this wasn't the case for many boys of his generation. He is the first to admit his mother was a 'soft touch' and he took advantage of her. In fact, he admitted in later life: 'I was a mummy's boy. I can't deny it, but it only made me more independent later on so I don't regret it.' He was very close to his siblings, sharing a room with Olive and hero-worshipping his elder brother Sam. They were both to play a major part in Tony's early musical development.

When his father bought a Baird television set with a 9-inch screen, young Tony's interest in science–fiction was stimulated further. One of his favourite shows was *The Quatermass Experiment*. One memorable episode showing two astronauts disappearing into their spacesuits found him hiding behind the sofa, not able to watch. Another of his favourite shows was *Three, Two, One, Zero*, about the atomic bomb. 'I have to admit that I found footage of the explosions terrifying and yet exciting. These were dangerous days with the total paranoia of the Americans fuelling the arms race.' A few markers were being laid down that would surface later on.

The family home was very cold in the winter and they relied on an open fire for heat. Tony's mum would have to hold up a page from the *News Of The World* against the surround of the fire to draw the flames from the paper and wood under the coals. Sometimes the newspaper would catch fire and she would be forced to take frantic action to put out the unwanted flames. Tony used the open fire in the front room to conduct chemical experiments. His party trick was to fart into a Smarties tube, put the cap on and throw it on the fire. It never blew up but it did produce a few colours.

Occasionally he'd visit his Auntie Olive and Uncle Tom in Teddington. He always got half a crown off his Uncle who worked at the National Physical Laboratory (which housed early computers) and would sometimes take his young nephew there. It may have been these visits that started Tony's interest in things electrical and electronic, coupled with an inquisitive nature that was to draw him to gadgetry. These boyhood interests would be essential tools of the trade during his later career.

Tony's father got a job in the Civil Service and things got better for the family. Soon after, he bought a motorised Bond three-wheel car – bike engines with a body built around them and two seats side by side. Like all bikes it was chain-driven and the chain was prone to coming off. One day the inevitable happened. Tony remembers it very well: 'It was the only

Tony's first school photograph. He was most concerned that he had been given a broken pencil.
TS Personal Collection

time I ever heard my dad swear! We were going up Franciscan Road, which is quite a steep hill, and suddenly he spat out "Shit!". We were going down the hill backwards, engine racing, as the chain came off the driving cog.'

At eight, Tony was quite opinionated regarding the ways of the world. One day he heard his mother say 'I don't like Atheists', but he had already come to the conclusion he didn't believe in God or any other deity. He had also firmly come to the conclusion that he was a socialist, so he was shocked, and disappointed, when he later found out that he was named after Tory prime minister, Anthony Eden. He remains an atheistic lefty to this day.

Things didn't bode well for Tony's eleven plus exam because it seemed he was never at school. He was always ill or bunking off, though he did suffer from recurring tonsillitis: 'My mum was a bit of a pushover on that score, telling me things like 'if you've got a sore throat, wrap a dirty sock round it. So there were many times she would walk into my bedroom and I would have a sock wrapped round my throat. The rest of the day would be spent reading the *Beano* and eating sweets; it was even worth suffering Mum's cure-all, a small glass of whisky with hot water and sugar.'

Eventually the Health Authorities decided he needed a week's convalescence at a facility in Whitstable with 20 other 'serially' sick children. He hated the place and nicknamed it Stalag 13. The upshot was that he caught adenitis there and had to have another two weeks off school when he returned home!

He managed to pass the eleven-plus and it meant that he had a passport to a grammar school. He chose the Bec, at Tooting Bec, but only because it was nearest to his home. The interview with Melhuish, the deputy head, revealed things not just about the school but even more about the class system in Britain at that time: 'He asked me to read a text about Victorian England and then asked questions about it. It was fine until he found out that I had an older brother and asked me if I cleaned his boots! I stared at him incredulously – of course I didn't! I was accepted and thus began the most influential and some of the most miserable years of my life.'

The first year pupils at the Bec were called 'weeds' whose initiation ceremony involved having your head stuck down the toilet. Fortunately, Tony was quick enough to avoid this fate. He eventually made a fruitful friendship with three pupils in particular, David 'Jim' Wetton, John 'Oscar' Wild and John 'Cakey' Weeks. These were to make up Tony's first band. He had known them for a while but they were brought together, as firm friends, by the musical revolution that was the happening thing.

It was 1955 and the UK was a very austere place. This was still the time of the rag and bone man, the chimney sweep, the rent collector and even the last vestiges of rationing, which had only just finished the year before. Even some of the streetlamps were still lit by gas! In among all the drabness there was no separate youth/music culture. The music papers of the time featured jazz, folk and the easy-listening pop music of the likes of Doris Day. Then along came Elvis Presley and things were never the same again.

Tony was lucky that he had older siblings who were buying records. Olive used to buy 78s to play on their record player (not many people had them then). One day she brought something different home; 'Rock Around The Clock' by Bill Haley and the Comets. The effect was inspiring, as Tony made clear: 'I was intrigued by the strange instrument featured on the record and asked Olive what it was. 'I think it is an electric guitar', she replied. My mind boggled. I sort of knew what a guitar was, but plugged into the mains?' He knew he had to have one.

In those days most of the artists in the charts were white. Black artists always had to battle

Second year at 'The Bec'. Tony is front row fourth from right, 'Cakey' Weeks back row far right.
Pic courtesy of Dave Wetton

with 'vanilla' cover versions of their songs. Pat Boone's version of Fats Domino's 'Ain't That A Shame' was a bigger hit than the original. Tony loved Boone's version and didn't hear the original for quite a while, but when he did he became, and still is, a big fan of Fats. By the summer of 1956 another classic had been and gone, Elvis Presley's 'Heartbreak Hotel'.

However, it was Presley's next hit that made a massive impression on him. He heard some schoolmates talking about 'Hound Dog' which he thought was 'Two Hound Dogs', a Bill Haley flip side he had heard and didn't think was that hot. He was informed it was actually by Elvis Presley and, as luck would have it, Olive had bought a copy. As Tony recalls: 'I was totally mesmerised by the two Scotty Moore solos, even though I still wasn't sure how the electric guitar worked. I just knew they sounded damn good!'

The first year at the Bec saw things going well for young Tony, who was fourth in his class overall. However, things were to go downhill rapidly the following year. A new headmaster was appointed by the name of Wilfred W Hore; it didn't take long for the boys to pun his name. He had a line in religious zealotry and delivered grace in Latin; typical of grammar schools in those days.

It's no exaggeration to say that the young Tony McPhee loathed this man and everything he stood for. Disenchanted, he rapidly plummeted down the class performance list. Tuesday morning was detention day (aka caning day) and Tony swore that he would never end up in the office under those circumstances; he never did! But plenty of buttocks were rendered black and blue by this arbitrary method of maintaining discipline.

Back in the real world, Tony's brother Sam was also bringing records home and providing another avenue from which to consider music. He was into Lonnie Donegan who was spearheading the skiffle movement. Tony recalls a television performance by Donegan on *6.5 Special* as 'one of the most exciting I have ever seen'. He soon realised his brother's tastes were well ahead of their time: 'He used to bring home Turkish music, what we would now call "world music". He used to get his records from Imhofs on Oxford Street, London.'

There was one more thing Sam was to initiate his younger sibling into, and it changed his life: blues historian Alan Lomax, who recorded the first blues that Tony ever heard in 1959 for the Library Of Congress. These recordings were intended to document the folk music of the Southern States artists from a social perspective. They were later released as 'The Blues Roll On' in the Southern folk heritage series.

But all was not well with Tony. It was at school that he first started to experience occasional minor psychological problems and would have panic attacks, as he related in an interview with *Penetration* magazine in 1973:

'I'd get this feeling of disembodiment somehow! Lots of detachment. It's incredible to describe. Lots of people have had this sensation, and when I was young I used to get over it by getting up and turning on the radio and forgetting about it.' He would still get these episodes occasionally into adulthood, culminating in an attack he was unable to forget about. It would provide the inspiration for the Groundhogs' finest musical hour.

Out of early youth culture came something that had darker overtones: gang violence! Tony remembers this period very well: 'One day in the playground I noticed a group of boys formed in a circle around "Fud" Campbell, from 3G, who was demonstrating his latest acquisition, a flick knife.' There had already been quite a lot of stabbings in the area and the young Tony was keen to acquire one. He never intended to stab anybody, his attraction to it was based on it being a gadget.

As he couldn't afford the 12s 6d he went halves with his friend, Christopher Webb, whose father was in the navy with Tony's father. In fact, Tony was far removed from the 'hard case' image he was trying to portray and, as one of the smallest boys in the class, was just trying to redress the balance.

In those days most of Tony's friends had a nickname and his was 'Mac': 'One day a teacher revealed that "Mac" meant "son of". I shrank below my desk as I could feel all the kids' eyes boring into the back of my neck. "Son of Phee!" somebody blurted out. The mathematics teacher didn't like me very much and, from that point, every time we were in a maths class and the teacher mentioned the word "fee", he couldn't understand why the whole class went into paroxysms of laughter.'

Tony's academic prowess was taking a hammering by the time he got to Class 3A (for arts stream) and he came 30th out of a class of 31 pupils. One of his friends, Johnny Bryant, had the dubious honour of being last. In fact, Bryant also made a mark on the entertainment industry by winning the very first edition of the TV talent show *New Faces*. As Tony noted: 'Isn't it strange how the only two people in our year to go on to be professional musicians were the most useless academically?'

It was no surprise that the subject that interested Tony most was science, but he ended up in the arts stream and was unable to shake off the accursed Latin lessons. By this time one of his best friends was Dave Wetton and they enjoyed the same types of music. It was 1957, a year in which they greeted the arrival of another big figure – Buddy Holly, to Tony one of the most influential white singer/guitarist/songwriters of all time.

Holly was the first consistent songwriter/performer to emerge to date. The number of artists that Tony admired was building up and the time was fast approaching when he would no longer be content with just listening to music. Up until now, though, Tony's grandfather, who played banjo, had been the only musician in the family.

Dave Wetton acquired an acoustic guitar and was the first of Tony's close friends to have one.

It had been a present from his uncle who had bought it while on shore leave in the Far East and brought it back with him when the war ended. It had a painted Hawaiian scene on it (scratched to blazes by plectrums) and Tony knew he had to have one. After much badgering it was agreed that he could have one for Christmas. It was 1958 and his mother took him down to Taborns music shop in Tooting to select his first guitar. He was 14 years old. He chose a Telesforo Julwe, a Spanish guitar and a good choice. His early guitar teacher even preferred it to his own.

His mother insisted on some musical education, so she booked guitar lessons for him with Sam Weller, who was based in Clapham, and Tony soon started lessons in earnest. But there were problems; first he couldn't get his head around the dots. This wasn't a total surprise to him as music lessons at school had been a mystery. Secondly, he had small hands and he couldn't cover the fretboard properly, so he stopped having lessons.

The next stage was to adopt a style he was comfortable with. It wasn't long before Tony and Dave Wetton got together to practice and dissect the latest sounds. They were listening to a lot of instrumental records, particularly the Shadows, the Fireballs and the Hunters.

The young McPhee honed his technique by playing along to these instrumental records, and seemed to have a knack for playing by ear. He was forging ahead rapidly and a regular three hours of practice a day was an indication of his dedication. He was very shy of girls and felt more comfortable staying in with his guitar.

Tony McPhee's first public performance in 1959 was his school's annual Christmas concert. It was quite informal and performances ranged from poetry to a piano recital or even snippets from the great plays. (1)

Dave Wetton recalls: 'Nine musicians on stage, including John Wild on banjo and Cakey playing a snare drum! We called ourselves the Worried Nine. As it turned out it was quite apt as John Wild was so nervous he played the same chord for the whole song. 'Worried Man Blues' was quite a simple

The first blues album Tony ever heard, bought by brother Sam.

Tony's first acoustic guitar. Despite those youthful looks, he really was 14.
TS Personal Collection

(1) A participant in the concert was a boy called Mike Scheuer, two years older than the Worried Nine. His party piece was an Elvis Presley impersonation. He later changed his name to Mike Sarne and had a massive hit with 'Come Outside' with Wendy Richard (of *Are You Being Served* and *EastEnders* fame) in June 1962.

First job, first wage packet, first electric guitar (the Futurama) – in debt ever since!
TS Personal Collection

12-bar song that could have lasted the whole afternoon if you wanted it to. I made a mistake as I started singing before Tony was ready! I had my dressing–gown cord tied round my guitar but he didn't have any support for his. We had to wait while he shuffled a chair forward to rest his leg on. But we got through it after that.

'They even used face make-up and painted sideburns to make them look older, which took ages to get off in the toilet afterwards. Tony doesn't remember much of that day, apart from the garish orange jumper he was wearing, but remembers what the Latin teacher, Mr Philpot, said to him: 'Don't you know you are wasting your time with that guitar! After that performance they trimmed back to a four-piece.

While they were rehearsing, the problem of amplification cropped up many times. How could they make their acoustic guitars sound louder? They couldn't afford electric guitars or proper amplifiers. It was here that Tony displayed his electrical ingenuity.

He owned some throat mics that were War Department surplus (similar to the ones used by wartime fighter pilots) and he worked on the idea of amplifying that vibration with a Ford ignition coil. The throat mics, strapped to the bridge of the guitar by their snake belts, had a cable going into the ignition coil and then out into the back of an old valve radio.

With only five feet of cable each, they were never going to move around like the Shadows. They stored the radio in the school janitor's room. Then one day Tony couldn't get the gear to work; and he realised somebody had pinched the valves! They never actually played a gig with that primitive set-up, but the friends, joined by Johnny Bryant, were now fired up to go a stage further.

They enrolled in a guitar night class held at the nearby Ensham Girls' School taught by a big man called Frank who seemed to have no trouble finding his way around the fretboard. There were no problems in making the class numbers up as lots of boys were trying to emulate their heroes.

Dave Wetton remembers those times very well: 'Frank used to play things like "Sweet Georgia Brown". It was all old tunes but there were loads of subtle chord changes and we all benefited. It gave us a good insight into how music fitted together. We all used to sit on the desk and strum along with chords he'd put on the blackboard' Later on they hired a separate room at the Ensham Girls School for their own use. They used it extensively and, in May 1961, rehearsed there as many as eight times.

Such was their love of the guitar that they all enrolled in an evening class in woodwork, intending to make their own instruments. They were made in the classic double cutaway shape (hollow but narrow, composed of ply back and front separated by wooden blocks, with thin ply laminate curved round the edges). But when Dave Wetton assembled his bass, the problems started: 'When I tightened the strings the whole thing fell apart and I had to rethink ways of making a more robust design.'

Tony McPhee left school in the summer of 1960, his only qualification a GCE in French – though he did have a near squeak in Physics and Art. At first it was thought Tony had done well, but his mother had opened the results letter upside down, and what she thought was a 'P' for pass was, in fact, a grade '9'! He decided, without telling his father, to have the full school holiday, but when his father found out he had left school he told Tony in no uncertain terms to get a job!

He saw an advert in the *Evening Standard* for a soldering job at Great Chapel Street and decided to go for it. He had learnt to solder at home and decided to apply. But when he got there he found the soldering team was made up entirely of women! He had many embarrassing moments and he confesses with a laugh: 'The women at the factory were really dirty!' He only stayed for a few months before he got a job at Post Office Telephones.

All this time Tony and Dave were still practising, but the fledgling band had a major obstruction that had to be overcome. Inspired by the Shadows they decided they needed a more practical division of instruments.

As Dave Wetton recalls, 'It was obvious that Tony was going to be the lead guitarist as he was so much better than the rest of us. We decided the rest by the toss of a coin, I lost and became the bass player and John Wild went to rhythm guitar. "Cakey" Weeks already had a snare drum, so he became the drummer.' (Cakey didn't get his first drum kit until 23rd May 1961).

At that stage they didn't have a name for the band. 'Cakey' remembers he suggested they call themselves 'The Four Horsemen Of The Apocalypse', but they preferred to remain nameless. At that point in time all the boys were members of the Shadows Fan Club. In fact, Tony's name on the fan club register was Elmer P Turner. They all gave themselves American sounding names in the way Hank B Marvin (Brian Rankin) had done.

One of the first things Tony bought when he started to receive wages was an electric guitar. The Futurama looked like a Stratocaster, but was made in Czechoslovakia. At fifty-five guineas, he couldn't afford to pay cash so he had to buy it on hire purchase, his father the guarantor. He didn't have an amp at that stage but he was over the moon with his new purchase, even though, as he remarked: 'From that point I was hardly out of debt.' Soon after this the rest of the band started to acquire electric guitars and amplifiers and started to think about playing gigs.

Rehearsal at Ensham Girls' School: Cakey, Dave Wetton, Tony and John Wild.
Pic courtesy Dave Wetton

It was around about this time they decided they needed a name for the band. Dave Wetton suggested the Talisman of Set, an icon in an HP Lovecraft novel about black magic that made the band sound very mystical. But in the end they settled on the Seneschals, Tony having found the word while thumbing through a dictionary. (It actually means a butler in a castle.) At this stage their repertoire consisted entirely of instrumental numbers, including Duane Eddy's '3:30 Blues', the first real blues tune that Tony played. (2)

The band was still going strong, and though they hadn't actually played a gig, that was about to change. Dave Wetton was travelling on the bus with his Burns Weill bass guitar, when a man approached him and asked if his band would play at his daughter's wedding. They were paid the sum of £2, which was a lot of money in those days. However, this was all used to pay for a drummer and the train and taxi fares that had got them there in the first place!

Back on the day job Tony McPhee enjoyed working for the General Post Office as a telephone engineer (this was before British Telecom was created). His old friend, John Wild, had recommended the job to him and had even coached him on how to pass the entry exam. He told Tony all about the quadratic equations that made up the test, so he learnt the formula by heart. He didn't really understand it but was determined to bluff his way through.

Tony recalls his problems started early on: 'The next question started 'Now use this formula!' I was stumped. The interviewer asked me why I hadn't answered the question and I just shrugged my shoulders. He then took me along to a panel of engineers and they started asking me questions about history, which I could not answer. Then one asked me the formula for Ohm's law and I rattled it off. They then asked me to apply it. I did.'

It was a very good job and he enjoyed the many perks; in the morning he seemed to spend most of his time in the café, then he'd do a couple of hours' work. After an extended lunch break during which he would saunter to the guitar shops in Charing Cross Road, he'd be back

to do another hour's work before going home. Tony liked his work, but there was no doubt where his priorities lay: 'The only thing I could think about was doing more music.'

As Christmas 1960 approached, something that had been on Tony's mind for quite a while came to a head when he was doing a job in the Smithfield meat market. The carcases had often repulsed him, but on this day he was working by a stall. He heard the stallholder say to a couple who had come to collect their christmas turkey 'Do you want the legs on?' The next thing he knew two legs landed right at his feet. This was the moment when he decided to become a vegetarian. (3) At the time it was so rare his family and friends were astounded – but showing the courage of his convictions was a trait that was to prove important to him in his later musical career.

The year of 1961 was a busy time for the boys, if Dave Wetton's diary is anything to go by. It certainly gives a strong flavour of the 1960s. He went to CND sit-downs, demos in Trafalgar Square against the bomb and still-active fascist Oswald Mosley, demos in Grosvenor Square and managed to fit in the Shadows and Chris Barber gigs. In October the Seneschals played their first gig at the Ensham Girls' School and on 10th December played the prestigious Castle in Tooting – but Dave Wetton noted in his diary that it was 'not so hot'.

They were investing in gear all the time. Tony had acquired his Truvoice amp and Cakey acquired his second set of Premier drums in early 1962. In the same year Tony bought a cherry red Gibson SG, paying one hundred and seventy-three guineas for it. This was the guitar that was to become his trademark to fans all over the world.

On 28th April 1962 the Seneschals played the St Thomas' Church Hall at Nunhead, South London, the first of many times there; Dave Wetton recalls the taxi fare was a whopping £5! However, a Wimbledon Park gig in June was a watershed for the band. Dave Wetton summed up the band's feeling in his diary 'not so bad as we thought – we need a singer'. The first they

(2) The Seneschals' early repertoire included Duane Eddy's 'Rebel Rouser' and 'Ramrod', the Scorpions' 'Riders In The Sky', the Shadows' 'Apache' and 'The Warlord', the Fireballs' 'Bulldog' and 'Foot-Patter', the Ventures' 'Walk, Don't Run' and 'Ram Bunk Shush', the Rockets' 'Gibraltar Rock' and 'Walking Home', Eddie Smith and the Hornets 'Up Turn' and 'Border Beat' and the Hunters' 'Santa Monica Flyer' and 'The Storm'.

After Ray Wade joined it was a more eclectic mix, apart from Rufus Thomas' 'Walking The Dog', Ritchie Valens' 'La Bamba', Chuck Berry's 'Sweet Little Sixteen' and Eddie Cochran's 'C'mon Everybody'.

(3) Tony's decision made a big impression on Dave Wetton, who was thinking of doing the same. He noted in his diary on 11th August 1962: 'I'd become increasingly impressed with Mac's moral stance on the subject and had simply been looking for the right opportunity to convince my grandmother, who did all the cooking, that I was sincere. For a while she saw it as a flash in the pan – but eventually she got the message.' Dave stuck to his principles and throughout the 1970s was Secretary of the Hunt Saboteurs Association. He also worked with Tony on a related project in 1975. He is still involved with the organisation.

13

Seneschals Tony, Dave, John and Ray Wade, with Cakey on drums, at the Castle, Tooting, 1962.
TS Personal Collection

(4) Cakey lived in Putney so he had to cart his drum kit on the bus in a big suitcase, into which it all fitted, apart from the bass drum. On one occasion it even rolled off the back of the bus. On another occasion, he got chatting to a fifteen-year old boy who was keen for him to be his drummer. Cakey refused his invitation – and Mark Feld went on to fame as Marc Bolan!

auditioned was a local lad called Graham Woollard who was very good at singing Cliff Richard songs but didn't seem right for the job. Then someone called 'Greek' John tagged along with the band for a while but was very brash, and didn't fit in. Barry Bethel, Reg Foreman and a guy called Dave were tried out in rehearsal, but Dave was the only one who actually got to perform with them in public.

Things looked up even further when they acquired their own transport. 'Cakey' Weeks' girlfriend's dad, Pat, offered his van and his services as chauffeur. This meant the days of carting gear on buses and trains was well and truly over. (4)

This was just as well because the ingenious Tony and Sam had built Dave Wetton a massive bass cabinet. There was even talk about going professional. However, there was a major problem on the horizon for the band as Cakey was getting engaged to Molly and he couldn't guarantee making all the gigs. His days in the band were numbered.

They were getting a lot of bookings at the Conservative Club Youth Movement, but on 25th August 1962 they played a gig at Kemsing, near Sevenoaks, their first gig in the van. By this time they had even acquired stage clothes of chef's

trousers, white shirts and black bow ties. They supported a band called the Dollarbills, featuring the talented Cruickshank brothers. Tony and John Wild worked with John Cruickshank as Post Office engineers.

In early September the Seneschals managed to get an audition at the Castle, but failed it because the promoter didn't think Dave the singer came up to scratch; he left shortly after. They put an advert in *Melody Maker* and a young man called Ray Orchard joined – but because there was Radio Luxembourg DJ of the same name he became Rocking Ray Wade. Dave Wetton recalls: 'He was older than us, he was very charismatic and he had a good voice.' Now they had a singer they could expand their material, adding Buddy Holly, Roy Orbison and Everly Brothers songs to the set.

By early November their gigs were going down very well and they decided to have another try at bigger venues. With their new singer in place it was time to secure another audition at the Castle – this time they got 'the thumbs-up'. Now they were on the circuit they played plenty of the bigger venues. but it was the Castle, which they played on 22nd and 29th November, that meant the most to Tony: 'When we played that gig I thought we'd made it. I always used to wonder why there were always guys standing outside the pub. It was only years later I found out it was also a brothel!' It also served as a boxing venue on Friday nights.

The Seneschals had another break when they were rehearsing at the Ensham Girls' School on 11th February 1963. A man came down from the nearby Bedford Hotel in Balham and said he needed a band to stand in for the Checkmates who'd cancelled next week's gig. This was a daunting prospect as, a few years before, they had a Number 1 hit with 'What Do You Want To Make Those Eyes At Me For'. The gig was a great success. Strangely, the Checkmates turned up late on, but were refused entry.

It was obvious that the Seneschals were beginning to be in great demand. Immediately after the Bedford Hotel gig they played three consecutive gigs. On 30th March they played the St Thomas Hall in Nunhead again, where for the cost of two shillings you could spend the night 'Dancing to the Fabulous Seneschals'.

As they got more gigs the band grew in stature, playing to bigger audiences. But how did a young, shy and innocent Tony McPhee overcome his reticence? Dave Wetton gave a clue: 'Tony was retiring but when you play in a band and you're playing good music and you are together as one, you acquire huge amounts of self-confidence. We were lucky because we'd played a lot together before we really started gigging.'

Tony McPhee had developed his own mindset for performing in public: 'I remember I was very apprehensive playing my first solo. However, when I played the first gig at the school Xmas concert I looked out at the audience and thought "I can do something you can't, you useless bastards!"'

Tony was always trying to advance the band in any way he could, as John Wild recalls: 'He was always the first at rehearsals, he would set everything up. He had this Swiss Echo tape machine and was always taping things off the radio for us to listen to. He knew what he wanted but he could never be described as a dictator. He was very persuasive and convinced us of his vision with the strength of his argument.' They would all learn how to play the latest hits of the day using this method.

Around this time Tony was starting to venture to the Marquee club in London on a Thursday with his brother Sam, the influence of Sam's records luring him to seek out the blues in the flesh. He later took Dave Wetton and John Wild and they witnessed the delights of the fledgling blues movement, the spearhead of which was Cyril Davies and his All Stars.

One of the blues artists that Tony liked the most was Robert Johnson. He particularly liked his slide-guitar playing. At the time a slide couldn't be purchased from any shop, so he had

to improvise and make one. He tried various bits of pipe but these would get stuck on his finger. He carried on in this haphazard way until a friend of his, who worked at the Ford Motor Company gave him a custom-made brass model.

After playing with the Seneschals for a couple of years came Tony's next career move. He had got to know Dollarbills singer John Cruickshank at work quite well, and when their guitarist left because he didn't want to turn professional. Cruikshank asked Tony to audition for the vacancy. He duly passed the audition, although he wasn't overly impressed by their name or by the fact they had a saxophone player; he didn't think the instrument was right for the band.

In April 1963 and shortly before Tony officially joined the Dollarbills, he wrote Dave Wetton a resignation letter, part of which reads: 'I'm leaving the group and turning professional with JC (John Cruickshank) and will be going to Germany soon. Roy Fisher, their manager, phoned me on Saturday saying that their lead guitarist finally decided not to turn pro.'

The Seneschals played their final gig at the Bruce Hall, just up the road from where it all began at the Ensham Girls' School. They'd done several previous gigs there and had always gone down well, so it was a good note to finish on. On Saturday 6th April 1963, the end of this era was played out.

Roy Fisher had already been associated with the Cruickshanks for some time. He recalls how it all started: 'In 1958 I was 18 and working as a photographic assistant, travelling to work in West London from South London. Everyday I would travel on the train with an Anglo-Indian guy called Phillip Holmes; he invited me to his wedding reception, and that's where I first met John Cruickshank (then 16) and his brother Pete (then 14).

John got drunk at the reception and I helped his brother carry him home. Arriving at their house too late to get my bus home, I was invited by their mother to stay the night, which was the start of my 45-year friendship with John and Pete.

Tony, Mr Hore and Dave Wetton at a school reunion. After years of planning what he would say to 'Whore', Tony found his childhood nemesis to be a little old man.
Pic courtesy Dave Wetton

'A couple of years later John got engaged, and his future wife's brother, John Lockyear, was learning to play the guitar. John Cruickshank had a good voice and Pete learnt to play bass guitar. They found a drummer called Dave Boorman and 'Eddy Troude' (John) and the Dollarbills was born. I could not sing and played no instruments but was good on the phone, so started to manage them.

'The few gigs that came along were laughable – the Nightingale Club at Biggin Hill and playing a couple of songs before the movie at the Lewisham Odeon Cinema which was a complete disaster as the rising platform didn't rise.'

There were no hard feelings towards Tony because, shortly after he left, the remainder of the Seneschals went to see him debut at the Cafe des Artistes, Chelsea, on Friday 10th May 1963.

The truth was that the Seneschals had been going in different directions for some time. Dave Wetton sums up the situation prior to the split: 'When we went to the London clubs, Mac was no longer coming with us and we weren't popping round to each other's houses, so we were beginning to lose the cohesiveness of those previous years.

'If I was pushed on the matter I'd say it was the visits to the clubs that got us all hooked on the blues to the point where we all started buying albums individually, rather than us buying the records first and then going to the clubs. It was a short sharp intro before the Seneschals broke up.'

However, they all remained friends and even though they did have a few rehearsals after Tony left, they

folded soon after. John Wild teamed up with some local bluesmen, while 'Cakey' Weeks later formed a band with Dave Wetton and Johnny Bryant called the Shifters.

They appeared with such luminaries as the Barron Knights, the Small Faces and Billy J Kramer and the Dakotas and appeared on ITV's *Ready, Steady, Win* competition. But, as Cakey remarked, life in the music business can be cruel: 'The odd thing is that the Seneschals were miles better but the Shifters got a lot more work!'

The small council house in Tooting where Tony grew up.
Pic by Joanna Deacon, TS Personal Collection

chapter 2
The House Of Blues

'He had a dramatic impact on the band.'
Pete Cruickshank's verdict on Tony joining the Dollarbills

'It is rock history's duty to attempt to make amends for all these lives of injustice and misery; while white rock musicians strutted in the hallways of five-star hotels earning money from music that was not really of their own making, the true composers were neither recognised nor recompensed.'
Chambers' Rock Music Guide

Apart from John Cruickshank on vocals, and later harmonica, the Dollarbills also featured his brother Pete, on bass, and John Lockyear on lead guitar, but John Cruickshank was the acknowledged leader. In joining the band, Tony began a lifelong association with John's younger brother. Peter Cruickshank was born in India on 2nd July 1945. His grandfather had gone to Calcutta to take over a mill and his father Jack was born on the voyage. Things didn't go well and his father ended up in an orphanage at the age of four. When he was older Jack joined the RAF where he met Pete's mother Marjorie, a teacher. They got married in India in 1955 and came to England in order to give their children a better education.

Pete's mother trained at the Royal Academy in London and there was always some sort of music going on in the household. He remembers hearing classical music and, although he didn't like it, it subconsciously made an impression on him. Elder brother John was interested in becoming a musician, but instead acquired a drum kit!

All his other friends had guitars and Pete also got one. However, being the youngest had distinct disadvantages: 'All the others were a lot more advanced than me. I was always making up ground. We needed a bass player, so I decided it would be something that would give me a unique identity. I paid £20 for a Tuxedo bass guitar.' The young Pete Cruickshank liked Gene Vincent, Elvis Presley and the Everly Brothers; one of his favourite tracks was 'Cathy's Clown' (April 1960).

The brothers rehearsed in their front room in Wallbutton Road, Brockley, South London. But this produced problems, as Pete revealed: 'My parents were incredibly tolerant. They did have people knocking on the door about the noise. They told us to turn it down but we would carry on playing. In fact, we had a "nasty" put through the letter box.' It was clear that the parents were giving the children as much artistic encouragement as they could.

Dollarbills poster 1963, Lee Grant an early John Cruickshank pseudonym.
TS Personal Collection

Young Pete Cruickshank.
Pic courtesy Pete Cruickshank

It turned out that John Cruickshank was a useless drummer, so he decided to concentrate on singing and drafted in Dave Boorman on drums. They came up with a name, the Dollarbills, in deference to the concept that 'all things American had to be good' as all the artists they liked were from there.

They played their first gig at the famous 2Is coffee bar in London and journeyed there by train and taxi. As Pete remembered with a big grin on his face: 'We thought we were going to be stars. We carried our gear around London without any covers! We didn't even have covers for the drums.' By this time John Lockyear was struggling as lead guitarist.

In 1961 Pete Cruickshank started work as an apprentice fitter. He didn't really have his heart in it: 'My dad forced me to sign the papers, he said "we are not going to leave this room until you do". However, when I'd served two years I packed it in. I was old enough to make my own decisions.'

The Dollarbills played the pop songs of the day, from the likes of the Coasters, Elvis and the Shadows. This was when Tony McPhee joined the line-up. He had just been offered promotion and loved his day job, but the chance to be a full-time musician was too tempting. He left the Post Office and turned professional.

The new addition immediately made an impression. Pete Cruickshank takes up the story: 'We were doing Shadows stuff quite badly. Tony was unusual in that he never copied songs note for note like everybody else. Even without an echo unit and Fender he still emulated the sound. He had a dramatic impact on the band.' Whereas Pete couldn't see them making it before John Lockyear's departure, Tony's arrival opened up new horizons

The Seneschals had played only local gigs, but the Dollarbills travelled around a lot more. They played places like the Top Hat in Worthing and Sophia Gardens in Cardiff. Tony knew there was a lot of competition: 'Sophia Gardens was huge and there would be many bands playing their 30-minute slot. In a way it was like a conveyor belt.' They appeared with Vince Hill on 31st August 1963 and, on another occasion, with Chris Andrews of 'Yesterday Man' fame. They also played the RAF base at Brize Norton, where they were asked if they could play a waltz – they could! They were getting around the country courtesy of John Lockyear's dad's Thames van. He was convinced they were going to make it and even started to arrange gigs for them. They approached Cana Variety agency to get them more gigs. They were told confidently 'If we can't get you gigs in England we can get them in Germany'. They had more than enough work at home so there was no need to go abroad.

Tony McPhee didn't just bring his guitar to the Dollarbills – he also brought every blues album he had ever heard. From this point the rest of the band would hear a lot about the movement Tony loved so much. As Pete revealed: 'We only knew of pop,

we didn't know where pop actually came from. Tony knew the background and, as it turned out, we soon came to love it too.'

In the early months after Tony joined, their repertoire started to change. Early additions included 'My Babe', influenced by Little Walter's version, and Jimmy Reed's 'Big Boss Man'. And, of course, John Lee Hooker and Muddy Waters songs were well represented in the set. There was a short period of inactivity as they honed their act to suit the new direction. Even though John Cruickshank was acknowledged as the leader of the band, Tony had other plans: 'I led from the back. I was happy to manipulate things from there.'

In an interview with *Record Collector* in 1993 Tony McPhee defined his early musical taste: 'I loved the primitiveness of the blues. I've never been into BB King that much; it's too city, too sweet. I prefer the rough, primitive stuff, country players from the 1920s and 1930s like Leadbelly and Robert Johnson – he's just a total genius. In the 1960s you mistrusted white artists playing the blues – I only wanted to listen to black artists. There wasn't anybody white who was any good back then.'

These black artists generally came from the Mississippi delta but gravitated north to Chicago to play the clubs. Leonard and Phil Chess owned one of the clubs and they snapped most of them up. In 1947 they founded Chess Records, the vehicle that would bring these artists to the attention of the world.

It wasn't long before a name change was on the cards in order to reflect the way the band had changed, and Tony suggested the Groundhogs, in homage to 'Groundhog Blues' from the 1960 John Lee Hooker album 'House Of

Before the Severn crossing was built, they had to travel up to Chepstow before the trip cross country to Cardiff.
TS Personal collection

SOPHIA GARDENS PAVILION
TEL. CARDIFF 32816
SATURDAY, AUG. 31
7.30 to 11.45 p.m.
WALES and WEST ENTERTAINMENTS LTD., INVITE YOU TO
ROCK TO THE STARS
WITH TOP POP SINGER—"STARS AND GARTERS" etc.
VINCE HILL
WITH THE SENSATIONAL
DOLLAR BILLS
WHO RETURN BY POPULAR DEMAND
plus
THE AFRO-CUBAN COMBO
LICENSED BAR and BUFFET
ADMISSION 7/6 :: LATE BUSES
EARLY DOORS
BEFORE 8.30 6/-
ANOTHER STAR ATTRACTION NEXT WEEK FROM "WALES and WEST"

The Blues'. Tony had perused all his Hooker albums to find the right name, but the decision process wasn't as straightforward as it seemed: 'Yes, it was Tony's idea for the name,' Pete elucidated, 'but my brother would have been involved as he was the leader of the band. John is a very forceful character. By that time we were all blues fans anyway, so that obviously helped.'

Tony wasn't the only one who disliked the name the Dollarbills; Pete found it a tad embarrassing. At the same time John decided to call himself John Lee and this was added to the name of the band. The Dollarbills had also been known as Lee Grant (a mixture of two US civil war generals) and the Dollarbills. Contrary to popular belief, John Lee Hooker did not influence his new stage name.

By late 1963 they decided they needed a piano player and put an advert in *Melody Maker*. Only two people applied for the job and only one turned up for the audition. That man was Bob Hall. As he outlined: 'I had applied for lots of jobs because I was desperate to get into a band, but I never had any replies. I had the audition above a pub in New Cross. As I was the only one who turned up I got the job.' Hall was able to open up the blues even more to the band, as he recalled: 'I had a friend (Dave Carey, ex-Humphrey Lyttleton drummer) who owned the Swing jazz record shop, located at 1b Mitcham

Lane, Streatham. The Swing Shop was dark and small, with albums downstairs and 78s up on the next level, via the spiral staircase. Even though Carey hated the blues, he used to get a lot of rare Crown blues albums in the shop. This was because he had an import deal for jazz records but could only have a certain amount per deal. This meant he had to make up the numbers with other types of music and the cheapest records he could get were blues ones. Bob Hall spread the word and took the band to the shop to check out the bargain blues section. To Tony McPhee it was manna from heaven.

In those days not many white people liked the blues and the records didn't get to the UK via the usual distribution channels. People would bring them back on the boats from various parts of the world. Consequently, the shortage of blues records made the Swing Shop a magnet for blues fans eager to pick up rare albums. But it wasn't just fans that frequented the shop, as ex-employee Len Tempan remembered: 'Many musicians came to the shop. They included Keith Relf, Paul Samwell-Smith and Eric Clapton of the Yardbirds. Later on Clapton brought John Mayall along and Jeff Beck also came in and a member of the Rolling Stones, I can't remember which one. One of these musicians asked about a guy he had heard about playing great blues slide guitar. I told him that was Tony McPhee.' It's

One of a series of very silly publicity shots. The shiny suits were tailor-made in lining material. From left: Tony, Dave Boorman, John Cruickshank (on floor), Jack (sax) and Pete.
Pic courtesy Pete Cruickshank

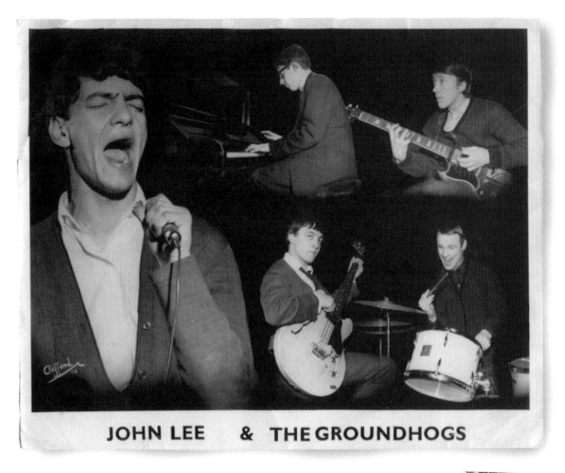

First publicity picture for the Groundhogs. Clockwise: John Lee (John Cruickshank), Bob Hall, Tony McPhee, Dave Boorman and Pete Cruickshank.
TS Personal Collection

JOHN LEE & THE GROUNDHOGS

(1) Jo Ann Kelly started out as a folk blues artist playing the local clubs, inspired by singers such as Memphis Minnie, Robert Johnson, John Lee Hooker and many others. The blues only had a cult following in those days, so to find a female blazing the trial was rare. Some of her earliest recordings were made for Mike Vernon but nothing came of them.

In September 1968 she took part in the first National Blues Federation Convention at the Conway Hall, London. The fact that she appeared with such luminaries as Stefan Grossman, Alexis Korner and Champion Jack Dupree illustrates the level that she had achieved. She performed with Canned Heat's Al Wilson and Bob Hite, who were very impressed.

She had a tremendous ability to get people behind her vision. In 1969 when John Lee Hooker was playing at the Festival Hall, she managed to persuade him and Big Joe Williams to appear with her at the Bridge House, a little blues/folk club in Borough, South London. Apart from Jo Ann, other regular performers there included Tony McPhee, Dave Kelly, Simon Prager and Steve Rye.

At the second National Blues Federation Convention she was asked to join Canned Heat, but declined. However, the word had spread across the pond and she was invited to perform at the Memphis Blues Festival. As a result of this performance she had a few offers but didn't like the hype that surrounded them. After that she mainly worked in the UK.

In the 1960s *Melody Maker* had referred to her as the 'Mother of British blues'. It was a great loss when she passed away of a brain tumour on 20th October 1990.

clear that Tony was starting to make a name for himself.

The Swing Shop took on extra significance for Tony, as this was where he met Jo Ann Kelly (1) sometime in early 1964. She made a big impression on him, as he outlines: 'I went into the shop and walked up to the counter where I noticed a girl bending down getting her purse out of her bag. Then she asked Len if he had a particular Howlin' Wolf album. I thought "Wow", but then I noticed she had a guitar slung over her shoulder. I knew I had to speak to this girl.' He did exactly that and struck up an immediate rapport. It wasn't long before Tony was appearing with Jo Ann at Bunjies Folk Cellar, as well as the Hole in the Ground at Swiss Cottage.

Jo Ann had a younger brother, Dave, who was also into the blues scene and later found fame as a blues musician: 'We were all into acoustic country blues at the time and generally had the impression that we were the only people in the country with that interest. We slowly found other pockets of country blues pickers in Bristol, Reading, Tyneside, Leeds etc. Jo, Mac, Bob Hall, Steve Rye and myself all used to hang around the Swing Shop in Streatham waiting for whatever blues releases came in. Jo worked a lot at the time with Mac and Bob Hall. I was still at school.'

Shortly afterwards, Tony taped an EP with Jo Ann in his Tooting home, using his Ampex recorder. She sang and played guitar and the songs recorded for side one were 'Long Black Curly Hair' and 'Boyfriend Blues'. The flip side contained 'New Milk Cow Blues' and 'I Looked Down The Line'. The first song was penned by Jo Ann, with the last three credited as 'Traditional, arranged by Jo Ann Kelly.' Tony took the finished tape to a place in the Old Kent Road where it was cut on a lathe, the swarf being sucked up by a domestic vacuum cleaner! In spite of the primitive technology the sound turned out very well. He completed the job by buying a John Bull stamping kit for sleeve information; only 99 were pressed and they are very rare items indeed. The EP was called 'Blues And Gospel'.

Things were going very well as John Lee's Groundhogs. They soon realised, to their delight, that Bob Hall was a very good piano player. Jack, the sax player, was now superfluous to their requirements. In true music business style they sacked him the day that Bob joined, taking his equipment and dumping it on his doorstep on their way to the next gig. These boys were learning fast! (2)

John Cruickshank was learning the harmonica, but he was lacking in one area, as Bob Hall noticed: 'John was a good singer but he didn't have the charisma that the girls went for.'

One of the things that inhibited John in this area was the fact he was married. However, the band centred round the Cruickshanks. 'We always left the van outside their house and their mother fed us on many occasions.' Around this time Tony struck up a relationship with younger sister, Jean, who was only 15. The relationship continued for two years.

Playing the blues was having a liberating effect on Pete: 'I could put my own bass lines with the blues, as you couldn't really hear it on the records. Furthermore, in those days there weren't many bands playing it and it made you feel you belonged to something special. It was like a cult. You would chat to most musicians and they'd never heard of the blues.' The first blues record that Pete really got excited about was Cyril Davis and his All Stars' 'Country Line Special'. In fact, one of his greatest regrets is that he never got to see the great man on stage (he died of leukaemia in 1964). However, a later visit to the Marquee provided him with his greatest inspiration: 'We went to see Long John Baldry and that's when I first saw his bass player. His name was Cliff Barton and he played slap bass, but on the electric bass guitar. His playing was obviously improvised and I realised that's how I wanted to play.' So he traded his Fender for an Epiphone EB2, the same bass as Barton.

The early part of 1964 was spent trying to build up support as a blues band. Their change of direction necessitated a change of venues too. They started getting gigs at places like Studio 51 and the 100 Club in Oxford Street; both hot R&B venues. Dave Wetton noted in his diary that he saw John Lee's Groundhogs support the Animals on 28th January at the 100 Club. On other occasions they supported Jimmy Powell and the Five Dimensions and Alex Harvey. But they ventured out of the capital on many occasions too. They played the famous Newcastle Club A Go Go and supported Long John Baldry

Howlin' Wolf with Dave Kelly in the late 1960s. Tony regretted selling a Harmony acoustic guitar to Dave; years later he was told that Wolf had accidentally stepped on and trashed it...
what a way to go!
Pic courtesy Dave Kelly

(2) The life of a piano player was not always a bed of roses. Sometimes the piano at a venue would be out of tune, in a state or non-existent! At a gig in Crawley they found themselves with no piano but, luckily, they located one just across the road. However, they were faced with the perilous job of manhandling it across the busy A23.

Dave, John, Tony, Bob and Pete posed around a soil-filled, empty flower bed. An early attempt at irony?
Pic by Roy Fisher
TS Personal Collection

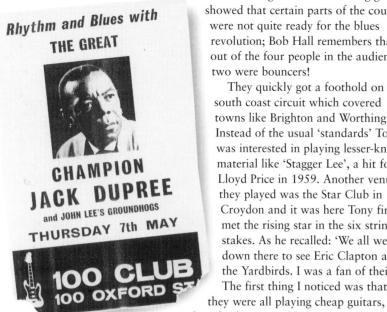

Rhythm and Blues with THE GREAT

CHAMPION JACK DUPREE
and JOHN LEE'S GROUNDHOGS

THURSDAY 7th MAY

100 CLUB
100 OXFORD ST

Jack Dupree was an affable guy who insisted on sharing royalties for the songs he recorded with Tony 50/50. Tony gigged and recorded with Champion Jack through the mid 1960s.
TS Personal Collection

jo-ann kelly
tony mcphee
same thing on their minds

Compilation of all the songs Tony and Jo Ann recorded together.
Pic courtesy Tony Sherratt

Jo Ann Kelly with Fred McDowell
Pic courtesy Pete Emery

(3) Roy Fisher met Arden's booking agent when he went round to his office in Denmark Street, London. At the time they had a temporary secretary working in the office. While he was waiting, a telephone was flung out of the office and landed at his feet. There was a look of horror on the temp's face. The agent was Peter Grant, later to find fame as Led Zeppelin's uncompromising manager.

at the Reading Town Hall. That gig showed that certain parts of the country were not quite ready for the blues revolution; Bob Hall remembers that out of the four people in the audience, two were bouncers!

They quickly got a foothold on the south coast circuit which covered towns like Brighton and Worthing. Instead of the usual 'standards' Tony was interested in playing lesser-known material like 'Stagger Lee', a hit for Lloyd Price in 1959. Another venue they played was the Star Club in Croydon and it was here Tony first met the rising star in the six string stakes. As he recalled: 'We all went down there to see Eric Clapton and the Yardbirds. I was a fan of theirs. The first thing I noticed was that they were all playing cheap guitars, I thought that was odd. We were invited by their manager, Giorgio Gomelsky, to play a few numbers in the interval.' The band went down very well in this impromptu gig. Tony's next meeting with Clapton would be more significant!

They played regularly at the 100 Club (including 10th and 31st March, again supporting the Animals). They got to know the manager of the club and it wasn't long before they started to press him about having their own slot. He wasn't keen on this, but offered them something else to keep them quiet. Bob Hall recalls, it was quite a consolation:

'He offered us the chance to back Champion Jack Dupree. The fact he was a piano player helped me because I played and he was free to concentrate on his act. This included dancing and telling bad and very dirty jokes. He was a great performer and a very nice man, but he was a bit of a bullshitter.' (The date of this was 7th May; Dupree had made his debut at the Marquee on the 3rd.) He was later quoted in *Record Mirror* as saying that John Lee's Groundhogs were the 'best band I've played with'.

On the back of this work they got the chance to back two more blues giants. Roy Fisher had prudently contacted their agents. They backed Little Walter on a one-off at a dance hall. Up until then most of his backing bands had not been up to scratch because he paid so little. The band was looking for a memorable occasion. But things didn't turn out as they had planned or hoped, as Bob Hall outlined: 'When we met Little Walter he demanded a bottle of whisky as it was the tradition of the backing band. We refused. He didn't like us after that and he wasn't a nice man anyway. He had no stage charisma and he had the cheek to blame us when he didn't go down

too well. We were probably the best band he had at that time because we knew his material.'

Tony didn't endear himself to Walter, either, as he recalled: 'I liked his "Just A Feeling" and asked him if he still played it. He replied "How do you know that?" We knew it because we liked the blues. When it came to that number in the show and we started playing it I suddenly realised I couldn't remember the riff. I thought "Oh shit!" He wasn't happy about "My Babe" either. I was playing it the way we usually played it but he was not like Hooker, who could ride over any hitch. He spent the whole song turning round and growling to me "E natural". Another reason why I didn't like him was that he took the piss out of Hooker – cheeky bastard! He wasn't a nice man at all; he walked with a limp because someone had shot him. I think someone finished the job when he got back home!'

Soon after this they played two gigs with Memphis Slim; one of them was at the Club Noreik, a converted cinema in London that the band hated. The gig was always at two in the morning and hardly anybody would be there. Slim was unlike most of the black artists of the day and was willing to protect his interests. He got into an argument with the promoter who was trying to rip him off. Bob Hall overheard the back end of the conversation. Slim told him: 'I am not one of those blacks who can't read or write.'

Success is often a matter of catching a lucky break and John Lee's Groundhogs got theirs in May 1964 when John Lee Hooker flew into the UK for a five-week tour. It coincided with his single 'Dimples' reaching Number 23 in the singles chart, his first hit in the UK. As was common in those days, no backing musicians accompanied him, as the cost was prohibitive.

As soon as manager Roy Fisher heard Hooker was coming over he went round to promoter Don Arden's office to make a pitch for the tour. He was too late, as John Mayall had beaten them to it, but when the tour was extended and Mayall couldn't make the last week Arden knew who could step in. (3)

chapter 3
Hooker & The Hogs

*'John Lee's Groundhogs are definitely my favourites.
They're tremendously nice fellows and
very good to work with.'*
John Lee Hooker

On 1st June 1964 John Lee Hooker opened his British tour with John Mayall at the Flamingo Club, London. John Lee's Groundhogs attended the show as fans. As the tour progressed Hooker got a lot of flak from blues snobs for 'selling out' his original roots. An infuriated Tony McPhee fired off a letter of defence to *Melody Maker*. It was published on 27th June and is worth quoting in full.

'John Lee Hooker and Howlin' Wolf are just as much bluesmen in their own right as Big Joe Williams and Sleepy John Estes. It's true that Hooker's later records are intended for R&B audiences, but his earlier discs contain some of the most forceful and primitive blues of all time. Wolf has always turned out good discs. His latest are exceptional.' Tony was not frightened to nail his colours to the mast!

Apart from the band grabbing a lot of interest, Tony himself was receiving his fair share. In June he received an offer to join Chris Barber's Jazzband. It was the first offer to join a name band he'd ever had; it wouldn't be the last. He was looking for his first electric guitarist (Barber had initially asked the guitarist from Them) but he was obviously impressed by what Tony was doing.

Tony never really considered joining, as he was keen to have his own band eventually. Chris Barber's next choice, John Slaughter, was more successful and at the time of writing he is still with Barber. It was a decision Tony's called the biggest mistake of his life: 'I would have had more money and been around the world several times by now.'

John Lee's Groundhogs' first gig with Hooker was later in the year on 5th July when the band journeyed to the Twisted Wheel club in Manchester to meet their hero. They were aware of most of the material Hooker wanted to play, but being major fans raised the tension, as Tony recalled: 'We were all very nervous, when I first met him I thought he looked mean, but it was only later that I found out he was still annoyed with John Mayall. It appears that Mayall's musical arrangements were not to Hooker's liking –

This turned out to be an eventful gig on the John Lee Hooker tour for less than appropriate reasons.
Pic courtesy Pete Cruickshank

he didn't like the wash of Mayall's keyboards, he preferred it simpler.' This was compounded by guitarist Roger Dean's inability to follow Hooker's idiosyncratic chord changes.

The band being fans of the great man created an edge – this gig was more than a pay cheque, as Pete Cruickshank remembered: 'We felt we could do it justice as it meant so much to us and I think we did. We saw him playing with Mayall and we wanted to integrate more and be part of Hooker and not just a backing band. We became very much a part of him on the stage.' It wasn't long before they realised the feelings was mutual.

Though they had no rehearsal, they knew the songs that Hooker played would be in E, as he only played in two keys – A when he played solo and E with a band. The opening number with Hooker was James Brown's 'I'll Go Crazy'. Hooker must have been impressed with Tony, as he knew all his licks and more.

Tony was disappointed with their performance at first, but he perked up when Hooker told the band: 'You boys really know my shit!' John Cruickshank explained how they hit it off with him: 'He never did a song the same way twice. But we were ready, as we knew his work. We knew he would go into a 12-bar but it might end in a 10-bar. I have to admit it was unnerving at first.' Flexibility was the secret of success – you had to think on your feet.'

Hooker was driven up to Manchester in an Austin Westminster, his designated transport for the duration of the tour. The driver was Pat Meehan, one of Don Arden's odd job men and a very dour character indeed. How Hooker got on with him one can only speculate. (In fact, Meehan became the manager of the Groundhogs in 1972 for a short time.) Meanwhile, the band were merrily travelling in their Commer van sampling the sights, sounds and smells of the English countryside, not to say the inside of the van! But the two entities were going to turn into one very soon, as Roy Fisher remembered in Charles Shaar Murray's book *Boogie Man*.

'John said that McPhee knew some of his old blues songs better than he remembered them, so therefore it wasn't a problem and it just went from there. Because he liked the guys and respected the way they played, he decided the very next day that he didn't want to tour with the chauffeur.' The social integration was completed hot on the heels of the musical integration and he finished the tour travelling in the back of the van! From that moment John Lee's Groundhogs ceased being a backing band. Now they were one homogenous unit.

The tour gained momentum very quickly and Graham Ackers captured the excitement generated in his review of the Savoy Ballroom gig, Cleveleys near Blackpool (8th July), for *Blues Unlimited* magazine: 'Hooker came on to a very enthusiastic reception – he rolled into "Shake It Baby" with great powe. Every number was received with enthusiasm to such a degree five encores were performed in all. A special mention is required for the Groundhogs, who

throughout played admirably. All in direct contrast to the "let's see who can play the loudest" approach of John Mayall. In fact, everything was just right – atmosphere, backing, amplification and temperature and everybody, including Hooker and the Hogs had a ball.' Other material they played included 'Night Time Is The Right Time', 'Hi Heel Sneakers', 'Boom Boom' and 'Dimples'. The latter was his current hit, although recorded in 1959.

Hooker was unfamiliar with the attention blues artists who came over to Europe had to get used to. The extent of the public's ignorance about bluesmen in the States was witnessed by Mick Jagger when the Rolling Stones were on their first tour there: 'The funny thing was, the kids had never heard of Muddy Waters. They've got the greatest blues singer living among them and they don't even know.' Hooker was a quiet and unassuming guy offstage but suddenly he had the spotlight on him. As manager Roy Fisher recalls: 'There were a lot of people, which he wasn't used to, and he'd get nervous when he had to go on stage if he had to push through a crowd.'

John Lee was confused when people asked for his autograph. Being illiterate, his immediate reaction to this was to refuse to sign, but this caused problems with PR. Tony and Roy decided to teach Hooker how to sign his name. Roy Fisher witnessed Hooker's progress. 'At first he was painfully slow. But because he wanted to get back to the hotel as soon as possible (usually with a girl) he started to sign JLH which got the queue down fast.' Hooker was getting lots of attention from the girls and it would increase

Tony, Bob Hall, Dave, Pete, John Lee and John (seated).
Pic Roy Fisher
TS Personal Collection

dramatically on the next tour. It would also cause a few sticky moments.

Hooker had many ways of disguising his inability to read or write. In the service stations he would pick up the menu, usually upside-down, and say 'Dave (Boorman), what are you having?' Hooker hated English food, but burgers and chicken were in short supply in those days. On the subject of food, he had never come across a vegetarian before and fired endless questions to Tony about it. The cultural differences worked the other way round too. Tony recalls that Hooker had a briefcase full of vitamin pills. He'd never seen that before.

As the end of the tour approached Tony changed his guitar style as the influence of Hooker intensified. This was the point when he slung the guitar strap over his right shoulder and abandoned his plectrum, just like Hooker. It was very strange at first but it wasn't long before he felt totally at ease with it. It is a style he still employs today and was a contributing factor to developing the unique guitar sound that was to pay real dividends in the 1970s. The tour climaxed at London's Beat City on 12th July. They then said goodbye to Hooker but it wouldn't be long before they met again.

The Hooker tour made John Lee's Groundhogs' name and in August they signed for Anglo-American Artists. They were booked for another tour with John Lee Hooker at the great man's request, 56 shows at £130 per week commencing on 1st October. In fact, it was only 28 venues as the contract stated they had to deliver two thirty-minute performances at each venue. By this time their workload was so heavy that Pete Cruickshank remembers his fingers were blistering.

Around this time they went into IBC studios to record a couple of demos for pop producer Mickie Most. They decided to do Howlin' Wolf's 'Wang Dang Doodle' and 'Rock Me Baby', but Most had other things on his mind. Bob Hall recalled this session: 'Most was going out with Marianne Faithfull at the time and she turned up in a mini-skirt with laddered fishnet tights. As the control booth was above the stage I spent most of the session looking up her skirt. Perhaps that's why the track didn't turn out so good.'

Most hated what they had done and he offered the master to Roy Fisher for £40. Bob Hall takes up the story: 'Roy didn't have the money so he borrowed it from me. I never got the money back.' For some reason the tape temporarily disappeared!

By this time Tony was getting some impressive notices. In an autumn edition of *R'N'B Scene*, an editorial waxed lyrical about two rising stars. Tony is described as: 'a really great guitarist whose work with a bottleneck has to be heard to be believed'. The second artist they mentioned was Steve Winwood, so he was in good company.

As October approached, the band started to prepare for the Hooker tour – and, with the tour being a month in duration, it was clear that Bob Hall would have to turn professional. But he was

unwilling to give up his career as a patent attorney. Keith Scott (ex-Cyril Davies) played a few gigs and was suggested for the tour, but in the end they recruited Tom Parker.

However, as Hall told Charles Shaar Murray: 'The guy (Parker) they got to play was a pub pianist! I had to teach him to play blues, which I did because I wanted to help, but he couldn't feel the way Hooker played.'

Hooker summed up the here and now to *Melody Maker* and his laidback style and politeness shone through: 'That John Mayall group and John Lee's Groundhogs are definitely my favourites. They're tremendously nice fellows and very good to work with. They try hard to do everything I want. I really was pleased to see those fellows when I arrived back in England.' The bond between Hooker and the Hogs was to get even stronger on the tour.

One of the early gigs on the tour was at the legendary Club A Go Go in Newcastle. They had an afternoon session for the teens but the fun started later. The size of the crowd dramatically increased Hooker's nerves. Roy Fisher related the course of events in Charles Shaar Murray's book: 'Most places were jam packed. In Newcastle it was big and there were about eight hundred people packed into this place. The dressing room wasn't at the side of the stage, it was in the back of the managerial offices.'

It was clear Hooker would have to push his way through. But as the band kicked into his intro music, he couldn't be found. Fisher was beside himself. All he could hear was the band

Contract for John Lee Hooker tour.
TS Personal Collection

Pete, John, Dave, Tony (with multiple zits) and Tom Parker (keyboards).
Photograph Roy Fisher.
Courtesy Pete Cruickshank.

(1) Bob Hall met Hooker again in the early 1980s. It was after a gig in California but Hooker's past shenanigans were, obviously, not far from the surface, as he explained to writer Bob Brunning: 'I walked into the dressing room and there was a sort of sea of people, you know, but Hooker instantly recognised me and I felt good about that because he's played with thousands of people. The first thing he did was to say "Hey, Bob, don't tell any stories about the old times – here's my new wife!" She was in her mid 20s!'

playing the intro repeatedly. Hooker was eventually found by a policeman in the toilet having wet himself. 'He used to drink a lot of whisky', Tony McPhee recalls 'but diluted with a lot of water. Consequently, he pissed a lot. But he was never drunk.' With the place so packed it was common for the band not to be able to get to the toilet.

A date at the Flamingo club on 23rd October was witnessed by Tony's old friend Dave Wetton. Another of the dates on the tour was the famous Cavern in Liverpool, attended by a couple of dedicated fans of the band. Bob Glass never forgot the magic of those gigs: 'I was going out with Jo Ann Kelly then; we had seen them in Manchester and were hitching a ride to Liverpool. But by coincidence the band's van turned up and we piled into the back. There wasn't a lot of room but we fitted in. I remember the fluidity of those gigs. Hooker would get requests to play on his own and he did. Also, Tony and Pete made a great rhythm team.' It seems odd today that the audience's main reason for being there was to dance.

Hooker was 47 and far older than most of the fans, but that didn't prove to be a barrier to him connecting with them. He was very interested in the many females that turned up and was always looking for a chance to chat them up.

Apart from the fact he was a star who had a hit single, he also had a stage presence that was utterly mesmerising and this helped in his quest to impress the girls.

It wasn't long before he was having success with some of them. But at the Dungeon Club in Nottingham he realised just how close he was sailing to the wind, even in the far more liberal United Kingdom.

Roy Fisher revealed how it came to a head: 'I came back into the dressing room and he was in a very, very upset state. He was stuttering away; it was obvious he was upset. I was trying to work out what had upset him and it was because he had found out that one young lady who had got through to him was only 15. He was a lot more careful after that episode.' (1)

After the gig the owner of a restaurant invited Hooker back for a meal. He agreed but he insisted the band be included in the offer too. The owner agreed, but it was to cause problems later on.

It turned out that the owner was a big music fan and collected artists autographs on his wall (at that stage there was only Ben E King). He asked Hooker to sign, but there was a problem as he still had difficulty signing his name. Hooker kept crossing out his crayon work because he was not happy with it until he had covered half the wall. They then sat down to their meal.

They naturally thought the invitation meant the meal was gratis, but halfway through Tony leant over to Hooker and said 'The waiter is writing things down.' With that, Hooker called over the waiter and said 'I want you to get a pen and paper and write down the club, the manager of the club and your name. I'm gonna tell all the papers about how nice it was for you to give us the meal'. There was a moment of tension as the waiter gave the paper to the manager. The manager came over and asked us 'Did you enjoy the meal?' And the band had their free meal.

Shortly after the tour started they appeared on BBC television on a program called *Beat Room*. Also on the bill were the Kinks and Tom Jones. Pete Cruickshank recalled the Welshman had an astounding voice, but it was the Kinks that made a bigger impression on Tony.

'Dave Davies had a small Italian Elpico amplifier which he plugged his guitar into, then he connected the speaker outlets of the Elpico into his Vox. It gave the guitar a very distorted sound, but when they started the soundcheck ("You Really Got Me") the recording engineer was confused by the horrible sound he was hearing and asked for the guitar mic to be checked as it was all distorted. Dave Davies just said "That's our sound!"'

The control booth was situated above the stage and Hooker seemed to be mesmerised by it, as he kept looking up throughout their performance. They played 'Boom Boom' and 'I'm Leaving' and, looking at the footage, now you barely get a glimpse of the band apart from their hands. Their segment was recorded very quickly, which was just as well as they went off to a gig afterwards. They even managed to record a session for *Saturday Club* at Maida Vale. The program was broadcast on 14th November and included the Isley Brothers and Freddie and the Dreamers.

The tour continued with Hooker in the van, and he certainly made a big impression on all concerned as Pete Cruickshank recalled: 'He used to get his semi-acoustic guitar out in the van. We'd be dozing but we'd soon wake up. Just hearing the travelling noises of the road and Hooker playing a slow blues like 'Waterfront' in his moving and meaningful way. It was the very essence of John and it would send shivers down your spine. If only I'd had a tape recorder.' John Cruickshank also has his memories of this time: 'There was a magic event on the road in the van. The whole band was sound asleep (save Dave Boorman, who was driving) after a gig when we were woken by JLH. He couldn't have been very tired as he was singing and playing his guitar. He could compose songs at the drop of a hat. We recalled later how we all gradually woke up to his singing, not wanting to interrupt him in anyway as the moment was truly magical. We were audience to something that was truly unique and to which tickets couldn't be bought.'

It must be said that Hooker also had some annoying habits. He tended to spit a lot in order to clear his throat. Spitting was perfectly normal

where John came from. John would be sitting in the single seat next to the window and they would feel a rush of cold air as he turned round, opened the window and spat out. But sometimes he'd not time it right so the side of the van would be encrusted with spit. At the end of the tour Pete drew the short straw and had to clean it all off. On another occasion they were invited back to Tom Parker's house where he proceeded to spit on the fireplace, only realising afterwards it was artificial.

The toilet problems continued at the Bure Country club, Bournemouth where Hooker pissed in the corner of the dressing room as he couldn't get to the facilities. Pete Cruickshank had foolishly left his new stage shirt in the vicinity. When he picked it up and complained the shirt was wet, Tony vividly remembers thinking 'I know what's happened here'. Another problem was the autumn weather. Hooker didn't like the cold very much. In fact, he couldn't tolerate it at all. As Roy Fisher recalled in Murray's book: 'He'd be up in the usual seat with a coat, a scarf and hat, a blanket over his knees, the heater on, and still complaining about the cold. We'd all be there in T-shirts saying "Oh my God", with sweat pouring off us.'

The tour's conclusion didn't end the association with Hooker as the Hogs were booked to make an album with the great man. But before that they had a single to record with a top American producer.

It now appears Hooker had been hustling for his erstwhile backing band. In an interview with Max Jones of *Melody Maker* he confided: 'I was so impressed with the Groundhogs on this tour I contacted Calvin Carter of Vee Jay (Records) right away with a view to recording them over here.

' I sent a demo disc of two songs by the group for him to hear (Roy Fisher gave the demo of 'Wang Dang Doodle' to Hooker). He phoned me back and then sent a cable saying he was coming over to London and would offer them a contract and record them here.' Carter was showing special interest in talented white artists and this was the band's chance to make a name.

Carter duly came over and the band picked him up from the Hilton Hotel in their van. By all accounts Carter was hoping to find a new Beatles, but things

Tour advert.
TS Personal Collection

Hooker with Epiphone, relaxing in a hotel bedroom.
TS Personal Collection

27

JOHN LEE HOOKER DIGS OUR R&B

GROUND HOGS— THE GREATEST

AS bluesman John Lee Hooker closed his second British tour on Sunday but remained in London in order to record for Vee Jay with his accompanying group, John Lee's Groundhogs. In this MM interview he talks to Max Jones about the tour and the British group.

As far as I'm concerned concerned this whole tour has been a complete success, and for their part the Groundhogs have been tremendous.

I'm bound to say that John Lee and the Groundhogs are one of the number one best blues groups that you have over here, and it fits in with my type of music perfectly.

DEMO DISC

Because it studies my style anyway, it knows how to work with me. Often the boys know what I'm going to do before I do it.

John Mayall has a real good blues band, too, but the Groundhogs, they fit better with what I do. Not that I'm taking anything away from Mayall. He has his own style, his own thing going. Oh, he's good.

Anyway, I was so impressed with the Groundhogs on this tour that I contacted Calvin Carter of Vee Jay right away with a view to him recording them over here. And I sent a demo disc of two ... by the group for him to hear.

John Lee . . too good to remain undiscovered.

He 'phoned me back and then sent a cable saying he was coming over to London this week and would offer the group a contract and record them here. He liked the acetate enough to want to record them with me and on their own.

PROUD OF THEM

So I'm staying on three or four days to do the recording. The Groundhogs will be backing me, and that's for Vee Jay who will release it in the States, also the Groundhogs' single.

What songs will I record here? I know one I'm going to do is "Seven Days And Seven Nights", a new one of mine. I got some more, too, but right now I'm undecided as to which to do.

I want to say this: "I'm very glad that John Lee and the Groundhogs have been discovered because they're too good a blues group to remain undiscovered."

I tried to do something for them, and did do something for them, and I'm proud of them. I am sure they'll become a great favourite of British blues fans, and they'll be known in America in a few months from now.

Naturally, there's been quite a lot of mix-ups during the tour over John Lee and John Lee Hooker. Well, that's life. I've enjoyed it all, and next year I'm looking forward to coming back this way.

REST UP

I'm bound to admit that it seems I can never give my fans enough — the more they see me the more they want, and believe me I love to work for them.

Sometimes, I'm ready to go on stage not feeling up to it, but a big push from them and it all passes over. Tiredness is forgotten when I start working.

The people have responded well, particularly in the North of England. We hit one or two spots down South where the people never quite understood what we were doing, but almost everywhere we've been very well received.

"Dimples", that's gone down well everywhere, and "Boom Boom" and "I'm Leaving", they're two they can hold on to.

Well, now I'm getting ready to go home to Detroit and rest up for a few weeks. Tell your ... I'll see them next

---

The Groundhogs managed to impress Hooker, not least because they could follow his 'unique' timings.
TS Personal Collection

When Calvin Carter came over to record 'Shake It' and 'Rock Me' for US release, he was looking for another Beatles!
TS Personal Collection

didn't get off to a good start, as John Cruickshank remembered: 'It was night-time and Carter was in the back. I was sitting in the passenger seat turning round talking to him. But I could see he was nervous and he clearly didn't want to speak to me. I thought it was odd but I only found out later he thought I was driving, as I was sitting on the left hand side.' After the initial awkward introduction Carter turned out to be very nice.

The recording session finally got under way at Philips studios in London on 19th November. They chose 'Shake It', which was really Fred McDowell's 'Shake 'Em On Down', and 'Rock Me Baby', which was played BB King-style.

The outstanding thing about these recordings is John

Booker Hooker

AMERICAN blues star John Lee Hooker is negotiating an American record contract for Britain's John Lee and the Groundhogs.

If the negotiations are completed it would mean that the group's records would be issued in America before Britain.

The Groundhogs, who have been touring with Hooker, guest in BBC-2 "Beat Room" on November 9 and have signed for "Saturday Club" on December 5.

Cruickshank's distinctive voice. In fact, as Pete Cruickshank recalls: 'Jo Ann Kelly thought he was a tremendous singer'. Bob Hall reflected: 'Tom Parker used my arrangement for piano because it's the same one I used later on Savoy Brown's debut album.'

The session was considered by all to be a success. But John Cruickshank had a shock when he finally received a copy of the single because he shared a songwriting credit with Carter. Carter was a canny operator and was well used to the techniques of getting round publishing credits. He knew that changing just a single word could facilitate such a transfer of rights. It was all rather shady stuff as it meant that, somewhere down the line, someone missed out on their due reward.

Calvin Carter was pictured in the 28th November edition of *Melody Maker* outside the studio shaking hands with John Cruickshank (the paper wrongly stated it was Jimmy Reed). The confusion was probably caused by the fact that, at the time the picture was taken, they were on tour with Reed. They got the tour through Don Arden, who was clearly impressed with how they handled Hooker.

They commenced the tour with Reed on 1st November at the Flamingo, London. But Tony expecially remembers the double-header in Birmingham at the Ritz and the Plaza, 30 miles apart: 'I remember as we packed our gear away to get over to the other side of Birmingham, I noticed that, even though he hadn't been

drinking, Jimmy was still confused and, when he was talking to the support band, congratulated them on the way they'd backed him!'

But there was a much more pressing problem on the music front, as Tony revealed: 'Reed had a habit of not tuning his guitar and we were coping well with that problem. However, when *Blues Unlimited's* review of the Guildford gig came out later they blamed us! I thought that was out of order because it was obvious where the problem was. They always hated us anyway. The only good review we ever got from them was on the first Hooker tour.'

Around this time Tony had a meeting with one of his heroes thanks to the timely intervention of Pete Cruickshank. They had played a gig earlier in the evening but managed to get back to catch a couple of numbers at a blues festival. Howlin' Wolf came off stage and Tony and Pete followed him. Steam was rising from Wolf's head but Tony was apprehensive about speaking to him because he had read in *Blues Unlimited* magazine that he didn't like white people.

However, Pete was not so shy in coming forward, as Tony relates: 'Pete didn't believe it at all and introduced himself: "Mr Burnett (Wolf's real name), I am the bass player in a band called the Groundhogs who play a lot of your songs." At that Wolf turned slightly to look way down at me and asked in his massive voice "Is this another li'l Groundhog?"

A Christmas card from John Lee, requesting a new lighter to replace the one the band had given him. JLH probably got someone to write the card for him.
Roy Fisher Personal Collection

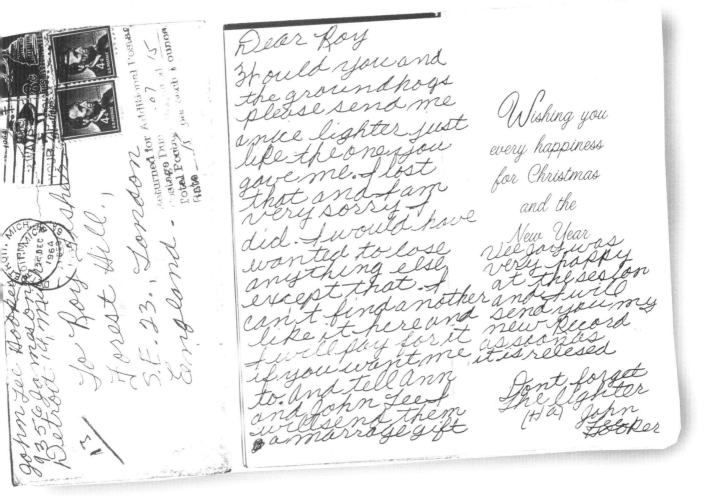

(2) There is no doubt that Bob Hall was exceptional and was a great loss when he had to leave John Lee's Groundhogs. This is what promoter Jim Simpson had to say about him: 'The number of (US) bluesmen that have told me that the pianist Bob Hall is the best piano player they ever worked with and that he's up there with Otis Spann are without number!'

Tom, Tony, Dave, John, Jimmy Reed and Pete outside the Twisted Wheel.
TS Personal Collection

Straight after Hooker, Jimmy Reed was very different to play with. For a start he seldom tuned his guitar.
TS Personal Collection

'Wolf invited us back to the hotel and as we walked into the foyer we couldn't believe it. (The artists from the festival) were all there. It was 1964-65 and all the waiters were white; you could tell that they didn't much like waiting on these black guys.

'Wolf had an acoustic guitar and he started playing "Down In The Bottom"; it was amazing. I still can't work out how he managed to put so much attack into his bottleneck playing, we just stood there stunned.'

So Tony spent the most memorable night of his life in the presence of Wolf, Sleepy John Estes and Hubert Sumlin. It meant that by the end of the decade Tony had played with or met the majority of his blues heroes!

The band later went to see Howlin' Wolf at Cooks Ferry Inn, London. Tony was just as interested to see his guitarist, Hubert Sumlin. The show was split into two sets and Tony recalls that Hubert was genius in the first set and only brilliant in the second.

At the end of the year came the inevitable comparisons between the blues artists they'd backed. Roy Fisher

summarised how difficult it could be as a backing band. Of John Lee Hooker, he said: 'He was a gentleman, always polite and in that way totally unique, unlike Little Walter and Jimmy Reed, who were totally uncouth! Walter was obnoxious and bad-tempered and got upset very, very quickly. Jimmy Reed was okay on stage when he was playing, but in-between times he drank too much and complained about absolutely everything.'

Bob Hall was in no doubt who was number one, as he recalled: 'I was later in the John Dummer Blues Band that backed Howlin' Wolf, but I think Hooker was the greatest of all the blues artists I was involved with.' (2)

Contrary to many reports, the Hogs did not record the album with John Lee Hooker at this time. It was discussed, but the reason why it didn't happen appears to have been lost in the mists of time.

Before he left for home Hooker gave a ringing endorsement to the band: 'I'm bound to say that John Lee's Groundhogs are one of the number one best groups you have over here, and it fits in with my type of music perfectly – I'm proud of them. I am sure they'll become a great favourite of British blues fans and they'll be known in America in a few months from now.'

For all Hooker's hopes it didn't quite pan out that way. The single appeared on Interphon across the pond and it bombed. That ensured a 'no profile' situation in America. However, the failure to consolidate the success of 1964 into 1965 is more inexplicable.

chapter 4
The Cold Wind Of Change

'The blues can be boring but I play things in different keys.'
John Mayall's pitch to Tony McPhee
to persuade him to join the Bluesbreakers

'The blues clubs were disappearing, so I accepted the situation.'
Tony McPhee on the switch to soul

John Lee Hooker came back to England in spring 1965 and John Lee's Groundhogs were favourites to cover the tour. But in the end they didn't get the job as John Mayall and the unknown Cops and Robbers did the honours. In and around Hooker's tour they recorded an album with him. In an interview with *Melody Maker* Hooker revealed he was not short of material: 'I know one I'm going to do is "Seven Days And Seven Nights", a new one of mine. I've got some more too, but right now I'm undecided as to which to do.' Hooker went into IBC studio with ten other songs.

There were problems, as Tony McPhee related to Bob Brunning for his excellent book *Blues: The British Connection*: 'Tom Parker wasn't

The Groundhogs
'big soul band',
Pete, Fred (sax), Colin
Huntley (drums),
John, Mick Humbey
(keyboards),
Unknown (brass), Tony.
Pic courtesy Pete
Cruickshank.

(1) Mike Vernon later founded the famous Blue Horizon label. He had a knack for seeking out home-grown R&B talent but he also was able to change with the times. He later produced successful acts from the late 1960s, 1970s and well into the 1980s. These included Ten Years After, Fleetwood Mac, Focus, Dr Feelgood and Level 42.

(2) In 1989 Pete Townshend released his 'Iron Man' solo album. The guest performers included John Lee Hooker.

able to vary the bar-counts, so what we had to do was let Hooker play his blues sequence, which was about 10 and a half bars and then he had to mark time until Parker had finished and then start off again.' Another problem was that Mickie Most insisted they record at low volume and this didn't help to create a live atmosphere. Tony thought that his guitar sounded more like a banjo at the low level, so he used a lot of slide in an attempt to give it more sustain.

The album sleeve indicates the sessions were held in May/June 1965, but Tony remembers only one session. Pete Cruickshank gives an insight into how the sessions went: 'Hooker would tell us the song we were going to do. He would sing the song, I'd sort out the bass line there and then, and we'd run it off. Most of the tracks were first takes, it was very impromptu. I listened to it recently and thought I could have done better with more time.'

Hooker aficionados believe the album was not a major addition to his catalogue, but it is a solid piece of work. However, as Charles Shaar Murray writes in *Boogie Man*, there are certain things that have to be borne in mind: 'Though the album may not have been the artistic triumph for Hooker, it was a considerable achievement for the fledgling Groundhogs, winning their spurs by keeping musical pace with an acknowledged master.' It was also an achievement given their relative lack of recording experience.

Some of the standout tracks are 'Little Girl Go Back To School', which is not a million miles away from Sonny Boy Williamson's 'Good Morning Little Schoolgirl'. Perhaps Hooker was still smarting from his experiences on the 1964 tour of the UK? It would also be tempting to connect 'Don't Go Messin' With My Bread' with his shenanigans with wayward promoters, but a cursory reference to the lyrics reveal the subject is a lot closer to home. The slow blues of 'Waterfront' evokes all of Pete Cruickshank's memories of Hooker strumming away in the back of the van. It is a beautiful slow blues, with the Hogs tastefully restrained backing working to great effect. The listener is transfixed as Hooker laments his 'five years of torture'. Strangely, the cut originally destined to be the title track, 'Seven Days And Seven Nights', doesn't stand out.

The album was released in the States under the title 'And Seven Nights' on the Verve-Folkways label and was quickly deleted. It finally got a UK release in 1971, probably because of the Groundhogs' success in the album charts. Sadly the album was thrown from pillar to post as all sorts of underhanded tactics manifested themselves. It was billed on one release as John Lee Hooker with John Mayall and the

JOHN LEE'S GROUNDHOGS

Meet JOHN LEE'S GROUNDHOGS! One of Britain's finest R&B groups. Famed for their fantastic backing work with Little Walter, Chuck Jackson and Memphis Slim they were hand picked to back both John Lee Hooker and Jimmy Reed on their entire tours here.
Now augmented to seven-piece with featured trumpet, sax and organ the group is regularly featured at London's famed Marquee Club.
You can count on the Groundhogs for up to 2½ hours of the most swinging R&B to be heard in Britain today.
For bookings please contact:
CANA VARIETY AGENCY, 43/44 ALBEMARLE STREET,
LONDON, W.1.   MAYfair 1436

Groundhogs (Mayall had nothing to do with the album). And, as Tony McPhee's sleevenotes reveal, even the music was changed to some degree: 'Although we did have a brass section later on in the original Hogs line-up, any versions you may have heard of songs from this album with brass had it added later by persons unknown.' In 1966, bizarrely, ex-Who producer Shel Talmy managed to acquire 'Mai Lee' and 'Don't Go Messing With My Bread' for his Planet label, but the single flopped.

John Lee's Groundhogs were now playing gigs at the famous Marquee club and it was here they met prolific producer Mike Vernon (1). He was impressed by their authentic blues and it wasn't long before he suggested they put a few tracks down at Decca studios in West Hampstead, London. They recorded 'Big Train Blues', 'Can't Sit Down' and Earl Hooker's 'Blue Guitar' and, although nothing came of these tracks, the latter ended up on a blues compilation in the 1970s.

It's important to note that in between Hooker's 1964 and 1965 tours the music scene in the UK changed in a way that spelt disaster for the blues. Another type of music had invaded these shores – it was called soul and it initiated big changes. Pete Townshend provided Charles Shaar Murray with the evidence: 'The irony was that they (US blues artists) all seemed too pathetic, John Lee Hooker in his checkered jacket, doing his cabaret...somehow they weren't able to attend to the quantum jump that we'd made.' (2)

But Bill Wyman of the Rolling Stones saw Hooker in 1969 and testified to the contrary: 'I took pictures from the side. He was an amazing performer, just him, and his guitar. He stood there with his chin pushed out, stamping his foot in rhythm – he looked like a god.'

One of the major attractions of soul was its dynamism and sex appeal epitomised by the godfather of soul, James Brown. Even the Rolling Stones abandoned their roots and it wasn't long before John Lee's Groundhogs did too!

The popularity of soul had the effect of gradually drying up gigs, as the blues clubs either closed down or jumped ship. This was especially acute outside London and, as Pete Cruickshank sums up, the band had no choice but to go along with it: 'We liked a track called "Further On Up The Road" by Bobby Bland, but we needed some brass to do it justice – so we acquired some. The soul period was my brother's influence; he liked James Brown a lot, it did put us on a more commercial path but we had to keep the work coming in.'

The shift to soul brought some problems to the surface in the band. Tom Parker left in early September to join the Mark Leeman Five (which included Brian Davison, later of the Nice). Short of a keyboard player, John Cruickshank phoned up Terry Goldberg, the previous Mark Leeman Five keyboard player, and offered him the job.

As Goldberg was looking for a gig, he accepted Cruickshank's offer and the informal transfer was complete. Goldberg's first job was to negotiate a week's tour of Scotland. But he never really settled down and only stayed a month. This ushered in a period when the band was without a regular keyboard player.

Around the same time that Parker left Dave Boorman vacated the drum stool. In fact, he was sacked. John Cruickshank reveals the reason why he had to go: 'Dave was a pain in the arse and by this time he was becoming very unprofessional.'

Roy Fisher, the band's first manager.
Pic courtesy Roy Fisher

Despite the apparently laid-back audience, at this time the Groundhogs were a dance band. Fred used to encourage this with wild dancing on the tables.
Pic courtesy Dave Boorman

DISC weekly

JANUARY 15, 1966   **6d**

WILL PAUL JONES GO SOLO?
see page 3

MICHELLE, SPENCER TOP!

THE UNTAMED
breaking in the charts with

"IT'S NOT TRUE"
c/w

'Gimme, gimme some shade'

PLF 103

PLANET

34 GREEK STREET,
LONDON, S.W.1.
REGENT 2148

JOHN LEE'S GROUNDHOGS
first release on Planet next week

"I'LL NEVER FALL IN LOVE AGAIN"
c/w

'Over you, baby'

PLF 104

Released on Shel Talmy's Planet label, 'I'll Never Fall In Love Again', had a positive reception... So did Paul Jones ever go solo?
Pic courtesy Pete Cruickshank

Single on the original Planet label.
TS Personal Collection

It fell to John to tell him he was out, but at least they didn't dump his drums on his doorstep! They even put a hilarious cover story out that Boorman had left to try his luck as a professional footballer. Delving into *Melody Maker* for a replacement, they chose Terry Slade, who by all accounts was a great drummer.

The shift to soul, although necessary, was not to everyone's liking. But Tony McPhee was quite philosophical about it: 'The blues clubs were disappearing so I accepted the situation. It meant I had a lot less to do, as I tended to play more rhythm guitar. I remember very well when John came round to my house and excitedly told me he'd heard James Brown's "Papa's Got A Brand New Bag" and it had got a great guitar part. But when I heard it there was hardly anything in there.' However, they never really did become an out-and-out soul band as they merged it with the blues.

In an interview with James Johnson of *NME* in 1972, Tony admitted that he was never totally won over by soul and he was always looking over his shoulder at other bands who were still on the original path: 'The point was the Yardbirds went on to become better while we got stuck into this soul thing. I was watching how well the Yardbirds were

doing while I was plugging along with "In The Midnight Hour". It was a bit sick.' In fact, the Yardbirds had bailed out from blues and were treading a path towards pop.

Shortly after their switch to soul they went into Regent Sound in Denmark Street, London, to record a couple of demos. They recorded 'Someone To Love' and 'Hallelujah'. The former is a rollicking adventure with brass to the fore

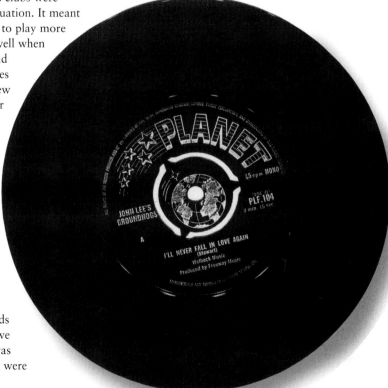

34

and John Cruickshank's expressive vocals. Bob Hall returned to play some piano for them. The latter is a lot more downbeat.

Years later someone suggested to Tony that he had written 'Hallelujah'. His reply was emphatic: 'I would never write a song with such a title'. In fact it was originally called 'The Storm Is Passing Over' and is an obscure track recorded by the Sensational Nightingales. Bob Hall had bought it when he was a student and nobody else had heard it before. It was, however, around this time that Tony started to think about writing his own songs.

Roy Fisher tried to get Shel Talmy, who was still trying to get his fledgling Planet label off the ground, interested in the band. Glyn Johns, who engineered the session, recommended they do 'I'll Never Fall In Love Again'.

It's a shame the single didn't make an impact because right from the first crack of Terry Slade's snare drum it's a tour de force. Again the brass is prominent. This consisted of David Ware on trumpet and Fred (they never did find out his surname) on sax and they sound a great combination. But it is obvious that Tony is less employed than hitherto.

Reviews were very good. The 28th January 1966 edition of *New Musical Express* filed it under 'Recommended' and trumpeted: 'One of our most underrated R & B groups...bouncy, full of the joys of living. Features the throaty, infectious tones of the leader with soul band.' *Record Mirror* weighed in heavily: 'One of the great sense of blues selling by the lead voice, with smartly laid down backing. Nice tempo; workmanlike all the way. Could catch on.'

Perhaps one of the reasons it didn't catch on was because of the saucy references to a 16 year-old girl. Talmy was uncomfortable with the subject-matter but it didn't stop the record being released. The significance of the flip side is that it's the first song written by Tony McPhee committed to vinyl and displays his acute sense of humour. The title 'Over You Baby' is a play on words and can be interpreted in different ways, a ploy he would use for future titles.

In early 1966 Terry Slade left the band. He'd had a better offer from a band called Sunshine who had got a deal with Warners and, after a short search, Colin Huntley became the last drummer for John Lee's Groundhogs. It was decided that they finally fill the vacant keyboard slot too. Mick Humbey duly took Goldberg's place in the band; he got the job because Terry Goldberg was always going on about the virtues of the Hammond organ, which was then very much in vogue, with Georgie Fame and Graham Bond making the instrument famous.

The Hogs were really keen to get Humbey, even though he was the least proficient keyboard player in their history. They told him that he could earn £8 a week and, on the strength of this untruth, Humbey went out and bought the expensive Hammond on hire purchase.

In early February 1966 Tony was invited to record with Champion Jack Dupree on a Mike Vernon-produced album, From 'New Orleans To Chicago'. Initially he was due to play electric lead on all the tracks, but the session was given an extra edge when Eric Clapton turned up. Obviously room had to be found for him and it resulted in Tony playing less lead.

John Cruickshank at the Marquee, Wardour Street, 1965.
Photo Leroy Artiste Publicity Ltd.
TS Personal Collection

Coincidentally, in August of the previous year Clapton had left Mayall's Bluesbreakers to go round the world with some of his musician friends (they got as far as Greece).

As Tony recalls, it all started at a gig: 'Mayall was playing at the Ricky Tick, Windsor. I met Eric there and he told me he had made enough money and wanted to go on a world trip. He mentioned that John was a megalomaniac. I wasn't interested. Mayall came to my Tooting home and offered me the job for £40 a week. He even said the blues can be boring but I play things in different keys. He then tried to get my mum to get me to join when I went to the toilet – I still wasn't interested.' It turned out to be a wise move in the end as Peter Green took the job but was kicked out as soon as Clapton returned.

The Dupree recordings took place at Central Sound Studios in Denmark Street, London. Tony plays slide guitar on two tracks, 'Third Degree' and 'Shim, Sham, Shimmy'. Clapton plays lead on both cuts with Keef Hartley on drums. Tony plays acoustic guitar on the rest of the tracks with Dupree on piano. Tony remembers 'Going Down To Big Leg Emma's' very well, and describes the impromptu nature of the sessions:

'Jack had written the song, but before we recorded it he wanted to improvise the lyrics. He started off with the first line and asked me to come up with something that would fit, but I couldn't do it. He was a very nice man and Clapton was very easy to work with.' The late Gus Dudgeon, who went on to fame with Elton John in the 1970s, engineered the session. The album was released in April 1966.

The extent to which John Lee's Groundhogs altered their sound can be summed up from an incident at the Cromwellian club, London. Tony painfully relates it: 'I thought the gig was dire and during the set the manager came up to me and said "What band's this?" I told him and he said "It isn't, I saw John Lee's Groundhogs play with Hooker and it isn't the same band", and told us to pack up.'

To Tony it was a blunt reminder of just how far he had moved from his blues roots. However, John Cruickshank had this to say about this

period: 'Tony was the only one in the band who was against the shift to soul. We were playing great and going down a storm most places we played.' To complete the misery for Tony, as they were packing away the gear a cocky young man with a Hohner Pianet under his arm told them to get off the stage. That man was Reg Dwight, later to become Elton John. Tony never did like him after that and, when a few years later, they were both on the same bill, he deliberately ran over time (the only time he ever did) just to annoy the headlining be-sequinned 'superstar'.

It was spring of 1966 and the band was going nowhere fast. They were even introduced by Rod Stewart at the Marquee as the Groundhogs Big Band! It was the final humiliation for Tony. It was difficult to believe that less than a year before they were backing the great John Lee Hooker on a major tour of the UK. The final straw was when John Cruickshank decided he'd had enough of touring. He was a married man and a father and didn't want that lifestyle any more. The last gig was an all-nighter at the Battersea Town Hall. Tony knew it was all slipping away long before all of this. He had had enough anyway, but he hadn't got a clue exactly what he was going to do next.

When Clapton took a sabbatical, Tony was asked to replace him. For better or worse, he declined.
TS Personal Collection

Ex-Yardbird joins John Mayall

Eric "Slowhand" Clapton, former lead guitarist with the Yardbirds, replaces Roger Dean who is leaving John Mayall's Bluesbreakers.

chapter 5
Have Guitar Will Travel

'Jo Ann Kelly was remarkable as a vocalist and guitarist who gained immense respect for her authentic grasp of a musical genre dominated by men.'
Tony McPhee writing about his dear friend

Just after the Hogs disbanded Tony went into the studio with Mike Vernon to record a couple of singles. Vernon had just launched his own Purdah label and was keen to increase the catalogue. But it was no ordinary label; it was more of a cottage industry. Only 99 copies were pressed of any single in order to avoid tax and that's why these singles are so rare today. Some big names succumbed to Vernon's charms including Eric Clapton, John Mayall and Savoy Brown. The Decca studio was technically at Vernon's disposal to audition new bands, but he used his initiative and launched his own concern.

These tracks represent Tony McPhee's first solo venture. He recruited his old mate, Pete Cruickshank on bass and another old mate, Bob Hall (piano) plus Vaughan Rees (drums). Tony didn't know Rees as he was brought in by Vernon. What gave the session extra edge was that Tony was taking lead vocals for the first time in his career. Considering the short duration of the session, these are assured performances. They recorded 'Ain't Gonna Cry No More', 'Someone To Love Me', 'You Don't Love Me' and 'When You Gotta A Good Friend' (Bob Hall is not on the last one).

The recordings were released as two singles in July 1966 (probably recorded in June). The standout track is 'Someone To Love Me' and this includes a great rhythm backing and some spirited lead from Tony. He purloined the riff off Charley Patton. Tony is the first one to admit that contemporary blues songs were rarely totally original.

The session with Vernon is also notable because this is where Tony acquired his TS moniker. It was Vernon's idea; he liked the idea of

Pete, Mike Meekham and Tony in a publicity flier for their first single. Regency jackets were high fashion.
TS Personal Collection

GET A DOSE...
...of HERBAL MIXTURE
FIRST Columbia DISC 'A love thats died' 'Tailor Made'
RIK GUNNELL AGENCY GER.1001.
47 GERRARD STREET
LONDON W1

DATE WITH 208

Hi there, folks. Well, the big day is drawing near and by n should have most of your Christmas cards and presents re: posting. Course, you're bound to have forgotten to send a someone, but you won't remember who it is until you rece from them. Then it's all down to rushing out, buying an ext and getting it posted. Don't worry too much, it happens to O.K., now on to the news of the week.

★ ★ ★ TUESDAY 13th ★ ★ ★

FIRST and foremost let's go straight in with the disc I've chosen for my pick of the week.

It's not, as you might have imagined, a Christmassy record. No, I don't go for all those mushy records that keep trying to convince you that there is a Santa Claus and he rides through the skies on his sleigh pulled by Rudolph the red-nosed reindeer. They're not for me!

Record of the week in Perry's book is by a group who call themselves The Herbal Mixture and they've come up with a rather weird thing entitled *Machines*.

One strange feature of this talented trio is that two of them, Tony McPhee and Peter Cruickshank, are both vegetarians and they're currently doing their best to get the third member, Michael Meekham to join them.

And, from what I hear they're slowly succeeding, even though it is just a little against Mike's will.

Reason for the vegetarian bit is that when Tony left school he worked for the G.P.O. and one of his first deliveries was to a slaughter-house. What he saw put him off the idea of eating meat and sure enough he's never touched it since.

Anyway now his G.P.O. days are over and Tony and his two mates could be well on the way to a big career in the pop business.

Your job is to take a listen to their disc on David Jacobs' show tonight.

Radio Luxembourg picked 'Machines' as their single of the week.
TS Personal Collection

(1) When Immediate Records was liquidated in 1970 Tony was approached by the liquidators and offered the princely sum of £43 for his contribution. He told them to shove it!

using initials for a stage name such as JB Lenoir, and asked Tony what his middle name was (it's Charles) but Tony didn't like that idea because TC was also the name of a famous cartoon character, Top Cat.

Vernon suggested TS instead, and Tony thought no more of it until the initials appeared on a US album sleeve. After that the name stuck. But when Tony later phoned Vernon about royalties, he was only able to speak to his secretary. She had a brief consultation with Vernon who told her to tell Tony that the TS stood for tough shit!

However, there is a postscript to the story. In 1968 the four tracks appeared on a best selling blues compilation album called 'Blues Anytime Vols 1 & 2'. (1)

Around this time Alexis Korner asked Tony to go on the road with him. Korner was still doing his *Five O'Clock Club* on television. This was an amazing show, and demonstrates what a smooth operator Korner was to persuade the BBC to include a blues segment in a children's television show.

He asked Tony to meet him at the Giaconda Cafe in Denmark Street in a 'couple of weeks' to discuss things. The problem was that Tony forgot to make the meeting and it turned out that Korner didn't forgive people who missed appointments. He heard later from other musicians that Korner had told them not to trust Tony McPhee. It didn't diminish the respect he had for the great old bluesman, however.

By July, Tony was struggling to maintain his professional status. In the nick of time he received a call from Dave Nicholson, who was manager of a band called Truth. He was looking for a guitarist. They had recently had a hit with a version of the Beatles song 'Girl' and their current single was a version of the Kinks' 'I Go To Sleep'. Tony was impressed with the single

and joined the band. Desperate times called for desperate measures! The nucleus of Truth was two singers: Frank Aiello, who ended up in Cozy Powell's Bedlam, and Steve Jameson, who had a hit as Nosmo King.

Tony was part of a backing trio that was made up of Ray Stock on drums and Dennis Taylor on bass. McPhee was in the band for a couple of months in total; he played a lot of gigs but never made any recordings with them.

McPhee's career was clearly lacking direction and his next job, though very interesting, illustrated the point. He got a call from Tom Parker, who offered work with Boz and the Boz People, which included getting paid 30 shillings for rehearsing. They had just secured the support slot for a Dusty Springfield tour in early September.

Boz later ended up in King Crimson and later became Bad Company's singer/bassist, but in those days he didn't play an instrument. Tony got on well with him and things were soon looking up. The tour started on 12th September at the Astoria, London, and initially they travelled in luxury in manager Basil Charles-Dean's Van Den Plas Princess.

However, later in the tour the car was 'misused' by Boz and they found themselves travelling in a Mini. At the tour's conclusion it was obvious to McPhee that he couldn't maintain his professional status. He was forced to go back to regular employment in September 1966.

Tony got a job with Pullmans who specialised in the maintenance of dictating machines. The company was situated in Old Street, London. But it wasn't long before he launched his own band, albeit part-time. The name Herbal Mixture was inspired by his vegetarianism and his interest in alternative medicine.

He didn't have to think about who was going to play bass. Tony had retained Roy Fisher as manager, so Fisher fired off a call to Pete Cruickshank. As it turned out Cruickshank was still playing pro, but in the most bizarre of circumstances, as he recalls:

'After John Lee's Groundhogs split up I got a job in a seven piece Jamaican band called Ossie Lane and the Red Hot Band. I can't remember how I got the job but I think it was because I had a certain pedigree. I was the only white guy and my nickname was 'Spooky'. We played Jamaican clubs and I had a great time.' The call from Tony put an end to that gig. Even though Pete had to go back to working nine to five, he'd had enough of Ossie's band anyway.

They recruited 17 year-old Mike Meekham on drums from the *Melody Maker* classified ads section. He had a Keith Moon 'I'm here' style, according to Pete Cruickshank. This was essential because playing in a three-piece meant they could not carry any passengers and Pete remembers Meekham as a fine drummer.

They started off doing soul, a lot of Sam and Dave numbers, which Tony liked. They also did 'I'll Keep On Holding On' by the Marvelettes. However, the psychedelic era of rock was kicking in and other influences would soon make their mark. They were quickly signed by Columbia and it wasn't long before they went into the studio. This was partly due to Bruce Higham, who Roy Fisher had approached to be the co-manager of the band. The recordings highlighted a few problems, as Tony wasn't sure whether to handle the vocals. At one stage Roy Fisher suggested they try out a singer he knew. Rab Monroe did indeed record a couple of demos but they got rid of him because Tony thought he wasn't very good.

They went into IBC studios, Portland Street, to record the McPhee-penned tracks 'A Love That's Died' and 'Tailor Made'. Both of these cuts are what could be called 'rockers' and the band is very together. The former has a great intro that sounds rather like Pink Floyd, except that this was months before the Floyd ever went into a studio. This might have improved if the haunting intro had been reprised. Still, it's a solid debut but clearly a band at the learning stage. The flipside is a really catchy tune, making it a value for money coupling. Norman Jopling reviewed 'A Love That's Died' in the 15th October edition of *Record Mirror*: 'Quaintly named, starts most promisingly but it deteriorates into a rather routine performance and song.'

The next single they recorded was a much more significant piece of work. 'Machines' is the first social comment that Tony ever wrote. It's a statement that there is more to life than working a machine in a factory. It underlines his determination not to succumb to that life. But as he remembers, there was another aspect to this song that the 1980s brought to fruition: 'In those days there was the idea of having a job for life. I didn't believe in lifelong security and I was shown to be right later.'

'Machines' is also memorable for an excellent guitar solo. The intro is very interesting as he played A and A flat together, creating a beat note, and, when fed through his self-built distortion unit in his Vox amp, this created an unique sound. Listening to this band's work the most satisfying aspect is that Tony establishes himself as a vocalist with a distinctive voice. Strangely, he was inspired later on by an unlikely source in his determination to be a singer, as he reveals: 'Hendrix had always said he couldn't sing, so I thought I'll do it too.'

'Machines' was released in December and *Record Mirror* was enthusiastic: 'Good bluesy sound on this jerky, somewhat unbalanced slice of earthiness. May get lost: but plugging could help it through.' Even better was *New Musical Express* who picked it as their record of the week! The review ends by urging people to listen to the record when it's aired on *Juke Box Jury*, which was the legendary television pop show hosted by David Jacobs, although it never got an airing as far as is known.

Glyn Johns was engineering the sessions; he also worked with the Who. He regaled the band with stories of Pete Townshend and Keith Moon ripping the towel dispensing machine off the wall and smashing mirrors in the studio toilet. Tony was baffled: 'I enjoyed the stories but my initial reaction was "Why?" I have never done anything like that on the road or anywhere else.' Although he enjoys the practical jokes, he was not into damage and demolition.

Tony with Harmony guitar.
Pict Sam McPhee
TS Personal Collection

Apart from the influence of John Lee Hooker, Jimi Hendrix and Hubert Sumlin, Tony's technique for writing entailed playing random chords until he came across something that sounded unusual. This is what interested him and ensured he had a better chance of creating something that was different. Well, that was the theory. It didn't always work early on, but this technique paid supreme dividends a little later. However, the lyrics didn't come easy. He usually left this to the last minute, but it was a bad move on the 'Machines' session, for which Glyn Johns was paid a stupendous £4 per hour.

Tony needed lyrics, and fast. He went to the toilet, sat down on the seat in the foetal position and had a brainstorming session. That later became a favourite place for writing lyrics. Tony wanted to fade out repeating the line 'vegetable matter' over and over, but Johns persuaded him not to. In this fledgling writing period Tony never was able to create a unique sound for Herbal Mixture, although he made a brave attempt.

As well as the material they recorded Tony had other self-penned songs they played live. 'Mr McGhee' was important because it was the first song that he wrote with an interesting chord change. The song's subject matter was the world of advertising. There was no Mr McGhee, it was a name that Tony plucked out of the air.

Another song was 'Eleven Year Old Man' and this one was about a rather simple-minded individual. 'Spontaneity' was another song they played live, but was never finished to Tony's satisfaction and every performance had different lyrics. As a result of limited studio opportunities, these songs went unrecorded.

It was clear they hadn't got an original sound that would put them ahead of the pack, so Roy Fisher set about giving the band an edge. Tony remembers his embarrassment when he recalls how it came about: 'I had a call from Roy who said we had a gig at Middle Earth. I said great, but then he told me he'd told them that we were different. He said we had to dress up like we did that time at Jo Ann Kelly's flat.' What happened then was they raided her wardrobe and put on some of her clothes for a laugh. Now they had to appear in public like that.

They got behind the idea and went to junk shops and bought pith helmets, beads, old ladies' hats and anything else they could wear. Tony even made himself a pair of Bermuda shorts from a cushion cover. However, as Pete Cruickshank remembers, it got worse than that: 'I had a green sparkly face and I dyed my hair

copper. My sister helped me on that one. Strangely, I met my wife when I had that face on. Looking back, it was all a bit embarrassing.'

Tony was still at the day job but he found solace in the work place with a strategically placed radio and this was to unexpectedly play a part in shaping the band's repertoire. Something came on the radio that hit him like a ton of bricks, so he turned it up full blast. It didn't last long at this level as his co-workers soon turned it down, but he thought the song was awesome. The record was 'Hey Joe' by Jimi Hendrix and it was soon incorporated into the act, along with Tim Rose's 'Morning Dew'. This was the time that they started to move away from soul, as a lot of bands were doing. Another band Tony liked were Soft Machine; they were playing the most incredible jazz-rock.

By early 1967 they were still raiding junk shops for unusual clothes. Now and again they would get the dreaded call from Roy Fisher, who was also a photographer. He would tell them that he needed more pictures. They'd drive to Hyde Park and change into their gear, emerging from the back of the van like bizarre butterflies. They would then spend the next hour skulking around having their photos taken not only by Fisher but also by bemused Japanese tourists.

Tony was still keeping busy on the session front. The Mike Vernon connection paid dividends as he was drafted in to play on an Eddie Boyd album. On 21st March 1967 he

Publishing contract with Jack Dupree.
TS Personal Collection

Publisher's Name **GETAWAY SONGS LTD.**

Address **Clifford House, 15 Clifford Street, London. W.1.**

Date **1st May 1967**

To the Secretary,
THE PERFORMING RIGHT SOCIETY, LTD.,
29/33 BERNERS STREET,
LONDON, W.1.

Notice of agreement to vary the division of fees, pursuant to Rule 5 (f) of P.R.S. Rules.

We, the undersigned, desire to notify you that we have agreed that all fees payable by the Society in respect of performances on and after **1st May** 19**67** of the work(s) entitled :—

"GET YOUR HEAD HAPPY" "NO MEAT BLUES" "TALK ALL IN MY SLEEP" "EASY IS THE WAY" "THERE'S A DEAD CAT ON THE LINE" "SNOW IS ON THE GROUND"

shall be divided between us in the following proportions instead of in the normal proportions specified in the Society's authorised plan of division of fees for British works, namely, for original works, two-thirds to the writer or writers and one-third to the publisher, or, for arrangements of non-copyright music, as provided in the plan of divisions for graded works.

	General fees	Broadcasting fees	Film fees
Composer share, or (if an arrangement of non-copyright music) arranger share	25%	25%	25%
Author share	25%	25%	25%
Publisher share	50%	50%	50%

and we hereby authorise and request the Society to act accordingly.

It is understood that the share of any signatory hereto who is not a member of the Society or of any of its affiliated societies shall in respect of all performances prior to the distribution period during which he is elected to membership of any such society, be paid to the publisher where the latter is the assignee of the performing right.

Signature(s) of Composer(s) or (if an arrangement of non-copyright music) of Arranger *[signature]* **JACK DUPREE**

Signature of Author(s) *[signature]* **TONY MCPHEE**

Publisher *[signature]* **GETAWAY SONGS LTD.**

NOTE 1.—This notice is subject to the rules 1 (e) and 5 (f) of the Society's Rules, which are as follows:—

Rule 1 (e) states that a "Publisher", in respect of any work the performing right in which has been assigned to or otherwise vested in the Society, means any Member who has acquired the publishing right or licence in the work and who has printed and published the work in the normal manner customary in the music trade or has himself otherwise exploited the work for the benefit of the persons interested therein.

Rule 5(f) states that in any variation from the normal basis of division the share of the publisher and/or proprietor of the performing right SHALL NOT EXCEED ONE HALF OF THE NET FEE, except in the case of a work being an arrangement of non-copyright music, in which case the share of any person interested shall not be less than three-fourths of the share attributable to him under the normal basis of division.

NOTE 2.—For the purposes of this notice, the word "performances" shall include broadcasts and transmissions by a rediffusion service; and "performing" shall have a corresponding meaning.

In order to get a gig, Roy Fisher suggested they 'dress up'...so they did!
Pic Roy Fisher
TS Personal Collection

played slide guitar on 'Dust My Broom' and 'Save Her Doctor'. The album was packed with luminaries such as Peter Green and John McVie. A lot of the recordings that big name blues artists were making at that time simply came about very informally. The way it worked was that a producer like Vernon would offer a couple of hundred pounds to make an album, so it was done in rapid time.

In April 1967 Tony teamed up with Champion Jack Dupree, Mike Vernon again producing. They went into a studio near Islington, London, where they recorded 13 original cuts. Apart from a couple, these tracks were never released and have since been gathering dust. The tracks were credited to Jack Dupree and Tony McPhee; although Tony didn't have any part in the writing, Dupree was generous enough to cede half the credit. The tapes have recently been discovered by Vernon and in 2004 Tony McPhee signed a contract with Dupree's daughter in order that they can be released. (2)

Gigs were always in short supply, although they did play the Marquee club four times. At the Roundhouse, they supported the legendary Jeff Beck Group which was making a dry run for Led Zeppelin in the blues-rock stakes. Luckily, by this time, the crazy clothes had been abandoned for Regency style, then the height of fashion. Tony was so broke he had to ask Beck if he had a spare first string, as he had snapped his.

(2) The tracks recorded were 'Get Your Head Happy', 'No Meat Blues', 'Talk All In My Sleep', 'Easy Is The Way', 'There's A Dead Cat On The Line', 'Snow Is On The Ground', 'Sick In Bed', 'Papa Told Mama', 'Who Was There A While Ago', 'Down In Clarksdale', 'Don't Cut Me Out', 'My Home In Mississippi', and 'My Baby Told Me'.

The band was drifting along now and seemed to be going nowhere. Worse was to come because Mike Meekham was infatuated with his girlfriend and she was always trying to dissuade him from playing the drums.

It came to a head when he was late for a gig at the Marquee on 16th December. The manager of the club, John Gee, went berserk and that was more or less it. The band limped on until the early summer of 1968 when Tony had an interesting offer to join the John Dummer Band. Dave Kelly, who played guitar in the outfit, recalls how it came about: 'I asked Mac if he fancied joining the Dummer Band. I'd joined about a year earlier as singer and slide guitarist. Then the lead guitarist was Roger Pearce, but he left quite soon as I don't think he liked the less 'modern' direction the band was going in. I thought Mac had nothing planned at that time, we (Dummer Band) had a record deal, and I thought we needed a lead guitarist, a bloody good one.

'Also we were friends. Mac shared the vocals, with myself in the band.' For a short while Tony was in two bands. But he was still loyal to Pete Cruikshank and Mike Meekham as he stipulated to Kelly that if Herbal Mixture took off he would leave to go full-time with them. But shortly after this Herbal Mixture folded.

As well as John Dummer on drums there was also Thumper Thompson on bass (they went on to form the rock'n'roll revivalists Darts in the 1970s). Dave Kelly was still quite young and inexperienced and his exuberance got them into trouble at a gig in London, as Tony recalls: 'We played a gig with Sam Apple Pie at their own club. At the end of their set they played an Elmore James number that we played in our set. Dave Kelly heard this and said "Let's show them how it's really done". My heart sank, as I don't like that sort of thing. I knew it would end in disaster and it did! We were total shit, we even started off in the wrong key.'

Dave Kelly also recalls these events: 'Yes, they were getting on my nerves, I thought they were pretty basic. I don't know why they bothered booking other bands as all their mates (90% of the audience) wanted to hear was them. However, longevity of career has proved my point I think.

'Was the Dummer Band shit? Probably not one of our better gigs; we had the ability to be absolutely brilliant or absolute crap and at the time I didn't know enough to put my finger on what happened to make the difference.'

In spite of the odd disaster the band was building up quite a name in the blues world and on 2nd July 1968, they appeared on a *Top Gear* radio session. Just after that session they recorded the album called 'Cabal'. Tony was pleased as Jo Ann Kelly was also involved and he always liked working with her.

The original John Lee's Groundhogs pianist, Bob Hall, Jack (sax) and Brian (trumpet) also joined the sessions. The songs are a curious mix of the old and the new. There are songs by John Lee Hooker, Little Walter and Willie Dixon, as well as new material by Dave Kelly. Even Tony's early solo Mike Vernon period is reprised with 'When You Gotta Good Friend', but at a faster tempo. Dave Kelly explains how he came to get a writing credit:

'This 'old song by Tony' was in fact a much older song by Robert Johnson. At that time Johnson's songs were up for grabs as the copyright laws weren't as protective as they are now. Presumably Mac had 'trad arranged' his version. The version by the Dummer Band was my arrangement.'

There's even space for some solid social comment in the 1930s song 'Welfare Blues' and this features a great vocal from Tony. The lead guitar duties were shared as Dave Kelly is an accomplished guitarist in his own right.

He recalls how they divided the solos: 'We had some songs prepared and busked some in the studio, some with Jo on vocals. I don't remember how we worked out who would play lead, it just worked out organically – horses for courses, etc.

'I remember more the recording of our first single 'Travellin' Man', which was a John Lee Hooker song, with me taking the Hooker lead vocal and Mac taking the middle vocal part a la Eddie Kirkland.' The highlight of Tony's contributions is 'After Hours'. It might not be the best track but it features a gutsy vocal and a storming guitar solo. Tony was into new territory on this album and he thought some of it was false. He remembers they did three versions of one track, then spliced the best bits of each one to make a hybrid. He wasn't keen on this.

'Cabal' was originally scheduled for a September release but it was delayed for a few months until January 1969. *New Musical Express* was gushing about it: '(the group) really gets an exciting, pulsating rhythm going, and the vocalist, Dave Kelly, really gets out his message. Great party maker.' *Melody Maker* added the good and the bad: 'The band achieves just the right balance and swing, handling even the difficult slow-medium tempo well. Though they have mastered the (blues) idiom, their influences are too obvious and they lack vocal flexibility.'

The record still stands up today and can be considered a great blues album. There are some top-class performances. Apart from the lead guitars, the music is superbly supplemented by Bob Hall's piano and John O'Leary's harmonica, creating a dense sound. Tony McPhee left as soon as the album was recorded because he had an offer to go to United Artists. His departure was so swift he doesn't even appear on the album cover, on which his place was taken by Adrian 'Putty' Pietryga.

When Tony departed the band he left with a new partner. Christine Payne had previously gone out with John Dummer and Dave Kelly. Tony wasn't even looking for someone permanent but they hit it off well. They were to be married a few years later.

The way Tony McPhee got involved with United Artists is the epitome of serendipity. Roy Fisher recalled that came about through his desire to rent a studio in Ebury Street, London, to shoot music videos: 'At that time music videos were starting to be the big thing but there were not a lot of video recording studios and I thought this place would be good for that purpose. I contacted the man that owned the building and, on meeting him, explained my plan for a video studio. He let me sign a six-month lease on the understanding that I would need time to raise the capital to develop the idea.

'It was on contacting companies in the entertainment business to see if they would be interested in investing in my plan that I met with Andrew Lauder, then head of A&R at Liberty. In conversation I mentioned managing the Groundhogs during the time they backed John Lee Hooker and he said he had seen a couple of the shows and asked what the band were doing now as he would be interested in offering them a record deal.' The rest, as they say, is history.

Roy Fisher immediately phoned Tony at work and asked for a meeting at a cafe near Green Park tube station, the conversation centering on re-forming the Groundhogs. Seconds after Tony heard the offer he effectively turned pro and didn't even go back to work in the afternoon. He handed his notice in with the Dummer Band, and then rescued Pete Cruickshank from a building site. They got Steve Rye, who was a friend of Jo Ann Kelly, on harmonica. The only slot left to fill was the drummer. But that would remain a problem until quite late in the day.

This offer was especially fortuitous because blues was back in vogue again, or a hybrid version of it. Fleetwood Mac had formed the year before and they were playing what was called blues-rock with great success and it wasn't very long before Jimmy Page formed Led Zeppelin from the ashes of the Yardbirds. It hadn't been long before that there was only John Mayall and one or two others on the original blues path.

Dave Kelly stayed in the John Dummer Band for a while longer. He went on to have a successful career, notably as a solo artist and in the legendary Blues Band with Paul Jones. 'Mac was the greatest influence on me in my early days of learning to play blues. He showed me how to tune the guitar to open tuning, gave me my first slide and sold me my first decent acoustic guitar.

'I loved, and still do, his quirky style of playing lead – totally unlike all of his contemporaries. He didn't do the usual BB/Freddie King style but I thought played more in the style of Hubert 'sublime' Sumlin. You ask me about Mac as a guitarist and my first feeling is the same when people constantly refer to me as a guitarist – what about the vocals?!'

With the formation of a new Groundhogs, Roy Fisher put into action some more projects: 'I originated the idea of the "Groundhog Series" of albums and put the idea to Andrew Lauder. I also

Old 'Mutton Chops' at Conway Hall in London, backing Champion Jack Dupree.
TS Personal Collection

devised the concept of each album and got the artistes together who recorded on them. They were mostly artistes we already knew from the London blues/folk clubs that Jo Ann Kelly was playing. Tony did the production work. We gave them the opportunity to record for a major label, then got accused of ripping them off because they didn't get any royalties. They did not realise that the albums did not sell enough to even cover the recording costs! They were only meant to help them get more gigs.'

The first of these projects was a compilation album called 'Me And The Devil' and it was scheduled before the Groundhogs went into the studio. The album was produced by Mike Batt (3) and was recorded at Marquee studios in September 1968. There was quite a talented roster of artists assembled, including Jo Ann Kelly, Dave Kelly, Andy Fernbach and, of course, Tony McPhee. Tony's original idea was get a small audience into the studio to give it more of a live feel. However, Batt didn't think much of that idea and, although the technicians tried a few claps, it was quickly dropped.

Tony appears on four tracks playing acoustic and slide guitar on the title cut, 'No More Doggin', 'Death Letter' and 'Rollin And Tumblin' – the latter was with Jo Ann Kelly who provides a riveting vocal performance. In 1998 Tony had this to say about Jo Ann in the sleeve notes of the re-issue: '(she) was remarkable as a vocalist and guitarist who gained immense respect for her authentic grasp of a musical genre dominated by men, and was almost certainly the only white British female playing acoustic slide guitar.'

The sleevenotes for the original album were written by Mike Raven and he asked the million dollar question 'How can a well-fed, well educated, young white musician ever do justice to a music originated by starving illiterate middle aged Negroes from the Deep South?'

The question was mainly pointed at the vocals. How, do you put across human suffering with conviction? At the end of the year Tony got his chance to answer the question in an interview with *Melody Maker*: 'I think you can compare it with the instrumental side of the blues. It's like copying Hubert Sumlin's sound on guitar. I don't put anything on for the blues. I try not to copy anybody in particular when I'm singing but I like the way Son House uses words and that influences me. It's a way of using words; you bend them like you do a note on a guitar. Really it's no effort for me. I couldn't sing any other way, not on blues, without having to think hard about it.'

'Me And The Devil' is a solid collection of songs but, much to Tony's disappointment, wasn't a sales success. However, he didn't have time to dwell on that as, with the Groundhogs' first visit to the studio due in the next few weeks, he would soon have to fill the drum stool.

The man he chose, Ken Pustelnik, was born on Friday 13th March 1946 near Blairgarry, on a farm in the highlands of Scotland. His grandfather had been a regimental sergeant major in the legendary Black Watch and a pipe major in the Scots Greys. He later played jazz drums and his uncle was also a drummer. Ken only recently found out that his father was an American GI and had been a guitar player.

The family moved to Bristol in 1951, where Ken was brought up. When he was about ten he started listening to great jazz Hammond organ players Jimmy Smith and Jimmy McGriff. At the time he enjoyed the sound. He also liked country blues and the mountain music of the Appalachian variety, the Carter Family being particular favourites.

But it wasn't long before percussion influences imposed themselves. He heard a record on Radio Luxembourg called 'El Watusi' by Ray Barretto and that knocked him out. Barretto's bongos are heavily featured, and two men arguing complement these furious sounds:

'That was a great track,' he remembers. 'Looking back, it was an early version of rap.' He later found that Barretto, who was inducted into the International Latin Music Hall of Fame in 1999, had recorded many film soundtracks.

Later on, Ken got into Miles Davis and Charlie Mingus. He clearly had a voracious appetite for music that was drawn from the four corners of the world. By the time he was 18 he had formulated a theory that music happens geographically and that rhythms happen due to temperatures.

Vietnamese and Indian music was at the top of his list then. One of the albums that had the most influence on him was 'The Drums Of India'.

At this time Ken Pustelnik sported long hair before it was fashionable. He was in Bristol city centre when a guy came up to him and said 'I love your image, I want you to be my drummer'.

(3) Mike Batt was working for a publishing company called Metric Music. It was some time afterwards that he moved to Liberty (which became United Artists). He has become a highly successful composer, conductor and producer, most prominently with the Wombles, Art Garfunkel's 'Bright Eyes', *The Phantom Of The Opera* and *The Hunting Of The Snark*.

He describes what happened next: 'I went back to his house where he opened his garage door. It was full of equipment. I told him I didn't play the drums but he convinced me. His name was Alan Clarke and was a dead ringer for the Hollies' lead singer...even had the same name.' He scraped together £50 and bought his first drum kit, a Premier, which lasted until the first Groundhogs album.

Although there is a certain Pustelnik family legacy, he is completely self-taught. From the first time he put the kit together he sat down and just played instinctively. It wasn't long before Ken was playing drums in Clarke's band and he started to bring in his friends such as Rob Freeman. Over the passage of time Clarke was squeezed out leaving them with a lot of equipment. This band developed into the Deep Blues Band.

It was 1962 and they were still playing exclusively in the garage. They were into country blues and skiffle. Robert Johnson and Lonnie Donnegan were the ones they most revered. The frustration of not having any gigs led them to desperate measures. They decided to form their own blues club. It wasn't long before they had clubs in Bristol and Gloucester. They didn't even have a name beyond 'The Blues Club'.

It was very egalitarian and they would have free and easy slots where members of the audience would be invited to perform. It wasn't all low key, the clubs were also booking name bands like Fleetwood Mac and the John Dummer Band – it's possible Tony performed there later. There were always big crowds for these gigs as the area was so starved of name bands. But that was part of the problem, they had no contact with London and that was where it all happened. But that was soon to change.

The Deep Blues Band were avid readers of the music press and, in late 1967, there were plenty of exciting things to read. It was here that they found out about the plight of Memphis Minnie. The story reported she was unable to pay for the medical treatment she desperately required. The article reported there was going to be a benefit for her at Club 51, London. Not being well versed in the correct etiquette of such things they piled into their van on the appointed day and drove to London, in true hippy fashion. There was nobody there when they arrived.

As it was still early they decided to set up their gear. Nobody challenged them initially but eventually somebody did ask if they were the house band, to which they replied in the affirmative. Ken Pustelnik recalls these events:

'As it got dark the stars came out. John Mayall came in and introduced his hot new bassist, Andy Fraser. So they both played with us. Then Bob Hall played with us, Andy Fernbach and Dave Kelly were also there. For some reason Tony wasn't there.' The evening was a great success and raised a great deal of money.

The Deep Blues Band played the blues in a totally off the cuff fashion. They were out of the mainstream London circuit; they made their

statement without reference to anybody else around. Ken explains: 'The Deep was paying blues in a rockabilly style. Ours was more like a hoedown in Mississippi. We were like skiffle but we had electric instruments. The London-based bands played Chicago blues with loads of technique. It was a culture clash.'

However, in the wake of the benefit the Deep's personnel was frequently being raided by London-based bands. Ken patience was wearing thin, but then he received a phone call from Tony McPhee. What transpired was quite odd, as he recalls: '(Tony) said "I want you to join my band". So I said you've never seen me play. He was quite willing to go on the recommendation of Dave and Jo Ann Kelly. I didn't want to join without an audition.'

The audition was duly arranged at Club 51. As well as Tony and Pete, Roy Fisher was in attendance at the back of the hall. Ken, who didn't like 'accountant-like people in suits', remembers the magic of that evening and also what he brought to the band: 'When we started playing it was like "bang". Pete and Tony were die-hard musicians, I was more into avant-garde like Andy Warhol and Stockhausen. I am a sophisticated music person but a primitive drummer. So when I played it didn't come out like that because I stripped it down to its elements. That's why I hated drum solos.'

It was his unorthodox approach that impressed Tony.

Tony left before the 'Cabal' album was released so doesn't appear on the cover picture.
TS Personal Collection

Not a studio set-up. Camped out under a tree, we can only wonder at his life story.
TS Personal Collection

Tony McPhee with guitar strap characteristically over his right shoulder, a style he 'acquired' from John Lee Hooker.
Pic Michael Hasted
TS Personal Collection

This is the magic ingredient that Ken brought to the Groundhogs. In theory it couldn't work, but this was to give them something no other band had. However, the selection process irked Ken. He was asked to come back the following day to the club and, after much procrastination, he was invited to the Marquee studios. There was just one problem – he had never been in a studio before!

He was now a member of the Groundhogs and in 1971, at the height of the band's fame, he gave an interview to *Record Mirror*: 'It's about the only magical thing left. I'm not terribly romantic any more – I've been through it. And I haven't any more illusions about pop. I value it for what it's worth – I still go out to see groups.

'Playing is an attitude, I guess. I never really grew up and never will. At school, (at 18) when I first saw the old Groundhogs playing, I wrote their name on my haversack and I'm still basically a fan.'

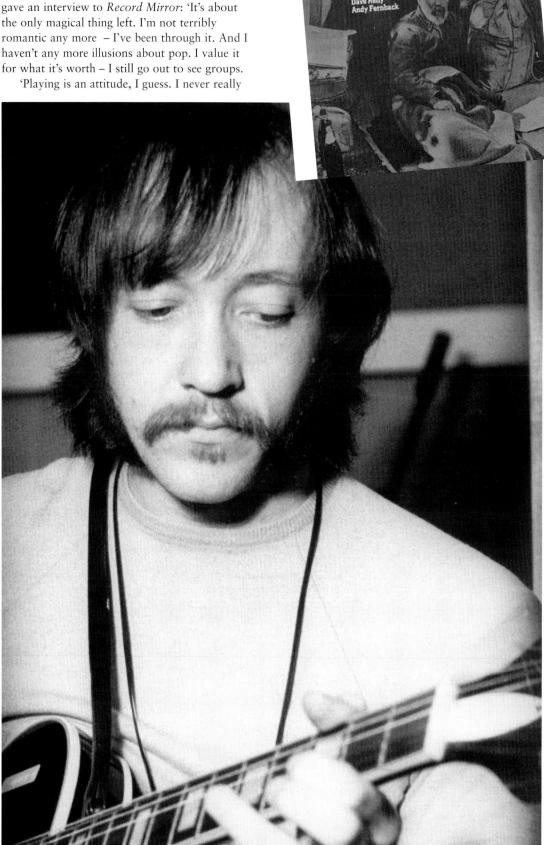

chapter 6
Light Was The Night

'I do think, and did then, that Tony is and was a superb talent, – very original and yet classic in his approach.'
Producer Mike Batt, 2004

'Tony is without doubt a genius and the best (bar none) bottleneck guitarist in Europe, let alone being a quite amazingly fast and accurate conventional guitarist.'
Journalist John Tobler writing in 1970

When Ken Pustelnik entered Marquee studios on 5th October 1968, it wasn't the only new experience for him that day, as he hadn't met all the band members. He was introduced to harmonica player Steve Rye just before they hit the first note. Unfamiliarity wasn't the only problem for the band as studio time was severely limited and, of course, they hadn't played any gigs together. The studio was four track (like most others at the time), and the situation didn't bode well for the new album. But with Mike Batt as their Liberty producer it didn't turn out so bad.

Tony McPhee was still in the early stages as a writer and only had two songs for the album. But this set up gave him the chance to develop fast. The first of his songs is 'Rocking Chair' and it's a solid opener with Tony's voice in fine form. In fact, he took all the lead vocals bar two. Steve Rye takes the lead on 'Early In The Morning', which is a traditional blues song. In listening to Rye's more conventional voice on that track, it does highlight what an interesting voice Tony possessed.

The other McPhee-penned track is 'Married Men'. It's odd because he can't recall why he chose that subject matter. He certainly wasn't married at that stage. The track is showcased by Rye's harmonica and Tony's restrained licks. Tony decided to resurrect 'No More Doggin' from the 'Me And The Devil' album. On that album he tackled it with his acoustic guitar, but here the band give it a new lease of life. It was played until the disbanding of the Groundhogs and remained a firm favourite with the fans.

The side two opener, 'Man Trouble', sees the rhythm section with its metronome recurring beat nailing everything down. Rye takes lead vocals again on 'You Don't Love Me', catchy but a million miles away from the album's final track 'Still A Fool', a great blues song with Tony singing about the downs of a relationship. 'Scratching The Surface' was released on Liberty in November 1968. Many years later it was reviewed by Dave Thompson of *Allmusic*: 'If you search for a fresh 'Cherry Red' or 'Status People' you'll probably be disappointed. But if you want to hear the blues sluicing

THE MAD FATMAN RIDES AGAIN!

THE **groundhogs**

HOPE HE MAKES IT TO YOUR HOUSE!

Christmas 1968 and any publicity is good publicity...

straight out of the Southern England Delta, there are precious few better introductions! "Scratching The Surface" ranks among the finest albums to emerge out of that entire period, a moody shuffle that includes an epic recounting of the Chicago classic "Still A Fool".'

The band has expressed disappointment with the finished result. It's true it isn't a polished album but what else could have been done under the constraints? Tony acknowledges there's a lot of mistakes on the album and describes it as 'conveyor belt stuff' but it does have its moments.

Mike Batt recalls the session: 'I remember the recording of the album at Marquee Studios, just behind the Marquee Club in Wardour Street. One of the songs was so long, and I was so tired, that I fell asleep over the recording desk during the take – so did the engineer – and we were woken by the band, who had finished the song and wanted to hear it back! Not the best way to show a band how much you care!'

All the band members recall that Batt didn't like the album. Andrew Lauder decided that it would be good to show the band in a pool of water. With that in mind they journeyed to Hampstead Pond with photographer Michael Hasted (1) and found a pool. It was freezing cold but the band waded in and proceeded to patiently pose for half an hour while the shots were taken. Pete Cruickshank looks like he's had enough and was taking steps to the bank – he really was on his way out!

However, Mike Batt was so impressed with Tony he decided to use him on his next project. Hapshash and the Coloured Coat was made up of the nucleus of artists Nigel Weymouth and Michael English who had made a debut album

described by some as a psychedelic classic. Interestingly, Batt pinpoints how good Tony was at interpreting what he wanted: '"Western Flyer" was recorded at Marquee Studios just after the first Groundhogs album. It was a bit experimental. I think I probably had "Music From Big Pink" (the Band) in my mind when I put that project together, as well as half a dozen other more psychedelic albums. I played piano, Tony played guitar.

'It was really exhilarating working on it, playing and producing. We would run through the songs probably once only, using chord sheets I'd prepared, and then we'd do a take, probably *the* take. Tony played some great stuff, very freaky, just right for what I wanted.

'Then I took the finished four-track tapes containing our rhythm-section performances, over the road to Trident Studios who had the only eight-track machine in town, and where the Beatles had just recorded "Hey Jude" – and we transferred the tapes to eight track, leaving four open tracks, which I used for weird-acid rocky effects like the girls singing and waving tinkly things.' The album was released in late 1968 but it didn't do very well.

Tony believes the value of regular sessions cannot be underestimated in his development as a musician: 'You have to think on your feet as you haven't got much time. When they start playing you have to follow. It certainly gives you confidence in your ability.' As Batt testified, Tony McPhee was a very experienced hand in the studio and most effective at doing exactly that.

The regular work continued when Andrew Lauder got Tony more work with another blues giant in the studio, but this time he was in a coordinator role.

(1) Michael Hasted had turned up at Andrew Lauder's office with his portfolio only a few days before the shoot, hustling for work. He was in luck!

Steve Rye, Pete Cruickshank, Tony McPhee, Ken Pustelnik. TS Personal Collection

Big Joe Williams was in the middle of touring the UK and had some free time between gigs. A deal was struck to record an album for Liberty. That it all happened so quickly can be judged by the fact that Tony had to borrow a Vox AC30 amp for Joe off Ken Pustelnik's flatmate Putty (Adrian Pietryga). He had been the guitarist in Ken's old band, the Deep. Roy Fisher recalls the casual nature of the session: 'We sat him in the studio, got the engineer to set up the equipment and let the tape run. He had half a bottle of Scotch and played non-stop till the bottle was empty and that was the album.'

As Big Joe was performing on his own, with no overdubs, Tony admits that there was not much work for him to do and, contrary to popular myth didn't perform on the album, although he wrote the sleeve notes. Tony describes the run-down nature of Big Joe's guitar in the notes: 'It is an incredibly dirty old Harmony Sovereign, which is the blues guitar next to the National, held together in parts with various forms of sticky tape.

'The three extra pegs required to make up the complement of nine strings are screwed to the top of the head. He uses a DeArmond pickup with volume control and a connecting lead which is patched up with insulating tape.' At the end of the session he told Tony it was the best recording he'd ever made.

Williams was a former cotton picker from the American South. He'd had a hard life and, clearly, had been treated badly for much of the time. His trademark was his walking stick, which had badges on of all the places he'd been to. He was quite a character and a nice guy, but he obviously overestimated Tony's standing when he asked him: 'Have you got a Model T Ford?' At the session's conclusion they had to get the amp and everybody else back home.

However, after they called one black cab they realised they needed another. Somebody suggested they call a minicab – on hearing this, the black cab driver indicated he wouldn't take them, there being fierce rivalry between the two types of hire car. An argument ensued and Tony recalled: 'Big Joe came up to the driver with his walking stick in hand and said "Get out of here!" The driver legged it!'

After all of these sessions it was time to get back to Groundhogs business. And what better way could there be than to re-acquaint themselves with John Lee Hooker? Hooker had written a letter prior to the tour asking for his old backing band for his first visit to the UK since 1965. Only Tony and Pete remained from the band that had toured with him previously, but Ken Pustelnik and Steve Rye were also to get on well with the great man.

The tour kicked off in late October 1968 and it was almost like the old days. Hooker had heard 'Scratching The Surface' (Tony took him into the studio and played him the whole album) and he recommended they release 'You Don't Love Me' as the single. They followed his advice!

Just after the tour started they played a double-header on 9th November. The early gig was at the Boston Gliderdrome, followed by a drive back to the Roundhouse where they were supporting Led Zeppelin – previously known as the New Yardbirds. Even though London was obviously the centre for all things, thanks to Ken Pustelnik's connections they were also getting gigs in the West Country. These were mainly in Bristol and Gloucester and some of these drew bigger crowds than the London gigs.

No-one could ever accuse Hooker of not giving enough 'air' for his band to breathe but that didn't interfere with him connecting to his audience, as Steve Rye once commented to Bob Brunning.

'I never saw him give a bad performance; there were good and extra good. He was very easygoing, very generous with solo time; he certainly didn't hog (pardon the pun) the stage in any way. But he had a lot of trouble with his tuning. In fact, Tony used to tune his guitar for him. Still, he was exciting, he always managed to win over young audiences.'

Hooker was a big character, but Rye was a bit of a character himself. Ken recalls him very well: 'He was a fiery bloke but he was an hypochondriac. He'd carry a thermometer round with him and he was always taking his temperature. We'd be in the back of the van coming back from a gig at four in the morning and he'd be shaking his thermometer around. One time he accidentally smashed it on the side of the van – he was distraught!'

All the travelling soon brought back memories as Hooker was up to his old tricks again, wearing layer after layer of clothing in the van, even though the heater was turned up full. Everyone else was frying! The band gelled as before but, as Tony relates, there was a little bit of a problem: 'Hooker didn't take to Ken's drumming. On stage he would sometimes turn round saying "Backbeat, backbeat." This was because Ken would invariably play on the on beat and Hooker didn't like that.' It was clear that this would happen as Ken's style was so eccetric, so there was no way that he could have fitted in with Hooker's basic requirements. But Ken's drumming would pay dividends when they got back to Groundhogs business.

Ken remembers that you got on the wrong side of Hooker at your peril: 'I went with him to buy a suit in the King's Road, Chelsea. You can imagine what they thought when this bloke came in their shop with a pork pie hat on. I whispered to the assistant "He's a famous American musician." You could see the pound signs on the assistant's face.' Hooker picked a suit he liked

'Scratching The Surface' was Andrew Lauder's fiendish idea for both title and cover shot.
TS Personal Collection

With John Lee Hooker during their tour. John, from the American South, was always complaining about the cold.
Pic Michael Hasted
TS Personal Collection

(2) When John Lee Hooker was touring the UK with Bonnie Raitt in 1990, Tony got back-stage passes from his friend, Barry Riddington, who was involved with the record company. Just like Bob Hall, Hooker never forgot a face. Even though Tony had changed a lot since their last meeting, Hooker recognised him without prompting and greeted his old friend with 'Hello, Mac!' They managed to speak for ten minutes. It was the last time Tony saw him.

TS Personal Collection

and asked how much it was in dollars. The assistant said it was about $25. They wrapped it up and it came to a little bit more. Hooker leant over the counter and said "When you tell me a price that is what I pay!" We came out of the shop and I understood why he was one of the first black artists to make sure he got his money back in the States.'

But Hooker, as well as being a tough negotiator, was also very warm and caring. Pete recalls an incident during that last tour: 'Just after our first child was born Hooker came to our house in Catford. We showed him the baby and he said "Oh no, it's a boy!" Next thing we knew he gave us a bracelet for our son. It was engraved "To Paul from John Lee Hooker". He still has the bracelet.'

The tour continued in early February 1969 when they were booked for a short six-gig tour with Champion Jack Dupree, Aynsley Dunbar's Retaliation and Jo Ann Kelly. The most prestigious of these gigs was the opener, held at the Royal Festival Hall on Saturday 8th February. Sound problems abounded, which made the job of the opening act a little more difficult. It just happened that it was the Groundhogs – minus Hooker. Their set included a version of Sleepy John Estes' 'Express Man' and Freddie King's 'Welfare Blues'. However, the band was later augmented by some welcome additions. Bob Hall made a joyous return for the tour and Jo Ann Kelly delivered powerful versions of 'Let Me Love You' and the old barnstormer 'Rock Me Baby'.

After that Hooker came out and played solo for a spell. Tony Wilson of *Melody Maker* describes the scene: 'Seated on a piano stool, John's mellow, haunting voice, backed by his distinctive amplified, semi-acoustic guitar filled the Festival Hall with "Serve You Right To Suffer" and "One Room Country Shack". The Groundhogs returned to finish the set with him and it generally went down well, in spite of the gremlins. They even recalled Jo Ann Kelly to help them out with "Boom Boom".'

There was a matinee tour that included the likes of Roland Kirk, Tubby Hayes and Philly Joe Jones and it was the latter that made an impression on Ken. He sat through a lot of these shows and was mesmerised by Jones's drumming. He'd never heard a jazz drummer bash his kit so much. But even though they were at the bottom of the bill Ken considered these giants to be the real thing.

The tour was a success and Hooker fired off a parting shot to *Melody Maker* that had a familiar ring to it: 'I wouldn't work with any other band. Before I came I sent a letter to Britain asking for them to work with.' It's an amazing endorsement

Hooker tours with Groundhogs

US BLUESMAN John Lee Hooker, due in Britain to-day (Thursday) to star in the Melody Maker's Blues Scene '69 concert tour, opening at London's Royal Festival Hall on Saturday (8), will make a 23-date tour with the Groundhogs.

Complete dates for the tour are Pontypool (14), Bath (17), Blackpool (18), Grimsby (19), Leytonstone

GROUNDHOGS

(20), Leicester (21), Colchester (22), London's Crystal Palace Hotel (23),

Newcastle (24), London's Klooks Kleek (25), Portsmouth (26), Southampton (27), Streatham (28), Bournemouth (March 1), Nottingham (2), Bishop's Stortford (3), Brighton (4), Tolworth (5), Welsh College of Technology (6), Plymouth (7), London School of Economics (8), Tunstall (9) and London's Royal Albert Hall (10).

considering all the bands he had worked with in the UK and elsewhere. As the band said their farewells to Hooker, Tony McPhee didn't realise he would only meet the great man one more time. (2)

By the spring of 1969 it was becoming more and more apparent that the traditional blues was going out of fashion. Most of the 'true blues' adherents were, in fact, mixing it with something else that later became known as blues-rock. Pete Cruickshank sums up the dilemma this transitional period presented: 'Tony thought sticking to the blues was very restrictive. There were many blues purists who didn't like this move. We wanted to say goodbye to being strictly a blues band.'

Towards late spring Steve Rye was becoming more and more unreliable, as Tony reveals: 'We had to play two sets at one gig. When it came to the second set we couldn't find him. (3) He was eventually found in a nearby pub, really drunk. It was just getting worse. So we asked him not to do any more gigs.' Later on Steve would work with Jo Ann Kelly, Sonny Terry, Brownie McGhee and Dave Kelly.

Just before the Groundhogs recorded their second album, Tony produced a multi-artist blues album called 'I Asked For Water, She Gave Me Gasoline' at Central Sound Studios, Denmark Street. Tony is on four of the cuts. (4)

After teaming up with Jo Ann Kelly for the opening. 'Oh, Death'. Tony closes side one with 'Gasoline'. For the next number he plugs the amps in as the Groundhogs utilise their talents on 'Rock Me', a lively, even foot-tapping cut featuring Jo Ann's expressive vocals. The final contribution from Tony is the self penned 'Don't Pass The Hat Round' which is a great blues song in its own right.

One of the artists on the 'Gasoline' album was Andy Fernbach. The Groundhog Series wasn't totally mapped out in 1968, in some cases it just happened, and Tony related to an American

magazine in 1972 how he came to produce Fernbach's album: 'The first one was "Me And The Devil" and that was just the initial one of lumping everyone together and seeing what came out. Some people were stroppy about it and some people weren't and Andy wasn't, he was the easiest to get on with so we decided to do an album with him.'

Tony produced the album just after the Hooker tour (it was released in June 1969). 'If You Miss Your Connexion' was unfairly slated, he emphatically insists: 'I thought it was a decent album but some reviewer called it the worst album ever made. After I read that review I went back and listened to the album and I couldn't see how that statement could have been made.' It was the first time that Tony received a totally negative review for something he was connected with. He didn't know it but it would be the shape of things to come. Pete Cruickshank and Ken Pustelnik played on the album.

Perversely, the departure of Rye gave the Groundhogs a new lease of life and they were becoming tighter than ever. It's difficult to imagine how Rye would have fitted in to their new musical direction if there was a decision to move away from the blues, Tony reflected to John Tobler in the re-issued album's sleeve notes: 'Well, it was made for us, really, because John Walters (BBC radio producer) decided that he hated blues. He decided that the Nice were a blues band! We figured it was time to get away from it.'

Just after Rye's departure, it was decided the time was right to acquire their first full-time roadie, Mick Hubbert. Up until then Roy Fisher occasionally helped with the shifting of the gear. He would also act as part-time driver and had driven the van up and down the country.

Hubbert liked the job: 'Roy showed me the way things were wired up. We all travelled in the same van, there wasn't much room but the band got on well together and there was no friction at all.' In June 1969 the

(3) The man who was usually detailed to find Rye was Mick Hubbert. He was a friend of Jo Ann Kelly and Bob Glass. He'd be there as a fan but later on he found himself as the Groundhogs' first roadie.

(4) One of the artists included is John Lewis, who was a fine piano boogie player. In the 1970s he became Jona Lewie and had a few hit singles, including the classic 'Stop The Cavalry'.
He was in Brett Marvin and the Thunderbolts, who featured on two cuts. Brett Marvin later became Terry Dactyl and the Dinosaurs, whose big hit was 'Seaside Shuffle'.

Tony on stage with John.
Pic Michael Hasted
TS Personal Collection

john lee hooker · groundhogs · pretty things
barclay james harvest · itys lightshow
edgar broughton blues band · rosa
feb. 26   south parade pier   · tickets 15/-

Poster for Portsmouth, where Edgar Broughton turned up with his mum driving the van and carrying the gear.
Courtesy Pete Cruickshank

revitalised slim-line Groundhogs went back into Marquee studios to record the follow up to 'Scratching The Surface'. This time Tony was producing the album and Roy Fisher had created a publishing company, Groundhog Productions. They were still limited by the four-track desk, but had a good nine months of gigging behind them. And it showed as they came up with a minor classic, the teasingly titled 'Blues Obituary'.

The opener is 'BDD', which stands for Blind, Deaf and Dumb. Tony remembered it from an acetate he'd heard of an old blues song, he liked the tune and put some words to it. It's a catchy number and was even chosen as a single, but the most interesting aspect of the track is Tony's playing. His style is so varied that you think there are two different guitarists playing. Strangely, it made Number 1 in Lebanon! Tony was miffed when Chicken Shack coincidentally released the rather similarly themed 'I'd Rather Go Blind' just before the Hogs album was released.

The second track, 'Daze Of The Week', is another example of Tony's play on words. As Ken Pustelnik explains: 'I'm the psychedelic freakout merchant. I'm very good at anticipating the right groove. We never played a track at the same speed twice. That's why we would sound like a different band by the end of a tour. Tony responded to it and we played off one another.' Tony remembers it differently: 'The first time I saw a freakout on stage was by the Yardbirds and I thought it was great. In fact, all three of us were into it.' 'Daze Of The Week' was the first totally unique song Tony wrote for the band.

'Times' is a number that Tony wrote based on a Blind Willie Johnson track, while 'Mistreated' is an old Tommy Johnson song that was to remain a firm favourite for 40 years. 'Mistreated' is a good example of how Tony was developing his own guitar sound, coupled with his convincing vocals. You really believe him when he sings 'Baby, what have I done that's wrong?' 'Natchez Burning' is a Howlin' Wolf song from the 1950s that tells the story of how the Ku Klux Klan burned down a church in Natchez, Mississippi. However, if anyone needed evidence of how far the band had travelled since the first album then the last cut would provide it.

'Light Was The Day', another of those McPhee wordplay titles, was lifted from a Blind Willie Johnson song called 'Dark Is The Night'. This featured a world-music intervention of epic proportions from Ken, as he outlines: 'I got a lot of Indian records off Andrew Lauder from the basement of UA. I listened to them over the weekend prior to going into the studio. I tuned the drums to highlight the Indian rhythms I was going to play. Tony had got a song called 'Dark Is The Night'. He plays a wailing spiritual and it has an African feel. In other words it is my

version of Indian drumming to a gospel.'

To say 'Light Was The Day' is a classic is an understatement. It is a track, more than any other on the album, that showed they were developing their own unique sound. It is an atmospheric delight. Tony used a nine-string guitar he got from a junk shop for just £15.

Journalist John Tobler, who witnessed some of the recording sessions, admitted he had heard a flood of bad reports about the band. He was there at Andrew Lauder's invitation. He recalled his experiences for *What's On Where* in 1970: 'The recording studio was really exciting. Efficient, perhaps, but the music was knockout, literally. It was such a surprise. I raved about the Hogs to all I met and gave them all the publicity I was able to at the time. Then I saw the Groundhogs on stage for the first time and yet another facet of their excitement hit me. It was just too much. That was at the Marquee, and they were probably playing second to somebody like the Taste and producing an incredible night for electric blues freaks.' But it wasn't just the band Tobler liked: 'Tony is without doubt a genius and the best (bar none) bottleneck guitarist in Europe, let alone being an amazingly fast and accurate conventional guitarist.'

This second album was a real step up from the Groundhogs' debut. There were so many more ideas and they were going in some interesting places. But what kind of band were they? What kind of music did they play? Ken sums it up: 'We'd got swing rhythm, it's a jazz thing, even trad jazz, folk-blues, electric blues and even free jazz is in there but it's in such small measures. "Daze Of The Week" was the shape of things to come. We didn't like to be defined. The press liked to control everything and they were always trying to shape musical trends.'

In acknowledgement of the musical shift the band were making, Roy Fisher came up with the idea of calling the album 'Blues Obituary' and the cover featured that concept. Roy Fisher arranged the picture shoot to take place at Highgate Cemetery, North London. They paid fifteen guineas for the privilege of a three-hour shoot. He also hired the clothes from Moss Bros and a classy 1919 hearse. Tony was transformed into a vicar with Ken and Pete as coffin-bearers. They even managed to persuade their friend, Hoss, from the band Screw to play the 'body' in the coffin. Tony is seen giving the last rites to the blues.

The book the Reverend McPhee is holding (his idea) is the bible of the blues, Paul Oliver's *Blues Fell This Morning* – he still has the book. Roy Fisher recalls an amusing incident from the shoot: 'The funny thing about the end result that is not widely known is that the pious look on vicar Tony's face was not so much from his acting skills but because the guy who volunteered to be the corpse was too tall to fit the coffin with his shoes on, and with them off he had the most evil-smelling feet that were wafting up under Tony's nose.'

When they finished the shoot something rather strange happened. Tony takes up the story:

'I, in my vicar's garb, walked off in front and after a while I realised that the hubbub of voices had gone, and I was in this cemetery, which was all overgrown, walking past these crypts with these little busted headstones, and there was this clap of thunder. I thought "Oh, I'm in the shit!" and I sort of dashed, hoping I was heading the right way. I did a big circle and found myself at the gates again, quickly donned my civilian clothes and buggered off.'

The album was released on 5th September 1969 and, to coincide with this, a publicity stunt was staged around the shooting of the album cover. Roy Fisher knew a freelance publicist who got his secretary to phone up the Sunday *News Of The World* newspaper complaining that she recognised a gravestone in the picture as her grandmother's and that this caused her a lot of distress! The paper fell for it hook, line and sinker and the story appeared with the lurid headline 'A Pop Group On Grannie's Grave', with a picture of the entourage standing by a number of graves. However, it didn't have a significant impact on sales.

The *Ipswich Evening Star* called the album 'strictly for the pure blues fan (and I say that with a guilty feeling). Good slide lead work and a wonderful wailing bass.' The *Allmusic* website paid special attention to one track in particular: 'The traditional "Natchez Burning," arranged by McPhee, fits in nicely with his originals while the longest track, the six-minute-and-50-second 'Light Is The Day' features the most innovation Ginger Baker-style tribal rant by drummer Ken Pustelnik allowing McPhee to lay down some muted slide work while Pete Cruickshank's bass drives along with the mayhem! Blistering guitar on the opening track, "BDD," sets the pace for this deep excursion into the musical depths further down than Canned Heat ever dared go.' Gushing praise indeed!

'Blues Obituary' was the last of the Groundhog Series of albums. It can be considered nothing less than a triumph. (5)

In 1969 they returned to the Marquee club, London on 7th February after three years and played another 12 times that year. Manager John Gee was a great fan of the band and called Tony 'a fine player in the bottleneck tradition.' Around this time Tony got to perform with Howlin' Wolf but, alas, his hero Hubert Sumlin wasn't in the band. Wolf was backed by Tony's old mates the John Dummer Band and, during the gig, he was invited on stage to play a number.

Just after they recorded the second album, Tony played an impromptu gig when Dave Wetton got married on 21st June 1969. He hired a band called Tangerine and, between sets, Dave and friends borrowed their instruments. The band, which included Tony on lead, plus future *New Faces* winner Johnny Bryant proceeded to play about half a dozen numbers, which went down a storm. As Dave adds: 'Poor old Tangerine didn't want to come back on again after that, especially the lead guitarist.'

On Saturday 8th August they appeared at the 9th National Jazz and Blues Festival at Plumpton racecourse. As usual there was a prestigious bill for the three-day event, with Pink Floyd, the Who and the Nice headlining. Ken recalls he watched the astonishing King Crimson, as they weren't too far from the main stage.

The Groundhogs played in a big marquee off the main arena in what was called the Village. The band played a short set featuring a bass solo by Pete. Paul Chitt, a lifelong fan, was seeing the band for the first time and was impressed: 'We came across a three-piece playing some really good blues. The guitarist was getting some incredible sounds out of a Gibson SG!

'We missed the beginning of the set but the music was so good it seemed to go on for ages! When a song required the use of a bottleneck the immaculate-looking SG was put down and a Fender Stratocaster that had seen better times was used.' By all accounts the small crowd was impressed.

They then embarked on their first trip to Germany, being booked for two weeks at the famous Star Club in Hamburg, where they shared the bill with Samson. It was no holiday as each band played alternate half-hour sets for the whole night. The crowds weren't that great either. Pete recalls even though they had well over a hundred people come in, there were only about 10 watching the gig at any time. The admission fee included a certain number of drinks. As soon as they consumed them they were off.

The highlight of the residency was when Vanilla Fudge played the club. The place was packed to the rafters. The greatest rhythm section he ever saw transfixed Pete. Not only were Tim Bogert (bass) and Carmine Appice (drums) great players, they had charisma and gelled impressively.

At the end of the Groundhogs' set, Tony was accosted by a journalist. 'He eventually mentioned "And The Beat Goes On" and I realised he thought I was with Vanilla Fudge. The conversation faltered and we both walked off bemused.'

Back in England they continued playing sporadic gigs; Mick Hubbert remembers one of them in particular: 'Ken lived in Earls Court with a guy who

Still in her 20s, Tony introduced Jo Ann Kelly as the 'Mother Figure' of the blues.
TS Personal Collection

(5) The Groundhog Series consisted of 'Me And The Devil' (various artists), 'Scratching The Surface' (Groundhogs), 'Hand Me Down My Old Walking Stick' (Big Joe Williams), 'If You Miss Your Connexion' (Andy Fernbach), 'I Asked For Water – She Gave Me Gasoline' (Various Artists) and 'Blues Obituary' (Groundhogs).

Courtesy Graham Vosper

synthesised mescaline (a hallucinogenic drug derived from the mescal cactus). Ken had taken a lot of mescaline and I had to carry him to the van to get to a gig we had somewhere in the Midlands. He played the gig but the following day he apologised to Mac for not playing the gig. He just couldn't remember it at all. He experimented like that.'

In late 1969, they found themselves supported by heavy rockers Earth (the future Black Sabbath) at a gig in Birmingham. Mick remembers seeing guitarist Tony Iommi inspecting the amplifier Tony had built for himself. Iommi was intrigued, as it was quite large and looked like a 1930s radio.

Hubbert invited him to pick it up. Iommi obliged, but his reaction was of surprise that it was so heavy. Initially Tony built his gear because of necessity but now he had faith that he could build something off-the-shelf models couldn't give him.

As he told *Melody Maker* in 1970: 'I like being totally involved; but it has a terrible effect on your time.'

Girl fan buys a new record and finds...

A POP GROUP ON GRANNIE'S GRAVE

By DAVID MERTENS

ANGELA WILSON got a shock when she looked closely at the macabre record sleeve of the new pop LP she had just bought.

For on it was a coffin, with someone in it—lying on her grandmother's grave.

The members of the pop group, the Groundhogs, stood around the grave dressed as undertakers, and one as a priest.

Angela, a 23-year-old secretary, of Ovington Square, Kensington, London, told me: "I was absolutely sickened. I bought the record after listening to some of it at a shop.

"And when I got home I looked more carefully at the sleeve. The coffin was lying on my grandmother's grave. It is disgraceful." She has complained to the record company, Liberty Records, who produced it, and asked for a written apology.

Top hats

The record, which is on general release this week, is called Blues Obituary.

The front of the "sick" cover shows a coffin being taken from a hearse.

Two long-haired members of the group are pictured as top-hatted undertakers taking the coffin from the hearse with a guitar placed on the "dead" man's lap. Beside it stands the long-haired preacher.

On the sleeve the record is titled "The Groundhogs Blues Obituary" featuring the Rev T. S. McPhee."

On the back of the sleeve, in the shape of the cross, are six other photographs. They show the journey to the grave.

Two of the pictures show an open coffin lying on a grave beneath a cross, with a man lying in it and the guitar on top of him.

Said Angela: "I recognised the grave immediately.

"My grandmother, Mrs

Louise Jones, died in her 70s about eight years ago.

"She was buried in Highgate cemetery and I have visited her grave since then on her birthday and at Christmas.

"I tidy it up and sometimes put flowers on it.

"There is no inscription on the stone but I know, from its position and the ornate decoration on the stone that it is my grandmother's."

Angela added: "I haven't dared tell my mother yet in case she gets really upset.

"Surely they would have to get permission or something to do this?

"I know there's not much can be done now, the record has been released, but I want to stop this happening to any one else."

At Liberty Records,

Miss Barbara Scott, the Press officer, said: "I have heard that this lady wants to make a complaint. But really there is nothing sacrilegious about these pictures.

"It could well have been this lady's grandmother's gravestone, but honestly who cares? We all have to die sometime.

"There was no identification on it. We can't expect photographers to check on unnamed gravestones.

"The whole idea of these pictures was to show that the group had finished with a certain period of music and wanted to forget it as dead and buried."

Miss Scott asked: "Don't you think the sleeve is really groovy?"

I said I didn't.

Mock funeral—but real grave

chapter 7

Thank Christ for the Groundhogs

'Without him it would have been just another album among many.
The album wouldn't have made it, no doubt about it.'
Tony McPhee summing up John Peel's contribution to the sales of
'Thank Christ For The Bomb'

'I hate the glorification of war.
I hate how people were duped into fighting.
Not much changed between World War 1 & World War 2
for the soldier.'
Tony McPhee

Tony McPhee spent the early part of 1970 writing the band's third album. This would ring in the changes on three fronts. The first was a complete divorce from the blues. Secondly, all of the material would spring from Tony's pen and, finally, it was the only time he went into the studio with all the material written beforehand: 'I wanted to prove I could do something away from the blues.'

Roy Fisher came up with a suggestion for the title of the album, as he recalls: 'I was sitting in Andrew Lauder's office and we were trying to think of a concept that Tony could write. That's when I thought of "Thank Christ For The Bomb" off the top of my head.'

The world was potentially teetering on the brink as the US faced the USSR, both armed to the teeth with nuclear weapons. Yet despite Tony McPhee's progressive views, the album took a different stand to the nuclear disarmers. It was a view that was based on the impossibility of both sides disarming simultaneously: 'I looked at the deterrent side of things. Some people came up to me and said "Did you mean that?" On this occasion they were my views.'

Pete Cruikshank outlines his views on this: 'It was a statement against all the ban the bomb marches. We would have had another war if we hadn't had them. We didn't welcome the weapons but while they were there it stopped others from starting World War 3.' Ken Pustelnik

Liberty's 'serious'
publicity photograph.
TS Personal Collection

TONY McPHEE and the GROUNDHOGS.

agency representation:
BRON AGENCY LIMITED,
29-31 OXFORD STREET,
LONDON, W.1.
01·437·5063.

managagement:
ROY FISHER - 01·699·2134.
ZAK MANAGEMENT.

LIBERTY

was equally succinct: 'It just might be possible that this was why there had been no major war since World War 2.'

Even before he finished writing all the music Tony had decided to instigate a new lyrical approach, as he explains: 'I told the band I wanted to make it something like the Who's "Tommy". They thought I meant a rock opera. I quickly told them I meant a concept album and they breathed a sigh of relief!' He had previously touched on social comment and the drudgery of the 40-hour week with Herbal Mixture's 'Machines', but now he decided to slant some of the lyrics in that direction. The new album would boast not one but two concept pieces and they both connected somewhere in the middle! Family's debut album 'Music In A Doll's House' had influenced him greatly, as he told *NME*: 'it really knocked me out. It gave me an inkling of numbers that could produce a feel or mood apart from the actual playing involved.'

As the title hinted, Tony kept coming back to the theme of war but he had an image of a World War 1 soldier copping a 'Blighty' injury, such as losing a foot, which would mean that his fighting days were over. When he actually started to write the lyrics they seemed to have a common thread running through. As he related on the liner notes of the 2003 digitally re-mastered CD: 'I realised that every song was about the way that, in a world crammed with people, there are levels of alienation, from individuals living isolated in one room through to communities which cannot accept individual differences and countries that are unable to communicate with each other.'

But the subject of war didn't cover everything that he wanted to express and so other areas were developed on side two.

Just before recording commenced for the album the Groundhogs went along to their first BBC radio session at Maida Vale, London and, on 7th February, premiered two new songs, 'Garden' and 'Eccentric Man', both destined for the new album. The other track they recorded was the outstanding 'Mistreated' from 'Blues Obituary'. The sessions were usually recorded in the evening and Tony always enjoyed them.

The first two albums had been recorded in the primitive Marquee studios, but for the new album, Tony wanted a different studio, one with all the latest technology. One of his favourite songs was Fleetwood Mac's 'Oh Well' and he decided the band would record where that was made. He found out it was at De Lane Lea studios, London. It takes more than studio equipment to make an album, however, and the in-house engineer was Martin Birch, who went on to work with Deep Purple.

Tony set about creating a unique sound for the band. Martin Birch really liked what they were doing. Tony had resurrected an old technique in the process of writing the new material: 'I remembered how I used to write stuff for Herbal Mixture and I used that formula of just hammering chords that shouldn't fit – notes that shouldn't fit.' However, as Tony reveals, these changes had the potential to create schisms in the band.

'I wanted to use the three-piece band fully. So I wrote the bass parts as well. I didn't want the usual root notes. I was writing different chord sequences and I wanted everything whirling about. I wanted bass parts that would coincide with everything else. Pete is a fine player and I did give him the opportunity of writing them, but he later admitted he couldn't do what I wanted.'

Recording began on 18th February 1970 at De Lane Lea and carried on into March (the last session was 3rd March). Tony had written four songs that made up the main concept. The opener, 'Strange Town' is unusual, as Tony reveals how he achieved it: 'Most riffs start with the root note. I decided to start the riff below the root note.' That's why it feels like you've missed the first few seconds of the intro! Tony's distinctive licks continually soar and descend and things are never on an even keel for long: this creates a huge dose of excitement. There's more

than a nod to Herbal Mixture's 'Machines' in the lyrics.

> I don't believe these people, spend all their time walkin' round lookin' so glum.
> They think that life is for workin' to secure their pension when retirement come.
> Ah, but they don't realise, it's right before their eyes, life is for livin', right now before you die.

The second track, 'Darkness Is No Friend', is a perfect example of the unusual bass sound Tony was after. Pete always interpreted what Tony wanted and really hits the button on this one. This time there's more of a hint of the inspiration for the band's next album, with its references to daylight and darkness bringing their own horrors in equal measure.

The chorus illustrates that Tony was prepared to take a back seat as Pete's bass dominates proceedings. However, it's the unusual ending that steals the show on this track. Tony had always liked Little Richard's abrupt endings and decided to put several of them together in a loop. This is how he got that swinging, jazzy 3/4 feeling to create a chunking effect.

'Soldier' is about men 'told by their country to go to war and nobody wants to.' 'Soldier' is set in the war to end wars, the First World War. The lyrics reveal an empathy with those unfortunate men, many of whom fought against their will, but is told through the eyes of someone like their sergeant major. The lyrics tell a horrible story and are worth quoting in full:

> Soldier, fix your bayonet before the enemy come,
> 'Cos you won't have time, when they start to climb the hill, y'know.
> Soldier, when you see 8,000 climbin' up on you,
> Don't see them as men, just see them as enemies of the King, y'know.
> Soldier, don't think of runnin', your death is just as sure.
> If you don't face it now, you'll face it anyhow in front of the squad, y'know.
> Soldier, stand firm in your trenches, don't let them break the line.
> Because these dirty Hun are all bastard whore sons not fit to live, don't you know.

The music was deliberately laid-back to contrast with the heavy lyrics, and much more effective because of it. Tony was making good use of the extra tracks available for overdubs and intertwined two guitar solos: 'I loved doing them. They were nothing to do with each other except for being in the same key. One was muted but then came out strong. I was looking for a change of colour as often as possible.' It was Tony's finger-picking style that gave this song an extra dimension: 'I feel I have an advantage with my pick style because if you play with a plectrum it will always sound staccato. But playing with your fingers you can use the thumb, the nail or even the fingertip and this gives you more tones.'

Another unusual aspect was provided by the vocal delivery, Tony inserting 'y'knows' at the end of the first three verses. In theory, it sounds absurd but it worked. In fact, he nicked this from a Beatles track, 'I Feel Fine' but stamped his own character on it. Many consider 'Soldier' to be the band's finest moment.

Pete had a testing time as, the night before they recorded 'Strange Town' and 'Soldier', his Gibson bass had fallen off stage at a gig at the Black Prince, Bexley and was broken. He borrowed a Fender Precision, the first time he had used that model for years.

The title track opens with some gentle acoustic guitar, the first time Tony featured the instrument so prominently on a Groundhogs album. Martin Birch accidentally wiped an acoustic intro from the beginning of 'Soldier', which in retrospect was no bad thing. As Tony put it, 'even the cock-ups worked'. 'Thank Christ For The Bomb' moves from the muddy trenches of World War 1 to the 'two big bangs' that were supposed to signal the end of World War 2 in a few *Dr Strangelove*-type lines, illustrating an economy in storytelling.

The acoustic section fades out and gives way to an upbeat march that belies what is to come next. This segment was inspired by seeing John Cruickshank's band performing a song called 'Reflections' that Tony had written years before and this was in the back of his mind when writing the title track.

Track sheet for 'TCFTB' with added interest!
TS Personal Collection

TRACK SHEET — DE LANE LEA MUSIC LTD. 129, KINGSWAY. LONDON W.C.2. tel: 01-242-2743/01-437-4252

EIGHT-TRACK ✓ FOUR-TRACK | NAB ✓ CCIR | 30 i.p.s. | 15 i.p.s. ✓

ARTIST Groundhogs | CLIENT Liberty Records | DATE 18-2-70. | ENGINEER M. Birch.

TITLE	TRACK ONE	TRACK TWO	TRACK THREE	TRACK FOUR	TRACK FIVE	TRACK SIX	TRACK SEVEN	TRACK EIGHT
1. DARKNESS IS NO FRIEND	DRUMS	BASS	GUITAR	DRUMS	LEAD GUITAR	TIT	VOCAL	BUM
2. SHIP ON THE OCEAN	DRUMS	BASS	GUITAR	DRUMS	LEAD GUITAR (2)	GUITAR (3)	VOCAL	FUZZ BASS
3. GARDEN	DRUMS	BASS	GUITAR	DRUMS	LEAD GUITAR (2)	LEAD GUITAR (3) (LEFT)	VOCAL	LEAD GUITAR (RIGHT)
4. STATUS PEOPLE	DRUMS	BASS	GUITAR (6)	DRUMS	GUITAR (7)	FUZZ BASS	VOCAL	GUITAR (8)
5. RICH MAN POOR MAN	DRUMS	BASS	(CLICK) (2) GUITAR	DRUMS	(CLICK) GUITAR (1)	VOCAL (2)	VOCAL (1)	GUITAR
6. ECCENTRIC MAN	DRUMS	BASS	GUITAR	DRUMS	LEAD GUITAR	VOCAL (2)	VOCAL (1)	FUZZ BASS
7. STRANGE TOWN	DRUMS	BASS	GUITAR	DRUMS	GUITAR (1)	LEG	VOCAL	LEAD GUITAR (cu)
8. SOLDIER	DRUMS	BASS	GUITAR	(CYMBAL HEAVY) DRUMS	LEAD GUITAR (1)	VOCAL (1)	ACOUSTIC GUITAR	(CLICK) VOCAL
9. THANK CHRIST FOR THE BOMB	DRUMS	ACOUSTIC GUITAR	ACOUSTIC GUITAR	ELECTRIC GUITAR (1)	BASS	GUITAR (3) VOCAL	LEAD GUITAR (4)	GUITAR (2)
10								
11								
12								

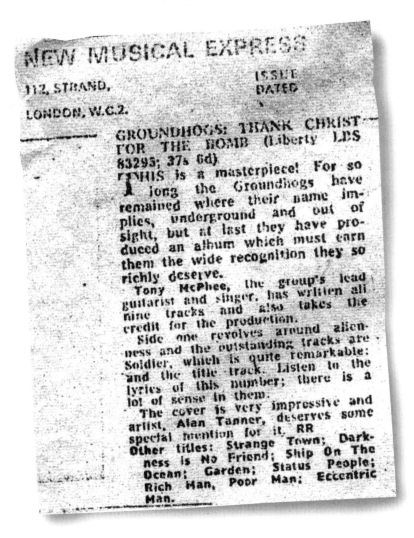

NME rave review.
Courtesy Pete Cruickshank

The procession soon gives way to freakout as the band careers towards its riveting climax of the two atomic bombs at the end of World War 2. Martin Birch had a friend who was working on an electronic symphony and Tony heard some of it, including big explosions Martin's friend said they could use. Pete remembers it differently.

'It was Martin's idea as he had seen two galaxies crashing into one another in a sc-fi programme.' It is clear that nobody thought about it representing the two atomic bombs which became the accepted interpretation. The coincidence of two explosions at the end of a song thanking Christ for the bomb led to fans believing they were hearing the US bombing Hiroshima and Nagasaki in 1945.

The sound quality far outstripped anything they had done before. Tony's idea to record at De Lane Lea had paid off handsomely. Ken outlines another factor that worked for them: 'We never had any arguments in the studios about music and that's floored many a group. There was a major technology change at the time. I remember for one section we wanted to move the sound around, so we had several people all lined up along the desk panning from one speaker to another. It was painstaking but we did it. We all had to turn a volume gain to make it run along the various channels and then we had to sequence it. It would be easy to do that today'

Tony related the intensity of it all to *Disc & Music Echo*: 'I really went to town on everything, double-tracked voice, overdubbed guitar, and the result was far more satisfying. I can't listen to the other albums.'

The second side also presented a concept but this was mostly overlooked with all the publicity surrounding the first side. In fact, Tony had deliberately buried it, as he told *Melody Maker*: 'I haven't made it blatantly obvious but there's a theme running through the second side: I just didn't want people to compare it with "Tommy" or something.' On the face of it, it is a bunch of disparate cuts telling the story of a man who becomes disillusioned about life. The first two lines of opener 'Ship On The Ocean' give a clue 'I'm like a ship on the ocean that's rolling from side to side, but I'm not drunk I'm just dissatisfied.' It's clear from later lines that the person is materially well off but lacking any direction in life. He is searching for something.

The next track, 'Garden', is one of the best on the album. Tony readily admits that he pinched the main riff from the Beatles' 'Come Together'; it's well disguised. Martin Birch suggested to Tony that he put the mic at the other end of the studio for the guitar solo; the slight delay gives it a fading sound. By now our wealthy man yearns for a return to the past in order to start again. Tony was critical that possessing wealth was not the be all and end all of things, as he confirms: 'If you have so much money what is there to strive for? I do believe in the work ethic. In a way I foretold what was to happen in the future. You see professional people giving up their high-paid, long-hours job and moving to the country, to live a more simple life. You didn't see that then.'

The lyrics make it crystal clear:
But I'm not going to cut a single blade of grass, my garden will look just like the distant past,
Before the days of agricultural land, before the time when pebbles turned to sand.
When I leave this house I'm going to stay, I'm forsaking my comforts to live another way,
Get my clothes from heaps, my food from bins, my water from ponds and have tramps for all my friends.

'Status People' starts with a bass intro that develops into a punchy riff with Ken in great form. Tony explains the mechanics of sounding different: 'The magic number of notes is 12 (the number in an octave) but I decided to group these notes in twos, threes and fours. On 'Status People' I grouped them in 3 x 4. It was a formula but I used it to sound different.' The track explores the searcher's current social standing and Tony is quite clear where he stands on this: 'You have these people that need to be part of something. Why don't you be yourself? People seem to need status, I think they must be shallow.' 'Rich Man, Poor Man' explores the essential differences in society which in the song is a 'cross section' of humankind.

The final track is 'Eccentric Man', a convenient label for society to put on a man that gives his wealth away. The journey is complete, from a Chelsea mansion to the benches of the Embankment. It's a crunching riff from the outset and climaxes with one of Tony's longest solos on record. It was no surprise that this was chosen as the single. The band didn't really harbour any hope of it being a hit, it was more of a ploy to get airplay.

When the album was being cut Tony and Ken went along to listen to it. At the end Ken said: 'I like that, I think!' Tony took an acetate (test pressing) home and put it on while he was eating his dinner. He found himself eating faster and faster. It was a sign of his excitement at what they had created. So much so he thought 'If this doesn't make it, nothing will.' It was obvious that the album was a great one. Tony was succinct: 'The album was like a jigsaw puzzle that came together.'

One of the things that occupied everyone's mind was the design of the album cover. Andrew Lauder knew of a design company called Clearwater Conception which had provided posters for various bands at gigs that he had seen. Tony was certain he wanted artwork and no photographs, so artist Alan Tanner came up with a brilliant idea. He took two famous photos from the First World War and re-worked them by superimposing the faces of the band. Even though the time frame of the images contradicts the title of the album, this does, in fact, make it more interesting. In discussions, it was decided to use poppies in some way but the way that Tanner used them is breathtaking.

On the inside cover is an old photograph of a group of men of the time of 'Soldier'. The photo has the quality of a negative. This emphasises their ghostly faces and invokes an idea of them situated outside a recruitment office. The plane above them is bombing them with red poppies because most of these men will be scattered in some field somewhere in Europe. Tanner also provided the emotive poem on the inside cover. One thing that was for certain – it was one the best covers of the year.

With the album safely in the can, the Hogs made their second trip to Germany. It was an eventful trip, as were all their visits. Ken got chatting to some US military personnel on the ferry and they opened a bottle of spirits. What he didn't know was it was spiked with LSD, and this had a dramatic effect on him. At one stage he ran through the lounge with a girl but he had her head under his arm because he thought he was the front of a camel. He remembers it like it was yesterday: 'I could see Tony walking towards me from a distance from the other end of the boat but he stayed the same size to me even when he reached me. He was walking like Popeye.'

The weather was about to turn and the boat, a last-minute replacement for the usual vessel, was too small to undertake such a long trip. Roy Fisher recalls the mayhem: 'Everyone on board was sick except for me and Tony. I went to find Pete, who we thought had fallen over the side. I found him in the toilet, which was awash in shit and seawater. He told me to fuck off and leave him alone. I guess he felt a little undignified.' Roadie Mick Hubbert took the drastic step of going down into the hold and spending the trip on the mattress in the van as it alleviated the seasickness somewhat. They wouldn't forget their voyage on the *Viking III* in a hurry!

In the morning Tony could see the vast estuary of the Elbe, but the ship had taken such a hammering in the night's storm that it was sailing at an angle so that he could see the river through the starboard window and sky on the port side. Every now and again the boat would lurch and all the breakfast rolls and plates would come crashing down.

After this eventful crossing they supported the rapidly disintegrating Nice at the Ernst Merck Halle, Hamburg, on 28th March. There was a riot when the organisers started showing slides advertising Coca-Cola, as the radical students didn't take to these corporate images. Germany proved quite different from anywhere else they had played. Ken related to *Melody Maker*: 'Managers and agents are illegal out there, so contracts don't mean very much.' The tour went well and they returned home via a less eventful crossing.

The Groundhogs were getting more exposure in the press now and Tony was fielding questions regarding the chemistry of the band. In one interview, Tony revealed: 'Politics is an issue

Ken's bass-drum skin supposedly depicting a Groundhog was painted by Paul Whitehead, who illustrated Genesis's 'Nursery Cryme' and 'Foxtrot'.
Pic Joanna Deacon
TS Personal Collection

between me and Ken. It is all down to me being a moderate and Ken being an extremist.' They did have more than a few lively debates. But there was never a chance of their political disagreements being an issue. But where did Pete Cruickshank stand in this? In an interview with *Zig-Zag* the following year, Tony gave a hint: 'Pete is basically very lazy – he plays because he likes it and it brings him a bit of bread – that's his philosophy as far as I can make out.'

Pete was keen to put the record straight: 'I was stuck between Tony and Ken squabbling pointlessly and, as I was not a political animal, all I wanted to do was play'. The organisation revolved round Roy Fisher, as Tony told *Zig-Zag*: 'I'm as lazy as Pete, really, and though I've got a lot of ambition to do things I don't particularly want to start them off. But Roy always manages to get us moving.'

In early May, the band played a gig in Brighton. The Brighton film festival had just shown *Rock Around The Clock* and *Blackboard Jungle*, so some of the Teddy boys wandering around the town ended up at the Groundhogs gig. As Tony was announcing the next song, he heard a cry from the back of the hall requesting some rock'n'roll. At Tony's retort 'we don't do rock'n'roll', a beer glass sailed over the crowd and landed on Ken's cymbal.

'A chair was thrown on the stage and it landed right in the middle of my bass drum. A kid from the audience got up and started to extricate it. I noticed from the gloom an arm come out and a beer glass was broken on the kid's head. All hell broke loose, so I made my way to the front of the stage. Pete was still playing, I don't know why! All I remember is a chair flying towards me. It hit me on the bridge of the nose. I was out cold.' The upshot was he

had to go down the police station to make a statement. His souvenir was two big black eyes and a permanently damaged nasal tube!

On 9th May, the day after the Brighton gig the Hogs made an appearance on progressive music programme *Disco 2*, BBC television's forerunner to the *Old Grey Whistle Test* and fronted by Richard Williams. But there was a problem; they had to mime. They mimed to 'Garden', but Ken was looking like an endangered panda with his black eyes. As he recalls: 'It was quite a small room but they had these big gantry cameras with hydraulic arms. The cameraman was seated on it and they zoomed right close to me. The cameras kept changing lens. That was all I needed.'

On 14th May the band was booked to appear on John Peel's *In Concert* radio programme at the Paris Theatre in Lower Regent Street, London. This was Pete's favourite venue, a fabulous theatre, with its plush seating and intimate atmosphere. Ken remembers the theatre for two reasons: 'We always played well there, we always seemed to be on the button. Also, I remember John Martyn supported us on one occasion. He was doing his soundcheck while we were standing on the side of the stage. I thought it sounded good so I thought I'd play my drums along with it. Soon after Pete started playing bass, it sounded good. But Martyn's body was getting more and more hunched in his chair. He was retreating into his shell – I thought what a miserable bastard!' (Tony later reflected that this was understandable considering it was supposed to be Martyn's soundcheck.)

In June, 'Thank Christ For The Bomb' was released to some critical acclaim, although more than that is needed for an album to make it. Just after the album was released John Peel played

Rare early live picture.
Pic courtesy
Andrew Lauder

'Soldier' on his Sunday afternoon radio show and the following week thousands left the racks. Peel waxed lyrical about the track – and he loved the 'y'knows'. Tony confirms that 'without him it would have been just another album among many. The album wouldn't have made it, no doubt about it.'

The album was released on Liberty and within a few weeks it peaked at Number 9. This represented a major achievement, and Tony sums up his feelings: 'It was exciting, but once Peel picked up on it I knew it was going to be a success.' However, in an interview at the time with *Melody Maker*, McPhee was keen to point out he wasn't going to leave his roots behind and was still in control of his career: 'I still enjoy playing the blues, and feature a couple of things on stage: 'Me And The Devil' and 'Groundhog Blues'. I still enjoy the odd acoustic gig which comes along once in a while but right now I'm purposely out of touch with the blues.' For the moment, it was only on vinyl that they had deserted the blues.

Melody Maker praised Tony to the hilt as producer and musician: 'McPhee has drawn on his long experiences in all facets of the music industry and he is one of the most original and calculating guitarists in Britain. He really used the bare minimum of three musicians to best advantage.' An unknown publication picked up on the sound the producer was looking for: 'Played during a period when little acknowledgement is given to a bass player (who) plays a far more rugged and imaginative bass than is accepted, thus succeeding the beautiful plunge down an octave or two, to depths where all notes are transformed into a naked, metallic grinding.'

Disc & Music Echo gave the album a four-star rating and emphasised: 'the effect of the counterpoint guitar phrases, with bass and drums well in the background, (which) is a change that other groups would do well to follow.' However, the *Jazz & Folk Blues Society* was less happy. 'It should be subtitled "And Thank God For The Off-Switch!" I'm sure that cavemen must have made better records.' It's clear some people still hadn't forgiven them for deserting the blues.

On 1st July 1970 the Hogs returned to Germany for a series of dates where audience reaction varied wildly: 'In North Germany they were very aware', Ken reveals. 'It is really down to the students. They want to hear political stuff. We played a University in Hamburg and we had representatives of the Baader-Meinhof gang coming in and asking us very seriously "What is this 'Thank Christ For The Bomb' about?" I thought I'd better be careful what I say here!'

They encountered the full spectrum of political views, playing a right-wing university in southern Germany where one promoter sounded them out about touring South Africa (then under apartheid)! On the border with Switzerland they played a casino where the gig consisted entirely of instrumentals because Tony had lost his voice. There was never a dull moment with the Groundhogs in Germany.

Pete Cruickshank.
TS Personal Collection

GROUNDHOGS – PETE CRUICKSHANK

Signed publicity photograph.
TS Personal Collection

They also played a festival in Essen, at an indoor venue with Black Sabbath. Its A Beautiful Day and Flock (the latter included Jerry Goodman who later joined the Mahavisnu Orchestra). There were two stages, one at either end of the arena, as one band played the other's gear was taken off for the next act to set up. Black Sabbath played their set but something was wrong with the other stage and Flock were unable to start their set. So Tony offered to play in order that the fans could hear a band, even though it put the running order out. Flock refused to do this, with the result that the Groundhogs never played because the police came and shut down the festival in the early hours of the morning. But at least they got paid.

The problems continued when they were stranded in an annexe at the Atlantic Hotel in Hamburg, a kind of theatrical bed and breakfast where all the bands stayed. The promoter was supposed to give then some money halfway through the tour but decided to do a bunk. The penniless band were reduced to cooking soup in their hotel room and sneaking round to the supermarket to get cornflakes. As Pete recalls: In the end we had to wait for our agency to send us some money.'

The tour continued but it was clear some venues weren't equipped to stage rock shows. At one place they had to get the gear in through a window! Roadie Mick Hubbert went absent without leave in the middle of the tour and left the band in the lurch. Then Pete had to do the driving! The Germans did get some things right, however. The band was directed to a cattle market, which they then found was the venue. The stench was vile and they thought there was no way they could play there, but four hours later the band played the gig and the smell had disappeared (the promoter had had the place sprayed).

Ken Pustelnik.
TS Personal Collection

On 5th July they played the Kiel Festival at the Oseenhalle. Also on the bill was Black Sabbath. It all went well until on the ferry coming back Ken and Ozzy Osbourne got locked up in the ferry's cells because they insisted on seeing an American film that had been dubbed in German. As Ken remembers: 'We thought it was great to hear a German dubbing John Wayne's voice. But they insisted we had to watch the other film being shown in English. That's how we ended up in the cells. To add insult to injury, our van broke down and we were towed off the ferry by Sabbath's Transit.'

Summertime brought the UK festival season and the band was booked for three. The first was the 10th National Jazz and Blues Festival, promoted by Harold Pendelton and the Marquee's own festival. The band had gone up on the bill since the previous year's appearance and, on Friday 7th August, they appeared third on the bill to headliners Family. In the programme notes it acknowledges just how far the band had travelled: 'Tony McPhee must have woken up one morning and suddenly realised where it really was. They are now so different and so much better that they could well be one of the outstanding successes of the whole festival. Thank Christ For The Groundhogs.'

The second festival was a week later at the inaugural Folk, Blues and Jazz Festival at Krumlin, near Halifax. Held over three days, it attracted a number of big names like Pink Floyd, Ginger Baker's Airforce, Manfred Mann and Fairport Convention. The two pound ten shilling cost of a weekend ticket was about the price of an album.

The band turned up at mid morning on the Saturday to be told they should have been performing the day before! Roy Fisher couldn't look at the contract as he didn't actually have one. Then Jo Ann Kelly (who was performing that day) came over and told them there had been many forged tickets. It also appeared that the local Yorkshire mafia had put the squeeze on festival traders and it was unlikely anybody was going to be paid. Tony recalls what happened next in his liner notes to 'Split': 'The promoter then decided that he could fit us in and our attitude was that, as we were only getting £100 for the gig and we were there, we wouldn't be losing a lot if we didn't get paid and we were sure the audience, who were sitting in a muddy field (yes, it was raining as well) would like to see something happening on stage.'

Their impromptu performance saw them appearing between folk acts Fairport Convention and Pentangle. Ken recalls the mood of the moment: 'We saw these people under a sea of plastic. When we started playing they went mental.' This positive attitude paid dividends because their photographer friend, Chris Richardson, took some shots of the performance which would be used to dramatic effect on the cover of the next album.

After the show they went to the bar where they saw bands that had refused to play like Pink Floyd. The festival was a complete disaster and the Sunday bill didn't even take place. The two promoters did a bunk; one of them was seen walking the hills mumbling about how much money he'd lost.

Even though 25,000 people had attended the Krumlin festival, the 1970 Isle of Wight festival, a watershed in such outdoor events, would completely dwarf that. The previous summers of love that had drawn the curtain on the 1960s were about to be shattered by a small section of the crowd who took the hippie ideal to extremes and insisted that 'music should be free'.

Joni Mitchell's set was interrupted as she was heckled with their slogans, while sections of the surrounding fences were torn down and thousands piled in for free. The Groundhogs were lucky they missed the mayhem, as they had performed on Thursday; this time they did turn up on the right day!

On stage at the Krumlin Festival – a photo taken at the same time as one used for the back of the 'Split' album.
Photograph by Christopher Richardson
TS Personal Collection

The Isle of Wight was the biggest gig they ever played in the UK. Tony recalls that they had almost missed the boat to the island. On the ferry they got chatting with the Mick Abrahams Band's drummer. Strangely, soon after they got there, promoter Rikki Farr asked them to go on early because the Mick Abrahams Band didn't have a drummer. The mystery of the disappearing drummer was never solved. Thursday 27th August was only a warm-up day but still a big crowd greeted the band.

It was a weird experience for Ken who had been there the year before as a spectator: 'We slept in a field that was by this big hotel and it was where we stayed in 1970. When we walked on stage the roar of the crowd was like a jet engine. It was so powerful it was almost primeval.' One of the music papers reported: 'the Groundhogs featured some really excellent bass guitar work from Pete Cruikshank on the splendid "Eccentric Man" from their new album.'

Many artists have to get over the fear of performing in public. It has already been noted that Tony conquered his with inner belief, but Pete had a different approach: 'During the Hooker period I drank whisky for Dutch courage. But I started to be sick a lot. You have to remember that everything was geared to the gig on the evening. I later went onto beer.'

At Mothers in Birmingham: 'There was a black DJ there and he came into the dressing room before the gig and offered us a smoke. I didn't want to say no, so I had a couple of drags. I don't know what was in it but everything was suddenly in slow motion.' The following day he asked the roadies what his performance was like; their reply was 'great'. As usual, Ken took a very pragmatic point of view regarding stage fright: 'I never really suffered with nerves. Stage fright is a condition. I like performing I like to see the audience response to what we do. That's why I never had nerves.'

Tony McPhee married Christine Payne on 4th September 1970 at Wandsworth Register Office, London. Master guitar maker Tony Zemaitis and his wife were witnesses. Tony knew Zemaitis because he was a friend of Jo Ann Kelly. But there wasn't to be a honeymoon.

Shortly after the wedding, the band embarked on a short tour supporting the great American blues band, Canned Heat, now labelmates to Liberty/UA Records. Pete recalls: 'Canned Heat were great and had lots of charisma. I watched them every night and learned a lot.' As the autumn leaves started falling they began to think about recording their next album. The seed for that work had already been planted in Tony's head. Trouble was, he didn't know it!

Tony 'TS' McPhee.
TS Personal Collection

chapter 8
One Way Split

*'I wrote "Thank Christ For The Bomb" and "Split" on riffs.
I knew my melodies were not great.'*
Tony McPhee

'The joke backfired on us when it became our signature song.'
Ken Pustelnik on 'Cherry Red'

*'Half of the Groundhogs' "Split" features
the musical tremors of a disturbed mind.'*
Notts Evening Post

Within just a few months of the release of 'Thank Christ For The Bomb', Tony was already fielding questions about the next album from sections of the music press. He had indicated as early as August that they were trying to find new songs. Burnout from the album-tour-album treadmill had not kicked in yet, but was not far away! However, the inspiration for the next album had already happened.

Tony McPhee's aberration of May 1970 was the inspiration for the lyrical content of 'Split'. Tony had tried dope once but it never really affected him. In fact, ex-roadie Mick Hubbert confirms: 'Tony and Pete were never into drugs that much.' On one occasion, Tony remembers Ken's mate, Putty, 'in an oozing lump' on the floor. Putty had been handing out some hash cake and was completely blitzed, but it didn't touch Tony!

During a gig in Huddersfield, Ken had been given some grass and they smoked it on the way home. Tony remembered thinking it highly amusing that the seeds had been left in and the joint would occasionally bang, like an exploding cigar. The next night Tony and Chris had been invited to Mick's house for a curry, and Mick's American lodger rolled a joint out of the remaining dust.

'I shared the joint with Chris and Mick,' Tony remembered. 'Mick's television (*Star Trek* was on) suddenly divided down the middle. Everybody else seemed to be having a good time, but I was feeling strange.

'I went to the bathroom. I needed something elemental and turned on the tap, but I started to grow like something from *Alice In Wonderland*. I tried to play the guitar to gain some focus but I was losing reality and all I could see was spirals. My heart was beating so fast I thought I was going to explode.

'Mick asked me to look at the curry as last time he looked it was growing out of the pan. I went into the kitchen opened a window and the garden looked like a Martian landscape. Mick's wife was there so I latched on to her because she was straight and I needed someone like that to get me through. I even started to pass out and after a few hours it subsided. I'm sure that episode opened the door a bit, which I couldn't close, to "Split".'

Just a few weeks later in May, Tony and Christine took their landlady's son, also called Tony, out for a walk in Green Park, London. It was a boiling hot day and later that night Tony couldn't get to sleep. It was then that he had a panic attack:

'I started to think and it came to me how on earth can I possibly exist, I still have trouble explaining it (Split Part One). It was a denial of existence, so I tried to run away from the thought, I ran upstairs to the top of the flats, it was too dark so I turned on the lights – too bright (Split Part Two).

'I couldn't get away from the thought all night; I tried stroking the cat to get my mind off it. We had this old fridge and I could listen to the sound of the motor when it started up.

'I eventually fell asleep through sheer exhaustion (Split Part Three) but when I woke up the feeling came back to me straight away. I used to look at the toilet bowls and they were alien, we were surrounded by buildings which overshadowed me – I was completely paranoid. Looking back, there were a few months when I would have believed anything; a door opened in my mind and I couldn't shut it. I don't fear it now, I used to.'

It was the morning after that he put it down to schizophrenia, but it was much later that he recalled the get-together after the Huddersfield gig and connected it with this incident.

As time went on, he realised that this was too big a thing to ignore with regard to his work. He started to think about incorporating this experience into the band's repertoire but had always found personal lyrics boring and self-indulgent.

Then something swung it in favour of recording these thoughts, as an interview with *Sounds* outlines: 'I know a lot of people who are getting the same thing; I was very confused at the time and I thought I was going nuts, so what I wanted to do was put that down to show anyone who's got it they're not alone.'

They entered De Lane Lea studios in November 1970 to record their follow-up to 'Thank Christ For The Bomb'. In the very early stages he still wasn't sure the theme was the right one to do, but when he found out that Martin Birch (who engineered 'Thank Christ For The Bomb') had suffered similar aberrations it confirmed his original idea. In order to write successful lyrics he found himself taking the rough mixes home and working the words out – a far cry from Herbal Mixture days sitting in the foetal position in the studio toilet!

All the preparations paid off when the album was completed in just a couple of weeks. The punchy opening of 'Split Part One' belies what's ahead, the double-tracked guitars and the steadiness of the band creating an ambience of

With Andrew Lauder in the UA offices.
Pic courtesy Andrew Lauder

66

calm reflected in the first two lines of the verse. However, as the track careers to its conclusion the band descends into freak-out. This is summed up in the last lines and cuts through to Tony's worst fears:

> *In the dying embers of a burnt-out day,*
> *When morning seems a thousand hours away,*
> *Dark prevails and the light gives up the fight*
> *to stay.*
> *The blackness thickens and surrounds.*

The second part of 'Split' starts with some frenzied wah-wah and tremelo work. Tony had acquired the wah-wah just after 'Thank Christ For The Bomb' because he liked the sound rather than it fitting in musically.

The riff to 'Split Part Two', one of Tony's finest, started life as something he played in the soundcheck. Then it graduated to being used in one of the improvisation sections at gigs. By the time he started writing the album it had developed sufficiently to be included. The middle-section solo refers briefly to the blues before the band really starts to kick. The impossible situation that Tony found himself in is summed up with the first lines:

> *I leap from bed in the middle of night,*
> *Run up the stairs for 3 or 4 flights,*
> *Run in a room, turn on the light,*
> *The dark is too dark but the light's too*
> *bright.*

There was a problem at the end of 'Split Part Two' because it was half a tone lower than 'Split Part Three'. Tony decided to open with a crescendo of noise and then make the change with a completely different instrument. He got round this problem with the Hammond organ – only because it happened to be there!

By using both hands to play chords, when he removed one hand he was in the correct key for the next part. 'Split Part Three' is really about the peak of Tony's aberration.

Exhaustion is reached and there are no more depths to plumb. There's a nice section where Pete plays a catchy bass line and everything else slots in around it. The end is manic with a raunchy solo from Tony.

'Split Part Four', which concludes the concept, opens with a juicy blues lick and continues in that groove. Tony delivers a great vocal with lots of references to the Almighty and salvation. The lyrics acknowledge that some people do turn to religion in times of crisis, although Tony didn't. Perhaps these lyrics confused some people.

Ken plays with a lot of feel and delivers some great snare drum work. In his role as producer Tony had instinctive ideas where to use light and shade and that's one of the secrets of his success in this field. However, as he confirmed to *NME*, these noises were not what they seemed: 'All the weird sound effects are accidental, really, and the closing section of side one we didn't even know we'd recorded.'

'Split' succeeds on many levels. However, as Tony reveals, he was aware of his limitations as a writer: 'I wrote "Thank Christ For The Bomb" and "Split" on riffs. I knew my melodies were not great' (although later he exclaimed 'I can't

Tony's beloved Zemaitis guitar.
TS Personal Collection

believe I said that'). In fact, the story and the riffs are so great the listener doesn't really hear any melodic deficiencies. 'Split' runs for twenty minutes but seems to fly by. The Hogs still had their unique sound but it was much more accessible than 'Thank Christ For The Bomb'.

Side two is made up of a number of disparate tracks. 'A Year In The Life' was inspired by the Beatles 'A Day In The Life'. The song, about the seasons and the passage of time, features some muscular drumming from Ken. The underrated 'Junkman' is an iconoclastic number, and like 'A Year In The Life', has many moods. The vocals were recorded at three in the morning when Tony was coming down with flu. The song is about modern food production techniques. Tony had been into health food for quite a while and had educated himself on the lamentable state of the

modern diet. He bemoans the removal of wheatgerm from bread and molasses from sugar; by implication, the best things are taken out. Although not in common parlance at the time it's interesting to note that Tony was using the term 'Junkman' in a song describing what is now commonly known as 'junk food'.

They had six tracks in the can, but were a little short of a complete album. In desperation, Tony turned to a number that he had written on the German tour in the summer, first tried out in a school hall on a day off. The track had since become a regular in the set, but nobody had thought about it for the album. Named 'Cherry Red', it inadvertently became their signature song. As Tony recalls, some things are way beyond the horizon: 'You can't really tell how a track is going to do. I had no idea it was going to

groundhogs

LIBERTY

be so big. In the end, it was a millstone round my neck and by the late 1970s I refused to play it.'

'Cherry Red' was recorded in one take and employed tricks they used on 'Blues Obituary'. It's a tour de force, with its wailing guitars, driving bass and crashing percussion topped by a weird, high-pitched delivery. Tony liked the idea of doing falsetto; it was another new experience.

With the backing track in the can and with minimal overdubs, Tony set about putting the vocals down. When Martin Birch put the backing track on, Tony was not quite in position and the mics were 20 yards away at the other end of the L-shaped studio. As the stunning opening kicked in Tony let out a shriek that is clearly audible on the record. Eyeing a cowbell, he picked up a drumstick and whacked it on his dash from desk to mic – and that was recorded for posterity too!

'Cherry Red' was actually a bit of a joke. Ken takes up the story: 'We sort of said let's do a piss-take. It was the Groundhogs plays Led Zeppelin, an in-house joke. We thought riff songs were good but simple. Originally "Cherry Red" was in the act before we recorded it but it was very bluesy. The joke backfired on us when it became our signature song.' They developed the riff idea to the full on that one.

There was another joke that was connected with the track and it concerned the BBC radio sessions. Tony was not averse to taking a short cut or two: 'We'd go in and (producer) Malcolm Brown would say 'All right lads, "Cherry Red" again? We've got a few of those'. We once used an old version of the track. Nobody noticed.'

There's a degree of the mischievous in Tony McPhee that belies his serious attitude to his music. In 'Split Part One' the lyrics portray the darkness of his flat. The working title was 'Nocturne In A Flat', although the song is in A major. 'Cherry Red' tells the story of a special girl he met who gave him the runaround. But who was this girl and where did he meet her? Did he see her again? The answer is simple; the whole story is bogus.

He remembers when Lester Bangs reviewed 'Thank Christ For The Bomb' for *Rolling Stone*: 'He had the lyrics of "Garden" and he dissected them believing he had found out their meaning. My attitude is fine, if that's what he wants to believe.' He gives a clue as to why some of his lyrics follow this path: 'Some phrases come out of your head. There is no pattern, they just fit. There is no creativity, it just happens.' When viewed in this way it can be dangerous to take his lyrics too seriously.

Even with the addition of 'Cherry Red' they still had five minutes to fill. This was the excuse that Tony was looking for, a return to the blues. There were already references to their roots on 'Split', but this was going to be a full-blown affair. 'Groundhog' is another old stage number they fell back on and Tony outlined to *Sounds* how it came about: 'As we were pushed for time I thought we'd put it down, and I think it works quite nicely with the rest of the numbers.'

Contract for the Rolling Stones tour.
TS Personal Collection

In some interviews Tony stated that 'Groundhog' was done because he couldn't get the vocals right on another track. That was a cover story as there was no other track. But it was more than that; it was Tony's statement that he still dug the blues. In order to get the sound he wanted he put the guitar through two amps and then used ten mics to record them. There are no drums on this track but Tony got a percussion effect by attaching some bottle tops to his shoe and tapped his foot against a wooden board.

This certainly fooled a lot of people. 'Groundhog' is John Lee Hooker's song and is Tony's tribute to the great man. It's quite a journey from 'Split Part One' to 'Groundhog' and as such, is a much more eclectic journey than 'Thank Christ...'.

By the time they had finished the final mixing it was early morning. The whole process had taken just two weeks. They were so elated they decided to give Andrew Lauder a preview. With the master tape in hand, they walked up Oxford Street, into Mortimer Street and the UA offices. They went into Lauder's office where Martin Birch put the mix onto the Revox machine – amazingly they hadn't made any copies! There was a moment of horror when the depressed play button brought forth a sound that could only have been described as rubbish. They looked at Martin whose facial contortions had changed to a sunnier side. He realised he put the tape in the wrong way! All was then revealed and it sounded great. It was a very strong album throughout.

However, not quite everybody agreed. Tony recalls: 'Around the time of "Split" I remember Ken saying to me "I've noticed that on every

(1) Part of the promo written to coincide with the release was a contribution by Martin Cerf – a UA executive in the States. It was decided to exploit the Groundhog Day connection: 'This year, to really add punch to this day, we call Groundhog Day, we are dedicating the entire year to the creatures and are sending you their latest album "Thank Christ For The Bomb" along with an exciting anthology book on the Groundhogs. You'll quickly realize these are English compositions. These are English Groundhogs, rare in these parts. The fact is these Groundhogs are rare: period, as you'll soon see! Enjoy!'

(2) Tony Zemaitis (1935-2002) started making guitars in his spare time, but it wasn't long before he was working 12-hour days from his home in Balham, London. He was apprenticed as a cabinet maker on leaving school. He learned to play the guitar and played semi-pro in clubs but he got into making guitars by stealth. He recalled in an interview at the time: 'It was over a good many years that I realised I was becoming a guitar maker. I managed to get a job that allowed me to work two or three days a week as a cabinet-maker and I used to spend the rest of the time on guitars.' His list of other clients included Donovan, Marc Bolan, Peter Green, Spencer Davies, Jo Ann Kelly, Ronnie Lane, Ronnie Wood and Greg Lake.

'Split' press promotion.
TS Personal Collection

album you put a weak track on." I thought "What?" I have never put a filler track on any album. Other people may have thought that but I can honestly say I never put anything on that was substandard to me.'

With the album in the can, they entered 1971 with the belief that things would get even better. In February 'Thank Christ For The Bomb' was released in the States. (1)

Around this time Tony decided he needed to upgrade his gear. He had shown interest in what Hiwatt (his existing gear) and Marshall had to offer, but by the end of March he'd gone over to Laney. The reason for the change was that his old gear had become obsolete. One of the problems was that although he had built his own amplifier, he had never bothered to house it properly. The rigours of touring had taken their toll, but as he told *Zig-Zag*, the new gear was not only up to scratch, it gave him more room to manouvre:

'There's not really much to choose between makes, but this Laney stuff gave out what it claimed to give out and seemed okay, though I've made some alterations to improve the tone because I'm as interested in getting a good sound as I am in volume.'

There was another factor in choosing Laney. He discovered his octave splitter (a device that could repeat a note Tony played an octave higher or lower, thus creating a new sound) worked better when using the wah-wah pedal. It gave him more tones than the others – he was a great fan of Hendrix's 'Machine Gun' and wanted to explore effects more fully.

Tony was also looking to improve his instrumentation and he turned to an old friend. He commissioned Tony Zemaitis, to make an electric guitar for him. Zemaitis had already made a twelve-string for Eric Clapton and was gaining a reputation for quality instruments.

Zemaitis turned the tables and asked Tony if he could improve on the performance of some Lawrence pickups he was using. Tony's reputation for his technical knowledge was widespread in the business. He had a go, but was unable to help on that occasion.

One day in March, Zemaitis showed Tony a guitar he had made. It was the first one he made with a metal front and he explained that it was only a prototype and he would make another if Tony didn't like it. It was beautiful. Tony was stunned and because it was quite early in Zemaitis's career, he only paid £175 for it. It was a real steal – McPhee still owns his prized guitar. It wouldn't be long before its value would go through the roof. Shortly after Tony received his guitar Zemaitis started work on a bass for Pete Cruikshank. (2)

In February Tony and Christine moved to a cottage in Haverhill, Suffolk. This meant the band lived quite far apart from each other but he made it clear to the *Suffolk Free Press* that was fine by him: 'Some groups live together but it doesn't work out.' As far as he was concerned a hard-working outfit like the Groundhogs already saw enough of each other and the rest of the band agreed.

Christine was also interviewed. The paper noted that she was also a vegetarian. However, she certainly didn't see her husband as anything other than a ordinary guy: 'Even when I go along to hear him play at gigs, it doesn't seem like Tony up there on stage.'

With the amount of travelling the band was doing in those days the result was a lot of boredom so to relieve some of the tension they devised silly ways of passing the time. They would have mock fights that sometimes got out of hand.

Once they were being driven by Charlie McLeod down the Charing Cross Road in London. Tony was sitting in the front and was turning round play-thumping Pete while Charlie had gone through a red light and was speeding. It wasn't long before an unmarked police car stopped them. The policeman asked the driver 'What's your name – death?' Charlie must have been impressed as he later joined the police.

On 6th February 1971 they recorded a *Top Gear* session for John Peel. The most significant gig they had around this time was at the Roundhouse, London, where they got a lucky break. In the audience was a certain Mick Jagger who was scouting for a support band for an upcoming Rolling Stones tour. The interest was so great that Roy Fisher was summoned for a meeting with Jagger and Trevor Churchill at the Stones' office the following day.

The deal was done and it was a good opportunity for the band to get more exposure, but it wasn't all roses. The contract was signed on 1st March with Chrysalis and the deal was £400 plus petrol for nine dates. The money looked even less however, when they realised most of the gigs had a matinee show. The tour started three days later at Newcastle City Hall.

Tony had seen the Stones back in the early days at Studio 51. In those days the crowds were

SPLIT IT'S BEEN WORTH WAITING FOR
THE NEW ALBUM FROM GROUNDHOGS

not that large for a blues band. In that period he also saw them many times at the Richmond Athletic club. He watched them grow, as he recalls: 'The Stones went from strength to strength, featuring on tours with Bo Diddley, etc, playing the big gigs like the Lewisham Odeon, whilst the Groundhogs had made it to Studio 51! So it was quite an honour to actually be asked to support them.'

Jagger remarked to the band that he didn't think they would do the tour because they were successful in their own right. Pete Cruickshank in fact, knew Bill Wyman who lived close by in Beckenham.

This was the first time the band had played to consistently large audiences and the atmosphere at these gigs was phenomenal. After the Coventry gig on the 6th there was a day's break so Tony went home to Haverhill. One of the reasons he went home was because Christine was heavily pregnant (their son, Conan, was born on 16th April 1971).

He planned to catch the train to Glasgow from London to arrive in good time for the Playhouse gig. Tony thought there was bound to be a train every hour. In this, he was seriously wrong because there were only two trains per day. By the time he got to the station he'd missed the first one and the last one was going to get him there after the first show started. He was pleasantly surprised to find Keith Richards on the train and they journeyed up together. Of course Richards was secure in the knowledge that he would make their first show. Tony missed his and a local band called

Merlin stepped in as support for the first performance. It was not their night, as their gear hadn't arrived – so Tony had to use Richards' Fender amp, which he hated.

The following day they played Bristol's Colston Hall, but Tony had some running repairs on his mind. He was wandering round the backstage catacombs with a soldering iron in his hand looking for a power point to effect some repairs to his amp. He came across a slightly opened door and pushed it, to be met with the sight of Mick and Bianca sprawled on the floor in a cloud of (coke) dust giggling.

It was also the first time Tony had seen an entourage. Keith Richards had a guy that followed him around. They called him a 'professional ponce' and all he seemed to do was to be at the beck and call of his mentor. That, no doubt, included fetching the drugs and taking the rap as the need arose.

Tony told *Sounds* he remembered Bristol quite well. 'The hairy audience gave us a good reception; however, as soon as the Stones came on, a dozen or so bouncers who were deployed around the hall lined up against the curved stage, facing the audience with their arms crossed.'

Tony playing the borrowed white Strat.
Pic courtesy Pete Cruickshank

Footnote

(3) Denis Knowles joined Liberty-UA in the summer of 1969; he came from CBS, where he had 52 vans at his disposal to cover the UK. However, as he related recently, Liberty was a much smaller operation: 'Philips (distributor for Liberty) had problems and needed to move to larger premises in Romford. The move happened the week before the release of "Thank Christ For The Bomb". They were unable to distribute any labels for over a week. At the time, Liberty-UA had just five sales vans, three in London and the suburbs, one in the Midlands and one to cover Manchester and Liverpool.'

The situation got worse further away from London: 'One Scottish dealer, Bruce Findlay, had five shops spread around Edinburgh, Glasgow and Stirling. Bruce rang me out of desperation, as he could not get the new Groundhogs' album ('Thank Christ') and demand in his shops was considerable. To cut a long story short I was able to ship him large quantities overnight via Security Express. We supplied other important dealers in the same way, all of which made returns to the album charts. The result was that the album shot in at Number 9 in the Top 50 album charts, which of course gave us more publicity and increased demand.'

When the Philips contract ran out after 'Split' they signed a distribution deal with EMI.

(4) In the 1990s *Mojo* magazine ran a regular item called 'Last Night A Record Changed My Life'. Karl Hyde of Underworld – their 'Born Slippy' became the anthem of the hit film *Trainspotting* – cited 'Split' as a seminal influence. In the article he recalls, at the age of 14, going to the Birmingham Town Hall to see them: 'I thought it was just incredible. Tony McPhee had a fantastic voice – he reminded me of Roger Chapman of Family. But his guitar playing was brilliant. I loved and still do his sense of syncopation. I still do things that I learned from listening to Tony McPhee.'

He was mesmerised by the pictures of the band on the album cover: 'I wanted to be on that stage, playing all those incredible guitar licks.'

One of gigs turned out to be quite un-rock'n'roll, as Tony related in his diary of the tour in *Sounds*: 'The Big Apple at Brighton is above a cinema. We were asked to keep the volume down for our set so it wouldn't disturb the filmgoers below!' With two and a half thousand backsides acting as sound absorbers in the floor, there was no real problem

It was then on to Leeds University for the Groundhogs' most famous gig. They had already been reunited with their one-time engineer Glyn Johns, who was recording the event for the Stones using their mobile studio.

They still owed him £20 for the Herbal Mixture session, but as Johns was now rich and famous he'd obviously forgotten about such trifles. He even offered to tape the Groundhogs' show for them. Though he said he couldn't tape all the set, a back-up tape was used as a fail-safe and a combination of the two machines recorded a blistering performance, led by 'Cherry Red' and finishing with a pulsating performance of 'Eccentric Man'. At the end of the night Johns got Jagger to present Tony with the tape.

The Stones were very approachable, although they never had much direct contact. Bill Wyman told Tony and Pete he envied them as he missed playing the smaller venues and being able to choose their own material.

Pete was disappointed that he never got to speak to Mick Jagger and Keith Richards, but Ken did: 'At Leeds the dressing rooms were upstairs above the stage off a sports hall. Their dressing room had tables of food but there was no one to eat it. Keith Richards couldn't get into the dressing room, so we took the lock off for him. He came back a few minutes later with a bowl of licorice allsorts as a thank you. It was a touching but pitiful moment.'

But, as Tony recollected: 'The Stones usually would have eaten before they got to the gig, so the rider was often plundered for far more than licorice allsorts.'

There was a lot of free time for the band on the tour, Tony being so bored at one stage that he built himself a drum kit made up of dustbins! The band was well received, but the Stones hadn't toured for a while and were rusty. Tony recalls one of the shows: 'Coventry was bad for them. They did "Midnight Rambler" and there was a part where Jagger took his belt off and hit it on the floor. At that point the band was supposed to hit their big note. Unfortunately, they were all out of sync and it ended up as a mess.'

The tour ended at the Roundhouse, London, where Ken recalls: 'At the end of the gig we walked into their dressing room, which was packed with all sorts of hangers-on. We made our way to the band to thank them and say goodbye. Everybody stopped and stared at us, they probably thought "Who the hell are these guys?"'

In an interview with James Johnson for *NME* just after the tour Tony noted what a culture shock the tour was: 'It may sound a little strange but what I liked about the whole thing was being organised. It was nice to have a tour manager

around, telling us what to do, how long to play and to get everything sorted out.'

But the two-show format caused a lot of problems for the band, as Tony recorded in his *Sounds* diary: 'It's just that on this kind of tour a second band is treated like a pimple being slowly squeezed out of its half-hour set because the house was late getting in, or the main band overran.' As he confessed later he was dubious of the whole thing, and expected to get slagged off by the music press for supporting the Stones given their own success at the time.

It was quite a surprise when Tony found out that United Artists was planning to put out 100 copies of the live Leeds recordings as a promo in the United States. These were distributed to DJs and quickly became collector's items. As he admits, he was bemused: 'I didn't know why they needed it as we had two albums out. I thought it was inept because they should have been promoting our last two albums more.' The album was actually distributed in anticipation of a tour, which never materialised. However, in 1979, when Tony found himself broke, he found out from a Canadian fan that copies of the album were going for £100. Tony contacted UA to see if they could find the tape (with the hope of making some more copies), but was told that the master was lost.

'Split' was released to coincide with the Stones tour and sold over 7,000 copies before the first week was out, and was well on the way to Number 5 in the charts. However, this could have been much higher because, as with 'Thank Christ', Liberty had pressing and distribution problems and didn't get the album in the shops which limited their success. (3)

Enthusiastic reviews appeared in the press. *Sounds*, while stating that it wasn't as good as their previous effort, made it clear that McPhee the songwriter and producer had come up trumps: '(He) has proved that he can take a basic theme – in this case the experience of a metaphysical psychosis – and it expand it cleverly.'

The paper also pointed out '(Tony) succeeds in capturing all his own guitar excitement and the driving rhythmic force of Ken Pustelnik and Pete Cruickshank which an independent producer might have failed to do.' *Disc & Music Echo* was just as gushing: 'In a way, the Groundhogs are the nearest thing we've got left to the now defunct Taste.'

The less mainstream *Music Business Weekly* marked the album down succinctly as: 'Definitely one to watch.' Their music was reaching far and wide now as *Capital Journal of Oregon*, USA, concentrating on Tony's success as a producer noted: 'The music is a superb example of how a commanding guitarist doesn't have to obscure an all-out drummer or an assertive bass player.' The album attracted many new fans of all ages! (4)

They had invested a lot of time in the sleeve and rightly so, as artwork was already established as an integral part of promotion and sales. However, Denis Knowles, who was in charge of distribution and promotion, remembers that the plans were becoming a little too ambitious:

'There was some delay in forward planning as Roy Fisher wanted a complicated sleeve consisting of several separate round photos, each diminishing in diameter, held together by a paper fastener in the centre.

'I looked at the feasibility but the practical problem was too great. We settled for photographing the diminishing photo discs as flat artwork, hence the final outcome. I can't remember whether this held up the sleeve supply, but sleeve artwork was always a big issue as it was an integral part of the product.'

As soon as 'Split' hit the shops it made a positive impact with its distinctive artwork. Chris Richardson's photography ranking with the best work of the day. (5) The sleeve worked out so well it could be looked on as a lucky break that Richardson couldn't do it. He'd taken the subject matter and made an inspirational cover that brilliantly encapsulated the concept. The starkness of the inside picture portrays the fierce intensity of the band. The shots were taken on that rainy day at the ill-fated Krumlin festival the previous year – some good had come out of that disastrous day.

The fact that Tony was photographed with a white Fender Stratocaster confused a few people. In fact, he had borrowed the instrument from his brother-in-law, Daryl Payne. He needed to change from the Gibson SG for some of the numbers as it worked better with his wah-wah pedal. Furthermore, the live shots of the festival reinforced the idea that, even though it was a studio album, you should come and see this band performing!

It was inevitable that Tony would field questions comparing their last two albums. In *Zig-Zag* magazine he started with 'Split': 'It's different! It creates a different mood to me. "Thank Christ" always left me feeling very satisfied; this one leaves me satisfied, but irritated too because it's so much more vicious and intense. All the numbers poke you somehow, whereas the last one relied on melody more and was comparatively relaxing.'

It's clear that the vibe that surrounded the concept of 'Split' had pervaded the music, and there is a lot more tension for that reason. But another factor that distinguishes the two albums is that 'Split' has a lot less overdubs. The arrangements are less complex and, consequently, it does have a 'live' feel to it. There are compelling reasons to believe that 'Thank Christ' is actually a consistently stronger album but it was this 'on the edge' feeling of the latter album that tipped the fans' vote.

In April, United Artist's publicity agent, Ronnie Bell, got them onto the long-running BBC chart show *Top Of The Pops*. He had been around in the business for many years and had a lot of connections at the BBC. When he heard about the new album slot he pitched in for the band. They performed 'Cherry Red' with Tony singing live over a remix of the backing track looking suitably embarrassed.

Ken caused the crew more than a few headaches. He was digging his heels in over being forced to mime and was determined that the band should play live. The plan was for Tony to sing live over a pre-recorded backing track. For playback purposes they had a one and half foot square speaker set up on a chipboard support – hardly hi-tech.

They ran through the song and it seemed okay but when the audience came in there were a lot of problems, the sound of their dancing feet

THE GROUNDHOGS "WHO WILL SAVE THE WORLD" UA UNITED ARTISTS RECORDS

Promotional picture taken on *Top Of The Pops* stage.
Pic courtesy Pete Cruickshank

seriously compromising the track. It was at this point that Ken took things into his own hands:

'I suggested I get a feed of the track on headphones and then I'd be in time. I wanted to see the producer but they said I couldn't. I made my way to the executive bar.'

On his way he had a stroke of luck as he saw John Dummer, who was doing a lot of work for the BBC. Dummer was able to sign Ken in and he confronted the producer, who must have had a bit of a shock. The upshot was he got his way but when they sat down to watch the programme all they could hear was Ken's hi-hat. He failed to hear it during recording because he had his headphones on.

Tony's version of the day is slightly different: 'I was given the job of picking Ken up; he lived in Chiswick High Street, above a butchers shop, which was empty 'cos the butcher had done a runner. We hired a Transit and driver to pick myself and then Ken up on the way to the studios.'

McPhee knew from experience it would be difficult to wake Ken. There was no point knocking on the front door of the flat, but there was an old broken greenhouse just below his bedroom window: 'So I risked life and limb and climbed up this rickety structure. Fortunately it was a casement window and it was open. I climbed in and he was lying there completely comatose.'

After much shouting and kicking the bed, Ken finally woke up fully clothed. Tony said 'The

(5) The US release of 'Split' had a different cover. It features three individual coloured pictures of the band members playing their instruments. In the background of each shot are artificially produced mountain/desert scenes. The inside cover features two Groundhogs standing up on a mound of earth. There are extensive sleeve notes that tell the story of 'Split'. This is how it starts: 'Screaming pulsating lead guitar riffs throw you into a rhythm track that creates enough motive for even the weakest muscle of your body to move sharply and involuntarily as if it were experiencing a spasmodic nerve attack, you have entered the first phase of "Split".'

van's outside to take us to the studio,' and left. Ken eventually followed: 'When we got there we watched Pan's People rehearse; it sounded like a herd of galumphing elephants, they were stomping and counting in time to fit the choreography. I really used to fancy one of them, but I wasn't impressed.'

At their soundcheck they had to mime to a backing track which Martin Birch had prepared. Tony's monitor was on the dancefloor some feet away: 'I was singing live and Ken couldn't help but hit his bloody drums. I was already having difficulty hearing the backing track in front of me and Ken's erratic drum hits behind were making it worse.

'I asked an engineer if the audience would be between me and the monitors, and he said they would. It was no good. I had to get them to move the monitors closer, and although they complained about possible feedback, they gave in in the end.

'We were introduced by Ed Stewart, who virtually apologised for us being there; he said something like, "Now boys and girls we are going to bring you something a little different tonight." "Wanker!" I thought. I played my Zemaitis on the show, but it was one of those wiped by Auntie – just as well as I was sporting a full beard, which seemed like a good idea at the time.'

The strange thing about this was the Groundhogs never released any singles from the album. The strategy, hitherto, had been to release singles for airplay. But then when they appeared on the premier singles show, nothing materialised.

In the early part of the year the subject of touring the States came up on more than one occasion. The band archive of 29th April gives a confident message from Roy Fisher's diary: 'See Tony for amps for US tour – size and weight'. However, by 14th May there was a negative, less sure, air about things.

'Pat Meehan said get Vince Romario – NY agent – to call him and put good word in for US tour'. Even as late as May, in an interview with *NME*, Tony reported the tour's structure was not quite right: 'We weren't happy about the tour anyway because we had dates that would be either Sacramento or San Francisco and we've learnt the hard way that you have to have something definite on paper.'

Ken elaborates as to why they were unhappy: 'Roy Fisher told us he had got us a tour in the US. But the problem was it was with the Beach Boys! I like them, but to tour with them would have been a complete mismatch. We all felt the same way. One of the dates we were going to play was Las Vegas. It was a great shame – the door was already half-open because we had a healthy level of import sales there.'

In fact, as Pete recalls, there were several misfires on foreign trips: 'We would have our passports ready only to find out the trip had been cancelled. So by the time we started to talk about the US I was in half a mind it wasn't going to happen.'

In June/July the band embarked on a headlining UK tour of concert halls and Universities. The gigs took up most of the month and it was a sign of the band's growing profile. As Tony related to Jerry Gilbert of *Sounds*: 'I'm finding now that the concerts we do are much more satisfactory. The clubs are hot and cramped and, although I'm nostalgic about clubs, there comes a point where you need the comfort of the concert halls.' *Melody Maker* was also there to witness the show at the Kinetic Circus, Birmingham attended by Led Zeppelin's Robert Plant.

On 4th August they travelled to Holland to support Canned Heat at the Paradiso, Amsterdam for £150 plus hotel and transport costs. However, the main attraction was that they were going to be part of a film being shot there about a girl 'finding herself' in a hippy community. According to Andrew Lauder, the rushes were not too good and the plot was corny. It was the first time dry ice had ever been used at a Hogs gig, but Ken hated it as he thought that it was more like Pink Floyd.

Pete remembers the audience were so stoned they were lying on the floor. For some reason the film was shelved, but, Tony mixed the tapes of the gig at Pye studios in late September and the soundtrack album was released in Holland. The only Groundhogs track used is 'Still A Fool', running at over eight minutes.

On 28th August the band played at the little-remembered Weeley festival organised by the Clacton Round Table to raise funds for charity. The Groundhogs appeared low down the bill and yet on the advertising poster they were second to the Faces – as they had just had a Top Five album that was still selling well.

A fan called Rich recalls seeing Hell's Angels being taken off the site in police vans. 'Me and six mates made our way straight to the front – not a good idea trying to wade through 20,000 people. We made it to about 20 ft from the stage where we tried to sit in a space about 3 ft square. From what I can remember of the music it was the Groundhogs (brilliant), Mott the Hoople (good), Barclay James Harvest (too long to set up) and King Crimson (brilliant).'

In the first weekend of September the band played festivals in Germany (Speyer) and Austria (Vienna). Two of the bands on the bill were Black Sabbath and Gentle Giant. Patrick Meehan, who at one point had been gainfully employed as John Lee Hooker's driver, managed both these bands with his son, who was also called Patrick. In the main, these kind of events blend in with all of the others, but on this occasion it was to have far-reaching consequences for Tony.

It was on the plane to Vienna, an old Viscount, that the problems started, Tony recalls what happened next: 'This thing started whirring away up the runway and took off and stayed three feet above the ground for about five minutes. I've never experienced anything like it before because you think this is really it! And you look at the other people sitting there with glazed eyes!

'Then this voice comes across saying "We are returning to Frankfurt airport, we have a little trouble, nothing to worry about" and then he banks so sharply that suddenly he's heading for this fucking plane taking off. By this time we thought well, what's the difference – either we hit the ground or the plane.'

It was an experience Tony took a long time to get over and was always in the back of his mind when US tours were mooted. It was something he wanted but when they were called off he didn't mind that much.

On 10th September they headlined the Buxton Festival, actually held indoors at the Pavilion Gardens, and the following day played the Queen Elizabeth Hall, London. For this they received £500, one of their biggest pay cheques to date. Tony Stewart of *Melody Maker* was there:

'Out of the many gigs I've seen (this) was easily one of the best! Tony, Ken and Pete still work well with each other, the arrangements are again loose, and so include a lot more of Tony's guitar improvisations! Ken drives hard with some complicated rhythm patterns, which build the number up to a fever of excitement, blended with persistent bass runs by Pete.'

They still played old favourites from the first two albums like 'Still A Fool' and 'BDD'. In fact, Tony was keen to put the record straight and he did so to James Johnson of *NME*: 'We are still playing the blues really. It is only on record we have changed. On stage 50 per cent of our numbers are blues and the ones we play off the album are those which have a blues feel to them.' However, Tony admits that the tentative move away from their roots opened up the band's potential – not to say his songwriting – because he did feel the blues was a little bit 'restrictive'.

Following the aborted movie gig, they flew out to Germany to support John Mayall for eight gigs. The tour started at Münster on 12th September and included shows in Munich, Düsseldorf, Berlin and Frankfurt. The Berlin gig turned out to be lively. Before going to the Deutschland Halle, a big sports stadium, they did a radio interview which went really well. A girl from UA accompanied them down to the gig but that's when the problems started.

They tried to get into the stage door on the side of the theatre but were told to go through the front. They couldn't get in the front either, so the UA rep tried to explain that they were the

Probably the only record of the Groundhogs playing on the *Top Of The Pops* stage.

support band. Roy Fisher takes up the story:

'Ticket prices in Germany then were high and there were a lot of militant students milling around protesting about the prices. When they let us through, the students surged through as well and we were carried along with them. It wasn't long before we met some more security but these had batons.

'Tony got lifted by both arms, kicked up the backside and thrown out. Ken got his hair pulled but Pete managed to get through. I also had my hair pulled and I was hit over the head with a baton. I couldn't understand what the security man was saying to me. It was only the girl that saved me.'

When they did get in they saw scores of police drinking coffee under the stage looking smug. As the band went on stage Tony explained to the crowd what had happened. The crowd reacted and the band, riding on the buzz, played a great gig.

The Groundhogs had been together for a long time now and from time to time the tensions rose, especially between Ken and Tony. Back in the hotel Tony noticed in Ken's room an old valve radio. As usual they couldn't wake him up so Tony turned the radio on behind Ken's head. It took a while to warm the valves up, but when they did it came on full blast. Ken sat up, startled, but then fell back on the bed. He wasn't too happy with that prank.

After the tour Ken gave his first solo interview to Tony Stewart of *NME*. It was suggested that someone other than Tony did an interview, and Ken was keen. 'We enjoyed the tour because it is too easy to play in England and get encores! In Germany we meant nothing at all and it has got to be good to be appreciated.'

He then decided to fire off a few bombs: 'We could have blown them (Mayall) off stage any night, we did blow them off.' Ken was aware of what he was doing: 'A lot of those interviews are very much the same. The journalist is looking for something extra so I gave it to him.'

Tony was furious, although he never said anything at the time: 'You don't do that if you want to get more work. I don't like that sort of thing, it disparages another artist.' Ken antagonised Tony further by referring to him as 'our guitarist' and saying that he 'has got an inflated ego.'

But he also realised where the inspirational element of the group was located: 'I'm not trying to kid myself that it's a three piece, co-operatively-written thing and whether I agree with (him) doesn't matter. My only job is to have a good time on stage and just hope everybody else does.' Ken wouldn't be speaking to the press again.

The idea of a US tour was still being worked on by Roy Fisher and Pat Meehan. They were trying to speak to Joe Smith from Warner Brothers Records. On 4th October it was noted in the band archive 'Vincent Romario – CMA agency of New York – interest to book US tour.'

On 17th November Roy Fisher heard from Mike Stuart of United Artists USA and had agreed a six-week tour of the States and major promo starting on 1st March 1972. It was also suggested that a new album be released on Groundhog Day in February, but nothing came of either idea.

chapter 9

Who will save The Groundhogs?

'Right you lot, cop this!'
Ken Pustelnik's approach to an unresponsive audience

'A lot of groups are in control but we're not – it must be amazing to see three very ordinary people crawl on stage and smash into it.'
Ken Pustelnik to Melody Maker

In early November 1971 the band embarked on their biggest tour of the UK, taking in dates to the middle of December. By then sales of 'Split' had passed the 50,000 mark and the band was in the ascendancy. They were supported on the tour by Egg and Quicksand, but there were rumblings in the camp about how the press viewed them. In an interview with *Melody Maker*'s Andrew Means, they had the chance to voice their concerns.

The headline was straight to the point 'Have We Been Fair To The Hogs?' One of the things that precipitated this was an open letter from Roy Fisher to the music press in which he accused them of ignoring his men and even floated the word conspiracy!

However, Means insisted that the band were partly to blame for any indifference by pointing the finger at interviews with too many one-word answers showing a distinct lack of enthusiasm. Ken admits that they never went to music-business functions and kept themselves to themselves. 'Everyone knew everybody else, but we were in a bubble!'

But this was actually one of the strengths of a band who never exposed themselves to trends, but just went out and did their own thing. And this was apparent in their approach to live shows.

The Groundhogs did not interact on stage like other bands. Sometimes Pete would follow Tony, leaving Ken free to follow his own thing. As Ray Telford noted in *Sounds*, it was this 'off the wall' approach that attracted the most criticism. Terms like 'self-indulgent' were bandied around, but to the band their style when playing live was their strongest card.

In *Record Mirror*, 'Split' reached Number 6 a week later.
TS Personal Collection

Disc and Music Echo—June 19, 1971

ALBUMS

1	(1)	**STICKY FINGERS**	
		Rolling Stones, Rolling Stones Records	
2	(6)	RAM	Paul and Linda McCartney, Apple
3	(2)	TAMLA MOTOWN CHARTBUSTERS Vol. 5	
			Various Artists, Tamla Motown
4	(3)	BRIDGE OVER TROUBLED WATER	
			Simon and Garfunkel, CBS
5	(8)	4 WAY STREET Crosby, Stills, Nash and Young, Atlantic	
6	(7)	SPLIT	Groundhogs, Liberty
7	(5)	MUD SLIDE SLIM	James Taylor, Warner Brothers
8	(20)	OSIBISA	MCA
9	(3)	HOME LOVIN' MAN	Andy Williams, CBS
10	(11)	RELICS OF THE PINK FLOYD	Starline
11	(10)	THE YES ALBUM	Atlantic
12	(12)	SONGS OF LOVE AND HATE	Leonard Cohen, CBS
13	(—)	EL PEA	Various Artists, Island
14	(9)	SYMPHONIES FOR THE SEVENTIES	
			Waldo De Los Rios, A & M
15	(13)	ANDY WILLIAMS GREATEST HITS	CBS
16	(—)	TARKUS	Emerson, Lake and Palmer, Island
17	(—)	SOMETHING ELSE	Shirley Bassey, United Artists
18	(15)	THIS IS MANUEL	Manuel, Studio Two
19	(26)	IT'S IMPOSSIBLE	Perry Como, RCA
20	(22)	FRANK SINATRA'S GREATEST HITS Vol. 2 Reprise	
21	(14)	AQUALUNG	Jethro Tull, Chrysalis
22	(16)	CLUB REGGAE	Various Artists, Trojan
23	(24)	PORTRAIT IN MUSIC	Burt Bacharach, A & M
24	(17)	BEST OF T. REX	Fly
25	(—)	LED ZEPPELIN II	Atlantic
—	(—)	SONGS FOR BEGINNERS	Graham Nash, Atlantic
27	(—)	THAT'S THE WAY IT IS	Elvis Presley, RCA
28	(26)	ELEGY	Nice, B & C
29	(18)	THE GOOD BOOK	Melanie, Buddah
30	(24)	AFTER THE GOLD RUSH	Neil Young, Reprise

Two titles tied for 25th position.

SOUNDS POLL AWARDS '71

Guitarist
1 ERIC CLAPTON
2 Jimmy Page
3 Steve Howe
4 Tony McPhee
5 Alvin Lee
6 Ritchie Blackmore
7 Rory Gallagher
8 Pete Townshend
9 George Harrison
10 Robert Fripp

Album
1 THE YES ALBUM
2 Sticky Fingers
3 Emerson, Lake & Palmer
4 All Things Must Pass
5 Atom Heart Mother
6 Deep Purple in Rock
7 Led Zeppelin III
8 Aqualung
9 Split
10 Wishbone Ash

nuances of winning an audience over: 'Sometimes its "Oh Christ, they're not into it, we are going to have to work with this. Let's get it by the throat and shake it." Or "My goodness, it was so easy that we didn't have to work at it." I like it when they are little bit resistant, when there is a bit of friction. That's when I say "Right you lot, cop this!" Or what I like to call our aural chaos.' Looking back, Ken is convinced that this is a complex interaction: 'You have to hit the audience at the level they operate rhythmically and emotionally and that's what we did!'

Tony had a slightly different attitude to this, as he told Chris Welch of *Melody Maker*: 'The Groundhogs today go out and play and we don't force anything. We hope that it works out. If it's a duff audience, nothing happens. But we play to enjoy ourselves. What's the point of playing otherwise? You might as well dig holes in the road.'

An important part of the strategy for Pete was to hit them from the first number to set the tone for the rest of the gig. To him, 'Split Part One' was a vital weapon: 'It was my favourite number and it opened the show and set the pace for what followed.' Interestingly, the band

Tony describes the fluid nature of the band on stage: 'It depends who was on a good night. I might find a riff but Ken could get a good rhythm going and we would follow him. Hopefully, we would come back as one in the end.' It didn't always work out like that but they never believed they should recreate the record note for note.

He told *Zig-Zag*: 'Ken wallops everything in sight and sometimes I lose him completely. I often come back during a solo and can't work out where he is – so I just have to play a note until we find each other.' Ken really did wallop his kit; there were many times when he cracked the cymbals!

Ken acknowledges his matter of fact approach: 'I hate the drummers who come to me and say "Have you seen the latest pedal? It goes 0.3 seconds through the air faster." My answer is "I just play them, mate!"' Ken was a unique drummer and he gave *Melody Maker* a clue as to why: 'I listened to other people's styles – which helps to expand technique – but didn't incorporate these into my own style. This destroys natural talent.'

The Groundhogs, in a way, was two bands. In the studio Tony had more control over what was played, at least on bass, but on stage Pete recalls: 'those bass lines were my own.' It was this element of improvisation that made them such an exciting and unpredictable live act.

There was, however, one major factor that gave this interaction on stage its tension. And it gave them an edge over most other bands. They hardly ever rehearsed, having tremendous confidence in their stagecraft. As they always seemed to be gigging there didn't seem to be any need.

But how did they interact with the audience? Ken gives an insight into the

Compiled from data reported from Roy Fisher diaries.
TS Personal Collection

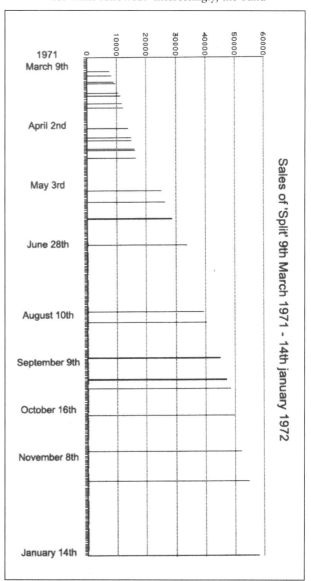

members each had different insights into how to achieve their goals.

As a band the Hogs had done more than their fair share of supporting top acts, but Tony recalled the recent Stones tour as unfufilling: 'If a support group muffs up something it is very easy to lose the audience completely. Actually on this tour the audiences were very attentive, so attentive they were almost too cool. At the end of every set everybody clapped politely, which was all right except that were never knew whether they were being polite or actually liking what we were doing. In some ways it is always better to play to a more critical audience with a few hecklers, because then you've got something to play at, something to draw you out and then the end result is musically much better.'

Well before the November tour, United Artists (with whom Liberty Records had merged) was banging on the door for another album. The problem was Tony didn't have any new material. However, in an interview with *Sounds* in late May 1971, he admitted he already knew what the next album was going to be about.

Ken.
Pic Terry Aldridge
TS Personal Collection

The original idea for the cover came from the band's love of Marvel comics. Roy Fisher suggested it would be a good idea to have a Marvel-type album cover. Their favourite hero was the Silver Surfer, which was drawn by Neal Adams. Pete recalls this period: 'Even though we were all into Marvel Comics, it was Ken who was into them in a big way. He used to collect them on the road.'

Roy Fisher tracked Adams down and secured his services by August. The idea was to portray the band as superheroes, taking on the world's problems. But things didn't initially go well as Adams fell asleep with the finished artwork in his briefcase on the New York subway. When he woke up it had been stolen!

Finally, on 17th November, the re-drawn artwork was sent to London from New York. With artwork in hand Tony set about creating the music and lyrics for the album. The trouble was they didn't finish their UK tour until mid December! He was a man that worked best under pressure but there was a limit.

Tony was 'Marvelous' McPhee, Pete was 'Quick' Cruickshank and Ken was 'Powerful' Pustelnik trying to save the world against pollution, warmongers and over-population. But these storylines were injected with a degree of humour, as 'Quick' Cruickshank accidentally sends the mother of overpopulation to India!

There's political comment, too, when 'Marvelous' McPhee fails to stop the polluting factories. Adams pictures an unholy triumvirate of the Church, the Army and a corrupt politician, with the Church mouthing: "Yes, yes, my boy! Pollution is the small price we pay to stave off the Godless Communists!" The punchline of the story comes when the superheroes are transformed into the Groundhogs, where they can accomplish more with their music.

The seriously overworked band finished their winter tour in Reading on 13th December 1971 and found themselves ensconced in De Lane Lea studios just nine days later. After the last two years of hard work the Hogs needed a break.

De Lane Lea had been re-located from Holborn to Wembley. The new studio was state of the art and they were the first rock band to use the facility. In theory it was going to make the recording process easier but, though the studio had 16 tracks, Tony thought it was sterile. And he was far from happy about the hurry to produce a new album when 'Split' was still selling well.

As luck would have it there was an array of instruments in the studio, but one in particular caught his eye. Sitting in the corner was a Mellotron, a keyboard instrument that recreated the sound of an orchestra. He was keen to use it, as he explains: 'Ken was listening to a lot of Yes (this would have been the 'Fragile' album) and I quite liked the sound of the Mellotron. I liked that idea of

different chords, so I thought I'll try it.' On the other hand, Pete was listening to a diet of mainly American bands like the Grateful Dead, Frank Zappa and Spirit. He was strangely disinterested in British bands. This probably explains why he wasn't too enamoured with the Mellotron: 'I felt it was a gimmick or even a toy. I was concerned because it was such a departure from our usual sound.'

Hitherto, Tony had been the only person contributing material, leaving it to the last minute to write the songs, so Ken decided to start writing himself. 'I had a guitarist friend called JD Fanger and I took him to the studio. I told Roy Fisher that I had a song and he picked up on the vibe. "Let's hear it", he said. "Good old Roy," I thought, so they ran through the song, but when it was suggested to Tony that they might use it, he replied "I don't play other people's songs!"' As Ken recalls: 'It had the desired effect as within a week he'd written half the album.' (1)

It was this pressure that provided the background to the opening track, 'Earth Is Not Room Enough'. The title came from a sc-fi book by Isaac Asimov and is another of one of those familiar wordplays that Tony loves. It inspired him to set the story from the inside of a gas chamber, somewhere in the USA. He especially concentrated on the American fixation of ritually executing its citizens.

He makes his case against the death penalty clear and recalled his childhood: 'This was the 1950s and they were still stretching people's necks on gallows; there was a lot to change and most of the worst would eventually be outlawed in the next couple of decades.' It's clear this was

(1) Fanger had been the guitarist when Tony produced Andy Fernbach's album 'If You Miss Your Connexion'.

Not happy with over- inflated prices, the band often insisted on capping ticket prices, typically under £1.
TS Personal Collection

CITY (OVAL) HALL-SHEFFIELD

Booking Agent: Wilson Peck Ltd.
CHRYSALIS presents
IN CONCERT
"THE GROUNDHOGS"
MONDAY
JUNE 21
at 7-0 p.m. (D. O. 6-30)
STALLS
50p
DOOR
G S33
This portion to be retained

**Designed by Neal Adams,
the famous Marvel
Comics illustrator.**
TS Personal Collection

in his mind when writing the album, but he also related it to the wider picture of mankind killing itself with pollution.

> Locked in a room, strapped to a hollow chair,
> Faint musty smell, odour of stale air,
> Sealed from the outside in a cage that is six-foot square,
> Eyes that are fixed in a glazed, disbelieving stare.
> Cyanide pills dropped in an acid bath,
> Froth forms a cloud as deadly as death's own staff,
> Lungs start to burst trying to hold your breath,
> But have the last laugh 'cos Earth is just a cage seven thousand miles wide!

The inventive Mellotron opening is used to great effect and continues throughout. As Ken comments: 'The Moody Blues never used it like this. Tony gave it an almost mournful, no-hope feeling.' The most amazing thing is the different amount of timbres he gets out of the unreliable machine!

The opening track is among the finest, with plenty of light and shade. The second cut 'Wages Of Peace', brings the mood down, but is an effective rocker about the ways nature can have harmful effects on mankind.

'Body In Mind' picks up on the subject of pollution but concentrates on the way people's minds can also be infected. It's quite catchy, with a great solo from Tony. 'Music Is The Food Of Thought' tells the story of how mankind has the potential to save itself. Tony particularly liked this one because the chord changes were reminiscent of the material they played in the early blues days. Its grave ambience is heightened, again, by some supporting Mellotron.

> To save the race
> We need to trace
> The source of power and fuse it!
> Enlightened minds
> All seem to find
> The vehicle is music

One of the album's distinctive features is the restrained nature of Tony's guitar playing, which creates a very interesting atmosphere. The opening track on side two is the wonderfully named 'Bog Roll Blues' – written while on the toilet! The guitar intro was collated from a tape of bits and pieces that Tony worked from and just happened to fit.

It shows the band in muscular mood and is punctuated by some tasty work by Tony. Pete loved the comedy of the lyrics. The theme is depressing but true, Tony believing that many people are not really interested in the problems that afflict the world. 'Death Of The Sun' rattles

81

along at a good lick and showcases two guitars, one an octave above the other.

Tony had bought a second-hand harmonium from an East End market and thought it would fit for 'Amazing Grace'. It was a song he had liked for a long time and ends with a scorching guitar riff. The album closer is the barnstorming 'The Grey Maze' and is a return to the old days. Ken remembers this track very well:

'The new studio was fitted upstairs with a bar and cafe. We were the first rock band to use the studio. When we started playing we had loads of complaints about the noise from upstairs.' The band is in truly inspired form as they have a chance to let rip at last. It's probably two minutes longer than it should be but provides a fitting counterpoint to the rest of the album.

The sessions also created a few problems regarding the dynamics within the band. One track in particular, 'Music Is The Food Of Thought' stood out because Ken was not sure he could drum to it. The way they usually worked was that Tony worked out both guitar parts and then Ken would come in with his part.

However, as Tony explained to *Sounds*, it sometimes didn't work out the way he wanted: 'I won't say to Ken the same because I know that what I'm thinking is a funky sort of drumming which he doesn't play. So I just hammer away on chords and Pete will do his bass bit and Ken will get some idea!

'As I said, this album has been a bit of a strain. On the last two it's worked okay because I was doing something that they could accept but this one was different.'

Tony admitted to *Melody Maker*'s Tony Stewart, the root cause of the problem was lack

of preparation: 'Because of the weight of work, I didn't get time to relax and write songs. In effect I'd used up the sort of formula I had for writing songs so I had to try and rethink the whole outlook.' For the time being, Tony had been wrung dry of inspiration!

Looking back on the album, Ken had this to say: 'It was too rushed and we were overworked but I like the sparseness of it, the depth and the weirdness. It suffers a bit from the ambitious notion that you have complicated ideas but then you are forced to approach them simply. The lyrics float nicely, though. The energy was phenomenal but it didn't come across on the record. There's a certain limpness about it.'

An example of this is on 'Earth Is Not Room Enough' where Tony's guitar does sound a bit feeble after the Mellotron opening. However, the album takes the band into new territory and even the band was not too enamoured with it but many Hogs fans rate it highly. It's incredible to think of the musical journey from 'Scratching The Surface' to 'Who Will Save The World'!

Incredibly, they were back gigging in the middle of making the album and played four concerts in rapid succession. On 8th January 1972 they played Leicester and two days later Jo Ann Kelly joined them at their Chatham gig. The day after they played Cheltenham Town Hall and *Disc*'s Andrew Tyler was there.

The band was in good spirits, with the new album almost finished. Ken was in especially buoyant mood as a friend of his had found several hundred pounds under his floorboards and given him half. Roadie Alan Laycock was busying himself by selling the signed black and white pictures of the band for 20 pence each.

After support band Writing on the Wall had finished their set, Tyler describes the proceedings: 'The Groundhogs open with "Mistreated" and the eyes immediately fall on Tony. On stage he is a transformed man – all energy and showmanship! By far the best thing of the evening is his solo "Groundhog Blues"! Cheltenham has gone wild. Several girls seem to be banging their heads against the front of the stage. Everyone is on their feet and the aisles are packed tight.'

They ran through their best material, although they didn't include anything off their new LP, and stayed in the dressing room for an hour after the gig signing autographs. The album was finally finished on 6th February with the master cut the following day. In mid February Roy Fisher went back to the States in the hope of finally securing a US tour. But by the time he got back things had slipped from his grasp.

For quite some time Tony had been dissatisfied with Roy Fisher's managerial performance, but it wasn't going to be easy to break the ties with him: 'We went to a solicitor because we (Tony and Ken) wanted him out. They told us you couldn't break a contract just because you think someone is bad at their job.'

By now Tony had built up a catalogue of grievances. The John Mayall tour of Germany in 1971 was typical: 'On that tour we played eight shows and got £750 between us. But Mayall used our roadies and our PA! I felt that we should be getting more money. I thought the Stones support tour was a good move but I wasn't happy we were supporting Mayall as we'd had a Top 5 album. We did another short tour of Germany later on supporting Gun, and I wasn't happy with that either because all they had was a hit single called "Race With The Devil".'

It was clear that Roy Fisher had made some smart moves in the early days but Tony was now looking for someone to take the band on to another level. He believed the Hogs had more to give. In fact, Tony had already come into contact with his future management on a previous foreign trip.

On the way to Vienna and Frankfurt with Black Sabbath and Gentle Giant the previous year (the trip that had precipitated Tony's hatred of flying) they had once again met Patrick Meehan who was the manager of both bands. It was his son, Patrick Meehan Junior, who was to play an ever-increasing part in the band's future.

Wilf Pine was a salaried associate of World Wide Artists (the Meehan family company) and had started out in the music business as odd-job man for tough-guy manager Don Arden. Later on he worked for Arden's former assistant, none other than Meehan Senior. But it was Meehan Junior who had a talent for spotting bands with the potential to reach the top, and had the silver tongue to convince musicians that they could take them there.

One of the early bands he poached was Black Sabbath. In Wilf Pine's recent biography, *One Of The Family: The Englishman And The Mafia*, a conversation is described with Meehan Senior:

'Listen, Wilf, there's a lot of talk going on in the record industry about Black Sabbath. Take it from me, they're going places and although we know that Jim Simpson's a lovely human being, who managed the group from the day they started, Sabbath won't stay with him forever.' This was how the Meehans generally acquired their roster of bands.

On the plane to Vienna Tony got talking to Pine and expressed his dissatisfaction with Roy Fisher. Pine was a fast worker who impressed the band at Frankfurt because he got them higher up the bill than Fleetwood Mac, much to John McVie's chagrin! But at that stage, Tony was not looking for other management. Wilf later attended a gig at the Queen Elizabeth Hall because Gentle Giant (a WWA act) was supporting, but he stayed on to watch the Groundhogs' set.

He describes it in his biography: 'Although musically they were wonderful, they were not so exciting to watch as Sabbath and they struck me as a very odd collection of individuals.' He describes Tony as 'standing there in the middle of the stage, in a pair of old tatty jeans, with long hair hanging down! But he had a great blues voice and what he could do with a guitar was incredible! I knew one day I was going to steal the Groundhogs.' That day was fast approaching!

Roy Fisher's company, Zak Management, was run in partnership with ex-John Lee's Groundhogs frontman John Cruickshank, who joined the company just after 'Thank Christ For The Bomb'. Zak also had Egg and Cochise on their books. They promoted the first Alice Cooper tour of the UK before they made their name but had a bit of bad luck with the New York Dolls when one of the band members died and they went back home.

It was later on that Cruickshank became a director and ploughed some of his own money in to the company. Obviously, this was a difficult situation for John as his brother, Pete, was in the band and losing the Groundhogs would have disastrous consequences. He recalls these events: 'We were initially approached by Patrick Meehan Junior who suggested we combine forces, but in reality I think he was trying to find information about us.'

It was early March and things were moving fast. When Roy Fisher returned from America he got a shock: 'Got a call from Wilf Pine, he said as from now we are managing the Groundhogs. I hung up.' That was all that was said. A few days later Fisher phoned Pete Cruickshank who told him he didn't know what was happening. One of the things that had happened was that Wilf Pine got wind that Wilf Wright of Chrysalis was being considered (they were the Groundhogs' booking agents) but Pine's advice to Tony was succinct: 'Don't go with Wilf Wright, you might as well stay with Roy Fisher.' He never did find out why he said that about Wright.

Shortly after this Tony, who was in Haverhill, Suffolk, had a visit from Wilf Pine. They drove to Ken's flat in London where Pine made a pitch for them to join WWA.

(2) In spite of the acrimonious split, Tony did work with Roy Fisher again. In December 1978 he asked Tony if he'd produce a 'black punk band' he was managing called Pure Hell. It was a clear indication that there was no bad blood between the two men, as Roy Fisher remembers:

'I have never been a person to bear grudges, so contacting Tony to see if he would be interested in producing the session was not awkward. He accepted and the results were fun although due to the band's US management contract the tapes were never released and have been in my archive box ever since. It would be good if they finally get to see the light of day.'

Tony journeyed to London on his motorbike. Roy Fisher recalls the session: 'Tony produced three tracks, "American", "Hungry Eyes" and "I Want Your Body", at Utopia Studios, engineered by Damian Korner, the son of Alexis.' He did the session and returned to Haverhill. The journey was tortuous as it was quite cold and he had to stop a few times to warm up in phone boxes along the route.

(3) Tony McPhee got his publishing royalties separate from performing royalties.

Ken was impressed, as Tony recalls: 'After Wilf had gone Ken said to me "I'm worried as I can't see anything wrong". I didn't know Pete's opinion on this as he was always reticent in coming forward.' However, Ken recalls it slightly differently: 'I wanted to go with Chrysalis but when Tony turned up at my flat with Pine and two big guys I could see he was already sold on the idea. I thought I'll try and change it from the inside, so I went along with it.' Pete confirms Ken's story: 'I was surprised when Ken changed his mind as I would have gone with Chrysalis if we had to change. I could see that a big management could open doors; I didn't know anything about WWA, but they were talking to Tony.'

The first thing the new management did was to take them off the road for a much-needed break. In an interview with *NME* later that year, Tony outlined the relief this brought: 'It had almost became a vicious circle. We needed the money from gigs simply to stay on the road at all. It became a very sad state of affairs. There were times when we'd go on stage sick of the whole set.'

It was agreed that up to the US tour the band would be paid £70 a week each. On 8th March Chrysalis (booking agents) was instructed by the band's solicitor (Canter & Martin) to work with World Wide Artists. The letter also undertook to pay all legal costs that might arise from the Zak Management dispute. The same day Roy Fisher took out an injunction against World Wide Artists on advice from his solicitor, Tony Russell.

Roy Fisher and John Cruickshank met with Patrick Meehan Junior and Wilf Pine on 12th March. By now, Roy Fisher was *persona non grata* with the band. A few days later he spoke to Pete Cruickshank who told him: 'I'm not supposed to speak to you.' A few days later it was all over and Roy Fisher noted: 'I agreed settlement out of court with Pat Meehan as I felt too much personal involvement to fight the Groundhogs in a long legal battle. I did not get or feel threatened by Wilf Pine but maybe this would have come if I had not agreed to settle for relative peanuts as compared with what the band could have made in the US in 1972.

'The new recording contract I negotiated and agreed with Mike Stewart, raising the royalty from 3% to 8%, plus 2% for Tony as producer, for UK, the USA, Canada and Japan was never signed. "Who Will Save The World" died a death as it was not promoted. My only regrets were the Groundhogs not making it big in the US. This would have put Tony up there with Clapton and Beck. And Wilf Pine getting my fucking gold album – still a sore point.' (2)

Roy Fisher was not quite accurate with the last count, as Tony confirms: 'We only got our gold albums for "Split" some time after Roy left us. Fisher was aggrieved because he had steered the band to the success and Wilf Pine had arrived at the tail end of it all. But Pine had to fight to get them the gold disc because we were a little short of the 100,000 required.' John Cruickshank had this to say about the end: 'Roy

accepted £2,000 as payoff, which was a ridiculous amount of money. As for me, when we lost the Groundhogs, our company was in trouble and I ended up losing my house. When we met Pat Meehan it was clear we were not in their league. Roy wasn't dominant enough but he worked hard for the band. He did have that personal touch which I think they lost.'

The finances for the band were organised in an odd fashion. The original contract they had with Roy Fisher stipulated that all performing record royalties be paid to him and not individually. This meant that the band never received individual royalty statements. It was Liberty's policy in order to avoid the confusion, in their view, of sending out multiple statements. They received their royalties from him. Their regular monthly payments made up of mainly gig money, were a curious mix too, as Tony explains: 'I lived in Haverhill and I had train bills to pay. So Roy totted my travel expenses up and paid Pete and Ken half of the total. The truth is I just went along with it like I did other things.' (3)

Despite the trauma unfolding behind the scenes, the band had to show that it was business as usual. 'Who Will Save The World' was released during this time and Tony had to do a string of interviews. In a preview, *Melody Maker*'s Andrew Means was positive about the new direction: 'The Mellotron translates McPhee's musical ideas on to a different plane. While his lead guitar work is directly stimulating and intensely subjective at times, the Mellotron gives the music more expanse.'

Across the pond, *Rolling Stone* writer Lester Bangs was more forthright. 'It's about goddam fucking time these Groundhogs started to get some recognition.' He mentions the two previous albums and, perhaps, anticipates the future: 'Those two albums were just good run of the racks heavy grunge. "Who Will Save The World" is that much more. McPhee's guitar work is as frenzied as ever, but much denser and more complex than before.'

The new album caused some confusion in the press about the inspiration behind Tony's music as an interview with *Melody Maker*'s Chris Welch revealed when it was suggested to him that he made 'Split' for the heavy/hard-rock audience: 'We never "aim" our albums. The music is not premeditated like that. As far as possible the album represents what we've been playing on stage. After "Split", we got fed up with hearing that type of sound, so we utilise ideas from the new album in our stage act... The music is very free and we get completely involved in every number. Every night it comes out different.'

One of the questions Tony was being forced to answer was the accusation that the band was being pretentious with their superhero image. Pretentious was, at the time, a very dirty word. Groups like Jethro Tull and Yes were bearing most of the flak. However, as Keith Emerson noted: 'You have to be musically pretentious to do something original.' Tony's answer to *Sounds* was very effective: 'I think a pretentious statement is something that's not quite so obvious. But it's so obviously pretentious that it's not.' For those who bothered to read the cartoon strip they would have seen that, in the end, they were not very good at saving the world anyway!

When asked if this was going to be the start of a new phase in the history of the band he was non-committal. The truth is that the album didn't appear to have many tracks that would translate live. Even though Ken was keen to play them it never really happened. Later on Tony was asked why they never really played the new album on stage. His reply consigned the album almost to oblivion: 'I made the album at the behest of UA. After it was finished it kept them quiet so we went back to playing "Split".' While it's true they didn't feature the album much in their shows, they did relent at a few gigs and played a couple of songs. The album got to Number 9 in the charts but disappeared from view.

The Hogs finally flew out to the States in early June for their long-awaited debut tour, a curious mixture of headlining and supporting gigs with some big names from both the UK and the US, including the Faces, Black Sabbath, Edgar Winter, Humble Pie, Black Oak Arkansas and Alice Cooper. In spite of Tony not being keen to tour there, he knew the States was very important regarding potential album sales. However, Tony and Ken detested flying and this tour was going to have a lot of that. The second reason was Tony thought that in some ways the country was backward.

The journey to Memphis, the first port of call, was a baptism of fire and the shape of thing to come. Arriving there via Washington involved a mammoth 19 hours' travelling time. Customs confiscated Tony's oranges, which his mother had packed for him, due to danger of disease, so he was annoyed about that. Pete had taken his wife, Jan, to her parents in Canada, and was making his own way.

'My wife's parents told me to be careful of all the rednecks, and to be honest I was shit scared. I was travelling alone in a country I didn't know. When I arrived at Memphis airport it was baking hot. I made my way to the Holiday Inn and promptly locked myself in.' It was only later he realised not only did he like Memphis, he also liked the people too!

Their first performance, at Stax radio's Ardent studios, turned out to be rather embarrassing, as Tony couldn't remember the

arrangement for 'Still A Fool' because it had been so long since they'd played together. They soon got into it but something else happened that Ken remembers well: 'Almost as soon as we started playing the audience starting clearing out. I thought we can't be that bad!' He later found out that this was one of the first stereo radio stations in America and they had gone out to the car park to listen to the gig on the radio. They were actually applauding in the car park!

After the recording a guy called Rusty, the rep for UA, asked them if they wanted to go to a club. They were all game so they went with him. It looked rather seedy outside but Rusty knocked the door and a sliding panel opened. 'We got UA artists here,' Rusty explained, at which the door opened and they made their way in.

Tony remembers hearing Dave the roadie say 'You must be fucking mad!' as he walked in the opposite direction; they didn't see him again that night. They were ushered to tables on the periphery of the stage. Tony heard a voice say 'Sit down, whitey!' It was then he realised the whole audience was black.

It was a big club, and Solomon Burke was

(4) Led by the charismatic
Malcolm X, the aim of the
Black Panther movement
was to achieve rights for
black people by violent
means, in direct opposition
to Martin Luther King's
peaceful tactics. Before the
1960s ended both men
were assassinated.

(5) This kind of
intimidation was not
uncommon in the USA. Led
Zeppelin played a gig at
the Forum, Inglewood, in
1970. Robert Plant makes
reference to the police on
a tape of the gig: 'All those
people with big sticks and
we don't care.'

performing on stage. He also remembers seeing
Wilson Pickett there too! It was only when they
were led to the side of the stage where they met
fellow UA artists that the ice was broken and
they were able to mingle without any problems.
They had their photo taken with Booker T's horn
section and in the end the evening was a success.
But Pete was under no illusion that if they'd have
been white Americans things could have
been different.

America was in race turmoil at that time as
black people were determined to claim their
constitutional rights. Pete recalls an experience at
another club where word got around that they
were a blues band, it wasn't long before they had
a visitation from a group of large black
gentlemen who shook their hands in a peculiar
way. 'They twisted their hand round and gripped
my thumb. It was only later I found out it was a
Black Panther handshake.' (4)

Two days after the radio show they made
their long-awaited US debut supporting Edgar
Winter at Overton Park Bandstand, Memphis.
The band, even though they hadn't fully
recovered from the traveling, had to contend with
the heat and humidity. Ken recalls the gig: 'Edgar
Winter was great. They jammed in the dressing
room all day and then went on with boundless
energy. I watched them from the side of the
stage.' But he had a surprise to come: 'One of
the first things that struck me about the States
was how many people knew our stuff.'

They played a memorable gig with Black Oak
Arkansas at the Vets Memorial Coliseum,
Jacksonville, Florida, where they were escorted to
their hotel and told to stay there until the police
took them to the venue. Ken recalls the weird
events: 'We got on stage with house lights on and
they stayed on. The police flanked both sides of
the stage and looked menacing in their shades
and arms folded. It was the worst atmosphere I
ever played in. (5)

'In the front row were a few Groundhogs
fans from Chicago and when we started playing
they started freaking out. By the end of our set
they had got the rest of crowd going. That was
one thing the police couldn't control. These
people were seriously repressed.' He loved the
headliners, Black Oak Arkansas, a bunch of
hillbillies who, when they travelled,
took their own little town with them
on the bus. They were a great live
act too.

In the early part of the tour the
Hogs had a few days' break, so they
decided to do their own thing. Pete
went to Canada to see Jan. Tony
decided he'd go back to Memphis as he
had befriended DJ Jon Scott and had
been made very welcome in his home
at 3744 James Road. Tony takes up
the story:

'I asked Ken where he was going
and he told me he'd come with me. I
was hoping he would have stayed with
the roadies. I told him he'd have to fly
but he was determined to come.' Both

Tony and Ken hated flying but it was the latter
who suffered most now.

When they arrived at 3744, he found out that
Stax were having an outdoor party and knew
Ken would have problems: 'I was having a bad
time but Ken was much worse. One of the things
that annoyed me the most about him was he
wouldn't admit to anything. He'd never admit to
disliking flying, which I knew he hated. He was
claustrophobic and agoraphobic. In fact, he was
everything! The problem for Ken was that Stax
had set up in the middle of a field. So I watched
him go round the perimeter of the hedge until he
got to the shortest point – then he made a dash
for it.' It must have made as odd sight to
anyone watching.

They flew to New York where they stayed at
the plush City Squires Hotel, where the doorman
was kitted out in what they thought was typically
English garb; red jackets and riding boots. Tony
remembers: 'He asked us if he could take our
luggage, but everything we had was in two plastic
bags! As he carried them through the foyer you
could see him squirming as the other bell hops
jeered.' On the evening they went to see a
Canadian rock band called Mama Lion. The
following day they were re-united with Pete, who
arrived from Canada.

After their break, they were booked for a
photoshoot just across the road from the hotel
but there was a problem in getting there, as Tony
recalls: 'Ken couldn't cross the road so we had to
get a taxi to take us round the block. I remember
he had got some pills off the doctor and his
hands were shaking so much he could hardly take
them. He was in a really bad way.' Pete recalls

those depressing events: 'I remember the photo shoot very well. Ken was on his knees, he was holding my ankles and he looked up at me and said "I can't cross the road".'

Ken's problems had been evident to Pete at the outset of the tour: 'We were playing gigs in intense heat and we had a lot of outdoor shows. But in New Orleans we played in a big warehouse and it was very hot. At one point he collapsed over his kit and a roadie had to help him. I knew then he was in a bad way.'

However, touring is a very artificial environment and Pete muses about the pitfalls of the road: 'Being on tour is bad enough. Your points of reference blow out of the window, especially in a place like the States. We all went off our heads to some extent. But Ken's problems were self-inflicted. He was taking a lot of things. I don't know how he got through those gigs; he was very shaky.' Tony confirms that Ken had always been pretty reckless: 'He told me he took a sweet off a guy that had some acid in. He couldn't have known what was really in it. He didn't even know the man.'

As far as Tony was concerned he had been having problems in coping with Ken. At the time of making 'Split', it wasn't only Tony and Martin Birch who'd had similar experiences. Ken had problems too, and, as far as Tony was concerned, never got over them. He remembers the German tour with Gun in 1971 as a watershed: 'I remember we played a gig where there were these plastic-backed chairs stacked up at the back of the dressing room. After we played our set Ken decided to go and see Gun's act. I don't know whether it was because he had to stand on the balcony to see them but he came back in the dressing room with his hands on his head. When Ken was having a bad time he thought his head was coming off. He called to our roadie, "Alan (Laycock), help me". So the two of them were wrestling each other, with Alan trying to get Ken's hands off his head. The result was they fell backwards into the piled-up chairs. I thought "Great, that's all I need." I knew then he would have to go.'

The Hogs moved on to Florida, but their plans were rudely interrupted by Hurricane Agnes which had already started to rip her way through the United States. It wasn't all play, as they were doing a fair amount of radio promotion. They were getting the Groundhogs' message across but the tour was short and the country vast.

It made sense to fly wherever they could but, when they left Florida for a gig with Black Sabbath in Virginia, they realised that going by air didn't provide all the answers.

Even though it was only a few hundred miles' distance they made several stops; it seemed to them more like a glorified bus route. Tony remembers he was in the toilet when he started hearing a harmonica:

'At first I was losing it, until I heard the pilot say "I'm going to stop playing now as it's a bit turbulent up ahead and I might knock my teeth out." His humour helped take the edge off my discomfort.' Next stop was Washington, two hundred miles away – and because both Tony and Ken were not really up to flying, they decided to ask Sabbath roadie Dave to drive.

They hadn't got very far in the wake of the storm before some of the roads were flooded. At one point the water was getting too high for comfort and a policeman approached their car. He said 'that dam up there is ready to blow' and directed them out of the area. They later made their way to Pittsburgh for the Three Rivers gig supporting Alice Cooper.

Ken recalls the misery: 'We were stuck there for three days, the water came up to the fourth floor of our hotel. Luckily our van with the gear was in a high-rise car park.' The Cooper gig was pulled and so was the following day's gig with Black Sabbath and Humble Pie in Akron, Ohio.

A few days later they made their way to Canada where they played the famous Maple Leaf Gardens, Toronto, with Humble Pie. They also played the Forum in Montreal with Marriott's men and finished off their mini-tour of Canada with a headlining gig at St Katherine's Ice Hockey arena. Ken was glad to get to Canada because the food improved dramatically.

The tour was extended in order for them to appear at the Pocono

Opposite the hotel. Ken needed a taxi to get 100 yards to the photo session.
Pic courtesy Pete Cruickshank

Hurricane Agnes put paid to some of the gigs.
TS Personal Collection

Music Festival in Long Pond, Pennsylvania, with ELP and Three Dog Night, as well as old friends Edgar Winter, Humble Pie and Black Sabbath. An estimated 200,000 people gathered for the event. The crowds were so great that they could only get in by helicopter. It was the biggest gig they ever played.

This time Mother Nature worked for them. They were booked as the second act on the opening day, 8th July. Folk-singer Claire Hamill opened proceedings and this low-key support worked perfectly for the band. As they went on stage the vastness of the crowd had an effect on Pete who was glad that the din drowned the sound of his knocking knees. By now they had revisited 'Who Will Save The World' and had played 'Music Is The Food Of Thought' and 'The Grey Maze' a few times.

The set was well received but, as they came off, Tony felt a drop of rain on his head. Within minutes the heavens opened and it wasn't long before the festival was stopped until the evening. This was a stroke of luck for the band because they appeared on news broadcasts all over the States. However, that's when their luck ran out! They didn't know it at the time, but it was Ken's last gig with the band for 30 years.

The day after the festival they stayed over and went horseriding at the suggestion of roadie Dave. There was an Indian Reservation shop at the stables and it had long lines of cowboy hats

That's buggered the wrist of the tour!
TS Personal Collection

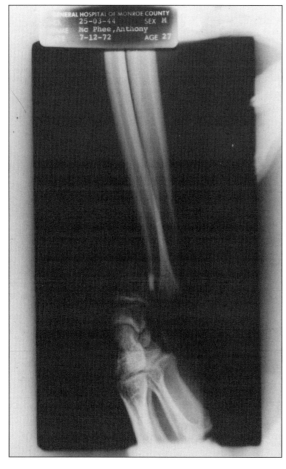

and riding boots. Tony treated himself to a native American hat. He had never actually been on a horse before and the whole band had a shock when they saw them. They were huge beasts!

Ken opted out but Tony, Pete, roadies Pete and Dave and a woman from the stable climbed on board. In the cold light of day it was a dangerous thing to do if only because a horse can sense when there's a novice aboard. They broke into a canter and Tony lost his hat; however, it couldn't have been too bad an experience as the next day they went again.

Tony realised after a while that the horse he was riding, Senator, was mates with the horse that roadie Pete was on. 'Pete's horse was always lagging behind and Senator would wait for him, then when the others had gone on ahead too far he would rush to catch up. Pete's horse was lagging and I noticed that the others had gone round a tight bend in the track. I thought "I know what's going to happen next." As I turned round to tell Pete to hold on tight round the bend, they galloped around the corner, but Pete fell off.

'I had no control of this animal but the others were waiting and I managed to tell them Pete had come off. They all went back, but Senator had different ideas – he started to bolt towards the direction of the freeway and I was getting battered by all the branches of trees along the way. I waited as long as I could for my horse to slow; then I leaped off.

'When I hit the floor I heard a crack, I looked down and my wrist was at right angles, I thought I'd dislocated it. I put my elbow round a tree and gave the hand a pull, but it hurt like fuck.'

In fact, he'd broken his wrist. They made their way to the General Hospital of Monroe County unaware that, due to the extension of the tour, Tony was not covered by medical insurance. It hadn't occurred to anyone in the new organisation to renew it.

Tony asked the doctor to do a good job and ended up with plaster up to his shoulder. During his two-day stay he was entertained courtesy of a roommate who had paid extra for a television set. The bill came to $237 and the tour they had sought for so long was prematurely ended in the worst of circumstances. The plaster was so comprehensive Tony needed to support its weight on a broom handle!

The rest of the tour was cancelled and it denied them visits to big cities like Chicago and Detroit. As Pete recalls, things might have gone better had they continued: '"Who Will Save The World" was just outside the Hot 100. It just needed more touring and we might have got into it. After that, who knows, but we should have done more to promote the album.'

As he flew home Tony had something else on his mind – what to do with Ken...

chapter **10**
The Emperor's New Clothes

'The time with Ken was special because it was three people with different ways of doing it but doing it together.'
Tony McPhee describing the unique chemistry of the band

'It is an extraordinarily good record that covers a wide expanse of ideas and sound.'
Melody Maker's review of 'Hogwash'

The first thing Tony did when he got back to the UK was to go to Addenbrookes Hospital where they reduced his plaster to more manageable proportions, at least to the point where he dispensed with the broom handle. The question of Ken's tenure in the band was uppermost in his mind. In the weeks to come he'd constantly wrestle with the problem.

Tony's broken wrist didn't completely incapacitate him, however, as he was offered the chance to produce an album. Wilf Pine had signed a group called Dancer to World Wide Artists. Wilf had heard some of the material that would make up the album 'Tales From The Riverbank', was impressed and drove the band in his white Rolls Royce to Olympic studio. The band recalls that Tony 'imposed strict discipline' in the studio. They recorded a 15-minute version of Soft Machine's 'Why Am I So Short?' which features Anthony Minghella on Mellotron. (1)

Wilf came up with the idea of naming one of the tracks 'Mac's Cafe'; this was intended as the single. But there were problems with the album; Pine went berserk when he heard they had taken 22 hours to record just the

(1) Anthony Minghella went on to become a film director. His credits include *The Talented Mr Ripley*, *The English Patient* and the American Civil War epic *Cold Mountain*.

Wilf Pine around 1974.
Pic courtesy Wilf Pine

(2) Hemdale produced the successful film *Women In Love* starring Oliver Reed and Glenda Jackson in the early 1970s. They also produced *The Terminator* starring Arnold Schwarzenegger, a massive box-office hit.

title track. The final straw came when the album's release was cancelled and, soon after it was finished, the band split up. It was the first time that Tony had access to a synthesiser and, being unable to play his guitar, he started dabbling with it; he was impressed.

The Moog synthesiser was very popular in the early 1970s and it was dominant in the market. However, by 1972 other makes of synthesiser were readily available and Tony started investigating them, especially ARP, as he really felt more comfortable with them. Even though he wasn't a keyboard player he was fascinated by the array of sounds that could be made. Furthermore, it had completely altered his way of creating music, as he told Ray Hammond of *Melody Maker*: 'I like to write my material on keyboards rather than guitar because I'm so familiar with the guitar that I find it limiting.' He still retained his method of looking for unusual chord sequences.

By the summer of 1972 Wilf Pine was sole manager of the band. Patrick Meehan Junior had negotiated a deal which saw WWA go public. They were now part of the Hemdale Leisure Corporation, which was owned by actor David Hemmings and a producer called John Daly. Hemdale had become the biggest independent group in the UK entertainment industry. (2)

The Meehans were now seriously wealthy and it was agreed that WWA would have autonomous status within the Hemdale Empire. Wilf Pine would become manager of the

Clive Brooks, Tony McPhee and Pete Cruickshank.
TS Personal Collection

Groundhogs, Gentle Giant, Stray and the Edgar Broughton Band.

The problem of whether Ken would stay or go was further complicated by several bust-ups with Patrick after the American tour. Meehan was having a go at the road crew at a gig and Ken told him to back off. Then Meehan had a go at Ken for wandering around New York. He told him: 'You don't do that, just call a limo.' His riposte was succinct: 'Listen, mate, I come from Bristol. Heavy people don't worry me as we have plenty of those back home.'

Shortly after he got back home Ken started having visitations from the road crew trying to get some of the gear back that he had stored. He knew his days were numbered, so he kept some bits and pieces he thought he was owed. He was holding back the gear as a negotiating tool. However, the truth was he was already out of the band.

A brief conversation between Tony and Wilf settled it. Tony recalls: 'I told Wilf that I couldn't handle Ken any more, he's got to go. I know the drummer from Egg, I think we might be able to poach him!' In fact, Tony had already sounded out Clive Brooks as to whether he would be interested. It was good timing as Egg had already split up, 'so it was down to Wilf Pine to tell Ken.'

Pete Cruickshank wasn't in the office that day but recalls conversations with Tony on the subject: 'Tony did mention Ken's possible departure several times. I recall when Ken got his medication on the US tour the doctor told him he

GROUNDHOGS

shouldn't be on the road. In that period at the end he was difficult to handle; nobody wanted to travel with him, even the roadies avoided him. I agreed he had to go.' It was clear to all that Ken wasn't going to make a miracle recovery. But as for Ken's replacement: 'I wouldn't have considered Clive – not because he wasn't a good drummer, but he was too clockwork.'

In spite of the tough reputation of the Meehan and Pine organisation, Ken Pustelnik was surprised by what happened next: 'I got a letter from their solicitor demanding money from me. I ignored that crap. I thought if a lightweight hippy can put them down, their reputation would be shattered.

'The truth is that by then I didn't care. We had all these ideals and it was reflected in our (sic) lyrics, but as far as I was concerned we were running with the enemy.' It must be reiterated that Ken had chosen to go with the Meehans when the band left Roy Fisher. (3)

It's true that Ken wasn't always the easiest person in the band to get along with, as he was the first to admit: 'People would come up to me and ask me to sign things. I'd tell them to go away as I wasn't working. I knew they'd think "what an unfriendly bastard!" When I'm off duty nobody owns me, so if they queued up outside the stage door after the gig I'd sign all the things they had. No problem. I will not compromise my morals for anything.'

It was clear that Ken was into drugs and the rest of the band weren't. But he felt that it was nothing to do with the band as long as he still performed on stage: 'Drugs was part of the hippy scene. I thought acid was evil. I couldn't have played while taking bad drugs. I had to be healthy. Drugs were a token. My music was serious and I lived for the few moments it all clicked into place.'

There is still no question he was a powerhouse performer and that nobody quite played the drums like him! Pete Cruickshank is very grateful for the part that Ken played in the Groundhogs: 'My playing would never have been the way it was if it wasn't for Ken. His approach to the drums made me go places I had never gone before, or since!' Tony McPhee had another way of saying the same thing: 'The time with Ken was special because it was three people with different way of doing it, but doing it together.'

The management put out a cover story that Ken's departure was due to 'musical differences'. Thus began the three decades of stories that Ken didn't like the 'Who Will Save The World' album and yearned for the return to 'Split'! For Pete, autumn 1972 was a dark period: 'I thought the band was in deep trouble. Tony couldn't play for three months, we had changed management, a large chunk of the American tour had been blown away by the weather and Ken had left the band. All of a sudden I was on my own and it had a huge impact on me. It felt to me like

impending doom. It's the kind of thing I woke up every day with it on my mind. I realised I had to make a big decision about staying in the band. But I had nothing else to go to, so I stayed and bit the bullet. I know that changed me a lot inside.'

That this classic line-up had something unique cannot be disputed, Tony himself had spelt out the consequences of a parting of the ways sometime before. In an interview in *NME* with James Johnson in 1971, he was quite candid: 'At the moment we have a kind of unwritten rule between us so that we have a way of dealing with each other. If one of us left, the group would collapse because there is just nobody who could fill in. We could only reappear as something completely different.'

Tony's words turned out to be prophetic; the Groundhogs never had another purely instinctive line-up that had such commercial success but there's no doubt Tony played/recorded good music with the Groundhogs afterwards.

Tony McPhee first met Clive Brooks on the Groundhogs' late-1971 tour of the UK. He got on well with him, so it was no surprise when he suggested him to Pete as Ken's replacement; no other drummer was considered. Tony had a good laugh with Egg and he recalls a trick he played on their bass player because he got on everyone's nerves: 'We were playing at some gig where there was an internal telephone system. So I phoned up the room where the band was.

'Clive answered the phone. "Is Montgomery Campbell there?" I asked

'He passed the phone to him. "Hello," said Campbell.

'I said "Are you Montgomery Campbell?" "Yes, I am," he replied.

'"Are you known as Mont?" "Yes, I am" came the reply.

'So I said "I am going to break your fucking legs!"

'Clive told me later that he really believed it and was shitting himself for the rest of the tour.'

At the time of joining the Groundhogs Clive

Clive and Pete, appearing on the internet...don't know where, don't know when!

(3) About a year after Roy Fisher was ousted he met Patrick Meehan Junior in a lift. 'He was telling me that they were having a hard time promoting the Groundhogs . To which I said: "That is strange, they had three Top 10 albums when they were managed by me." We reached the ground floor at this point; I went one way and he went the other saying no more.'

In 1975 he formed a management company, Snazz International, working with Bowie's ex-band the Spiders From Mars, the Flamin' Groovies, Rab Munro and Russ & Lee who went on to become Imagination. Another project was negotiating the lease of Stonebridge Park television studios from London Weekend Television and raising a million pounds' investment capital from Richard Branson to develop the facility for music video production.

In 1986 he moved to Los Angeles and started freelancing as a designer for party and special event companies. He continues to work in the industry.

Tony at the Mellotron.
TS Personal Collection

(4) In 1995 Mick Stones, who ran the *Hogs Feedback* magazine, went to Memphis to seek out Tony's old haunt; it was not as he expected it: 'As many people know "3744 James Road" is not just a track on the "Hogwash" album but an account of Tony's first impressions of America, flying and the warm reception the band received when they first arrived on US soil. It is also of course the address of where they stayed in Memphis.

'I can remember waiting for the taxi in the hotel lounge to take myself and my wife over to said address and the look on the cabbie's face as if to say "Well, there's nothing out there to see." It was indeed in a remote part of Memphis not far from the freeway surrounded by fields but very peaceful. It was not what I expected. It looked like a building rich in history with a long drive surrounded by deep green lawns. The one thing that stood out in particular was a plaque at the gateway with the house number that was perfect for documenting the occasion with a photograph.

The cabbie must have thought I was nuts to have come all this way to have my picture taken in a gateway in a remote suburb of Memphis, We visited Gracelands and had our picture taken in the gateway there but for me 3744 James Road, Memphis, Tennessee, is my special memory of visiting America. Unfortunately more recent visitors report that the house has been torn down.'

Brooks had played the drums for eight years and had been with Egg, his first 'name' band, for three.

He told Ray Telford of *Sounds*: 'My style developed itself fully when I was with Egg. Everything was on a fairly rigid musical level and I reckon only about ten per cent of the material had any room for improvisation. Basically, the group broke up when the bass player (Mont) decided he couldn't work any longer in a rock group.'

Tony liked Clive because 'he was a very basic drummer, different to Ken who used to fly all over the place. I wanted to change the direction of the band. It turned out he was a little bit too basic, but he was very good.'

Pete recalls the choice was a strange one: 'I didn't really like Egg, though they were good musicians. They were into time signatures and everything worked out beforehand and we were the complete opposite.'

It was clear that Tony was fired up again and relished the challenge. Brooks didn't have much time to prepare but as soon as they played together they gelled. Clive told *Penetration* magazine how he found it at the time: 'It was awkward at first because the first thing we had to do when I joined was an album and it was very difficult trying to fit in. I wish that first we'd done a tour.'

After the struggle over 'Who Will Save The World' at De Lane Lea, Tony decided to record his next album at Advision studios. The change meant the relationship with Martin Birch ended. However, the studio engineer they met in September 1972, was just as good. His name was Martin Rushent.

Tony's arm was in plaster for a total of three months, but he had already started writing the new material before the plaster came off, with the help of the Mellotron. And to his immense relief he felt the wrist had made a good recovery. The subject matter of the albums was always interesting, but this time he chose a novel approach. When a journalist asked him what the next album was going to be about he got a strange reply: 'It's going to be about rubbish.' The title of the new album was to be 'Hogwash'!

The opener, the intriguingly titled 'I Love Miss Ogyny', had its origins in Tony's dictionary-surfing. The moment he saw the word misogynist he realised he could use a lot of puns: 'I thought it's strange that the word isn't 'mr-ogynist'. I got an idea and I rattled off a lot of contradictory lyrics. As a result it was so easy to write.'

The subject matter inspired Tony to go deeper and darker and there are even references to committing murder. The delivery is so convincing that many thought that it was autobiographical! The first four lines set the dark tone:

The days that you're gone, I can't stand the silence,
The hours that you're here, I can't stand your presence,
The starlight that shone from your eyes in the beginning,
Now blinds me with hate for you and all women.

It's clear from the outset that Clive is more solid than Ken and there's more than enough evidence on this track to show that it's business as usual. Interestingly, Pete's Zemaitis bass exhibits a lot more 'top' than had been discernable on 'WWSTW'. 'It had such an individual sound and was very easy to play. I bought it for cheaper that I would have got a Fender Jazz Bass but mine was custom-made. I don't have it any more as I gave it away to my son, Paul, as incentive for passing his O and A levels.'

The opening track is especially poignant for Pete as he explains: 'The bass behind the opening vocal is lovely and also Tony's patterns in the middle gave the bass more of a free rein. I just went for broke.' But these moments were few and far between: 'On the whole I thought we were getting too technical, whereas before we had done a lot of things on instinct. Until recently we were a blues band and now we are playing on technique and not feel.'

The next track 'You Had A Lesson', known to Tony as 'You Adolescent', is about brother-in-law Daryl Payne: 'He was a typical teenager with the whole world on his shoulders.' Tony had frequently borrowed his white Fender Stratocaster when he started playing 'Split' live. Daryl was part-time roadie with the band but fell in with a bad crowd and died very young a few years later after he injected strychnine-laced heroin. The track was destined to be a live staple and features some punchy Mellotron from Tony.

Tony's word games continued with 'Ringmaster'. The Ring Modulator is an electronic device that is good for creating percussive noises like clanging bell sounds. He was keen to use it on the album: 'I asked Clive to play a drum solo. He was surprised by my request, as he didn't have one. He said "Fucking hell" and it's just audible on the album. So he played one there and then and Tony added the Ring Modulator sounds to it.' Tony's love of gadgets was coming into its own with the plethora of electronic devices that were being invented at the time. One critic even called it the first 'space-age' drum solo.

The next track is straight down the line with no puns, word games or hidden meanings. Tony hadn't forgotten the house in Memphis that he had returned to on days off during the US tour. '3744 James Road' is his tribute to Jon Scott and his generous hospitality. But it's also about the trip in general with its trials and tribulations. Tony's manic count-in belies the way in which the music starts off. (4)

The main riff was another from his famous ideas tape, which he decided to make more interesting by playing it live in the studio without overdubs: 'I'm in awe of guitarists who play riffs with their thumb and do other things with their fingers (Bert Jansch and Blind Lemon Jefferson are two). I could never figure it out properly. But what I could do was a simple thing with my thumb.' The opening sounds a little plodding, but when the infectious riff kicks in the song becomes an anthem.

There are some great moments on this one, including the fantastic guitar solo, but Tony was also concentrating on the drum sound just as much as the guitars when they recorded it: 'I always wanted to get a sound like John Bonham. He had the best drum sound I ever heard in my life, it was in your face! The drummer in the pit at the London Palladium had a fabulous sound. It was just two stereo microphones and that's what we tried to do.' Out of all the tracks on the album this was

the one Tony knew would work best live.

The first six letters of the side two opener 'Sad Is The Hunter' spells 'sadist'. This song, a barnstormer in live performance, is unusual as it features two guitar solos. The song reflects Tony's anti-foxhunting stance and brought out his playfully devious side: 'I like to put things in that might not be seen at first but are there to be discovered later.'

His old friend Dave Wetton was heavily involved with the fledgling Hunt Saboteurs who were yet to organise nationally, but the song is also about what a predatory creature man is. At an anti-hunt meeting that was reported on the television Tony noticed someone with 'Sadist The Hunter' on his T-shirt. Perhaps he was a fan ?

The first and third verses are worth quoting in full:

'Hogwash' advert...not quite the truth, as neither Pete nor Tony used picks.
TS Personal Collection

*Read about the Spanish
inquisition,
Read about the witch-hunts of
those days,
Things have only changed in
outward appearance,
Cruelty is integral in man's ways.*

*Hunting is the vehicle for
some men,
To satisfy their baser needs,
Sport is the label for
this depravity,
A distortion of the need to feed.*

'S'one Song' (it's alternative title is 'Swan Song') is spit into two. In the first part Tony 'dies', making the raunchy second part his swan song. The lyrics betray a deep resentment of his schooldays when he was bullied and the lyrics can pretty much be read at face value.

The penultimate track on the album is the moody and magnificent 'Earth Shanty'. Its curious title came about when Tony thought 'there's a sea shanty, so why isn't there an earth shanty?' It's a question he was so convinced about that he created one. The big Mellotron opening creates a stunning ambience supplemented by the rushing of the wind, a sound achieved on the ARP synthesiser. In fact, it's one of Tony's best melodies.

Martin Rushent suggested Tony use the Yamaha acoustic on this one and it turned out very well. Along with 'I Love Miss Ogyny', this track is one of Pete Cruickshank's favourites because there was a more organic feel to it: 'I played the intro with the Gibson and got a nice rounded sound; after that I used the Zemaitis with a lot more top. With regard to the album I thought, playing-wise, it was less of me.'

Towards the end of the album Tony started to think in 'Split' mode. He had ended that album with an acoustic blues, but this time it would be different. His thoughts turned to John Lee Hooker, so he set about writing a song dedicated to him. He called it 'Mr Hooker, Sir John'. Back in Detroit, Hooker's hometown, they called him Sir John Lee Hooker.

The song, a moving tribute, is delivered with conviction:

Your music is timeless as a mountain and as earthy as the clay.

However, some people were still hearing things that were not there. Tony was told by one fan 'I didn't know Hooker was a surgeon', while the opening track convinced some that he hated women. Tony felt he could play around lyrically as the words didn't have the highest priority: 'For me an album should be listenable. I don't write a song for the lyrics that's why the music comes first.' On the meanings of the lyrics he was just as forthright: 'It's like saying every song that people sing they mean it. That would make it too limiting if true.' Tony's vocal delivery was more precise than previously as most of the lyrics are discernible; that had always been a problem.

Tony was still applying his technological knowledge to further the band's sound, as well as

Melody Maker **profile. TS would like to make it known his birthday is in fact on the 23rd of March.** TS Personal Collection

making life easier. One of his favourite guitars was a very early Gibson SG. The original model was fitted with a side-action tremelo arm which he decided to remove. In its place he fitted a re-designed scratchplate in order to include some effects of his own. One of these was a pressure switch that enabled him to achieve a wah-wah effect. Another was to use one channel of the stereo output jack to control a special effects unit.

This enabled him to operate the special effects locally and do without foot pedals. The Synthi Hi Fli consisted of a main processing unit mounted on a stand. It had an impressive complement of effects including ring modulator, vibrato, two phaser modes, three wah-wah modes and several other controls. Tony would soon have a chance to test his new equipment as Wilf Pine organised a big tour of the UK to promote the new album.

Fellow World Wide Artists acts Gentle Giant and Stray were supporting, with Badger also appearing at selected dates. Hogwash was released on 10th November, just in time for the fans to get their hands on it before the first gigs.

The press were very positive. *New Musical Express* called it a 'fine album' and heaped praise on the new dimension of the band: 'Tony McPhee has really come to terms with both Mellotron and synthesiser and knows how to use them to dynamic effect.' 'I Love Miss Ogny' and '3744 James Road' were cited as the outstanding tracks.

Even the more pop-orientated papers were positive. '"Thank Christ" is still the best album the Hogs have made. But "Hogwash" comes a close second. The addition of synths and Mellotrons has made the band far more palatable than they have been for the past couple of albums and if they keep this up there's a good chance that they will add thousands to their current horde of worshippers,' gushed *Record Mirror*.

Disc paid the ultimate compliment for any band worth their salt: 'You can never predict which way the music is going to go next. I think the Groundhogs are searching for something different.' In the States *Rolling Stone* was equally praising and, like Lester Bangs before him, Gordon Fletcher was just as mystified:

'Why have the Groundhogs yet to make it big in America? Bands

with half their talent, taste and heavy-metal intensity seem to be top-billed at Madison Square Garden every weekend.' Fletcher was convinced that 'Hogwash' was their best album.

On the eve of the tour Tony told James Johnson of *NME* that the addition of Clive Brooks had injected a fresh enthusiasm: 'I'm pleased with the way the new album and the new

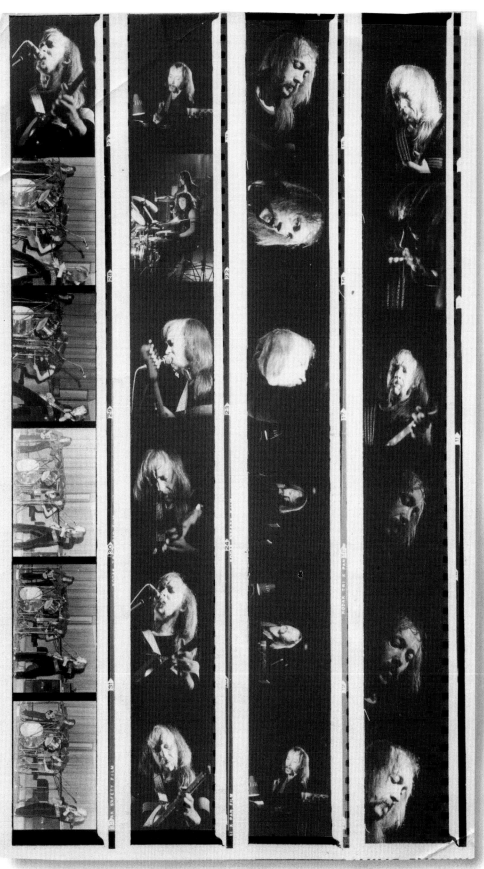

In action at the Rainbow Theatre, Finsbury Park.
TS Personal Collection

numbers have worked out. On "Who Will Save The World" I was really striving to write lyrics, when obviously I'd prefer it if they came naturally. This time, though, I got out of that notion I'd had about discarding anything that sounded remotely like anything we'd done previously. I found that the album didn't take long to make.'

This confidence clearly translated to the prospect of the tour working out just as well. For the first time, Tony was touring with a Mellotron and ARP synthesiser and to project them properly he wanted them to be put through the PA rather than a guitar amp. As a consequence there was going to be more variety and texture.

More than a few people were puzzled as there was no interruption in the sound when Tony switched to the Mellotron; he'd programmed his synthesiser. Most bands had technical personnel to do all of this, but in the Groundhogs Tony did more than his fair share of the work.

The opening gig was the Birmingham Town Hall on Friday 17 November 1972. Jerry Gilbert of *Sounds* was there: 'The crowd surged to the front of the hall to greet the new Groundhogs, just as they would be doing at all the other venues on the tour!

'For Tony McPhee – notwithstanding all those fan letters that constantly exult his talents on a comparative level with Hendrix and Clapton – is the new brains behind British rock music. And in a day when such accolades are two a penny, I would add that I do not make such a statement lightly.'

They presented 'Split' in its entirety, plus '3744 James Road', 'Soldier', 'I Love Miss Ogyny' and 'You Had A Lesson'. They prospered with 'Earth Shanty', while 'Mr Hooker, Sir John' reaffirmed their roots and changed the mood nicely. The show was a lot more balanced than hitherto. And there was yet another major change to take into account, as Tony told *Sounds*: 'In this band, because Clive is a clearer drummer, the lyrics seem to be clearer. In rehearsals I've managed to hear every word where they used to be lost and people are beginning to take notice.' Gilbert wrote a very positive piece on the band but the headline, 'The Emperor's New Clothes', was puzzling.

Wilf had taken the initiative and instigated something that raised eyebrows in some quarters. The Groundhogs had stage clothes! All the band members had boots custom made at Granny Takes A Trip in the Kings Road, London (Pete still has his!). Unfortunately Tony's never fitted properly. Pete Cruickshank had a cream suit made as the colour always worked for him.

Pete recalls the stage clothes: 'I wore a frilly shirt from Geoff Banks. I thought the management were trying to make us something that we weren't. I never felt comfortable with them. This concept didn't suit us, as we were not an image band; the whole thing confused me. It seemed to me they were trying to make us into pop stars.'

Tony had a velvet shirt and trousers. At

Clive Brooks in action.

Brunel University, where the stage was so high a chair was used as an impromptu leg-up, he heard a ripping sound. 'I thought maybe it didn't split but when I got up on stage I felt a draught. I nodded to the roadie and backed up to the amplifier so he could put a safety pin in. But velvet doesn't lend itself to that very well and it quickly ripped some more.'

The shirt was no better because there were no buttons on the front so he had to put it on over his head. By the end of a gig the shirt had stuck to him with all the sweat, so Pete and Clive would have an arm each in order to pull it off. At least the most undignified moments of the tour went, in the main, unseen by the fans.

On 1st December they played the Manchester Free Trade Hall. Lifelong fan Steve Thompson vividly recalls the excitement of the event: 'The electric hiss and humming coming from the speakers, the power of the amps was just awesome. On they came to rapturous applause. I moved to the front to get some close-ups of Tony in full swing. Tonight was the first time I heard the haunting song "Miss Ogyny" which had the theatre spellbound with its lyrics especially as it merged into "You Had A Lesson". A medley of "Thank Christ...", and "Split" followed.

'My personal moment of the night was the rendition of "Earth Shanty" with Tony playing his synthesiser like a god on stage; the sound of the sea and the power brought goosebumps to my whole body (it still does). This was the Groundhogs at their best and I think the best concert ever. A final encore brought them on for "Cherry Red" and as we left the theatre everybody was stunned with the power of the performance.'

The tour was turning out to be a value for money trip. Stray were getting good reports and the prodigiously talented Gentle Giant would have given anybody a run for their money. There was no taking it easy on this tour for the Groundhogs. But things got a lot harder for Tony at the Playhouse date in Glasgow. The dressing rooms were directly below the stage and got very warm and he noticed heaps of rat poison in all corners of the room. It wasn't the best of atmospheres. However, Tony's pre-gig preparation was interrupted by a loud bang.

'There was a raked stage, and our PA was quite high. I noticed in the soundcheck that it was leaning over a bit. I thought the whole lot had gone over, but it turned out that Stray had set off a thunderflash in a dustbin for maximum effect.

'Our roadies, Charlie and Pete,

came down with my Mellotron and all the keys were black. All the soot from the ceiling had rained down on the keys.' Luckily after much cleaning and testing it worked – no thanks to Stray, who were oblivious to the problems they had caused.

Tony had been keen to introduce the Mellotron for live performances but it gave him constant technical problems – soot raining down from the ceiling notwithstanding. The original models had endless tape loops but the one he was using had only eight-second tapes. The idea was that the springs in the workings pulled the tape back down again at the end of the cycle. However, this didn't happen every time, so he had to have the front off in order to pull the string back whenever it got stuck. He even had

the manufacturer come down to look at this, but of course it then worked perfectly! Everybody who used one cursed its unreliability.

A key Mellotron number was 'Earth Shanty', one of the highlights of the show. But Tony suffered a crucial lack of timing with the new technology at the Caird Hall, Dundee. As he told Jerry Gilbert of *Sounds*: 'I couldn't quite get the synthesiser together – there was a slight mismatch between synthesiser and amp and in "Earth Shanty", just as it went down to the quiet bit, someone shouted in a broad Dundee accent "Have you finished tuning up yet, Jimmy?" – and it brought me right down.

'I didn't know I could be deflated so easily, although it's a good thing really because it gives you something to strive for.'

Picture from 'Hogwash' tour brochure.
TS Personal Collection

The tour came to its conclusion with a gig at the Rainbow, London, on 22nd December. The year of 1972 had been one of considerable difficulties but most of those problems appeared to have melted away. Clive Brooks had settled in well and they had recorded an album that was up there with their best and had been released to enthusiastic reviews. It was depressing, though, when it failed to chart. Tony put the failure down to 'Who Will Save The World' because, even though it made the Top 10, many of their fans melted away after buying it, not liking the new direction. The new album did, however, make it into Kid Jensen's chart on Radio Luxembourg.

Even though the band was doing well, it was clear to Pete Cruickshank that this was a different band without Ken Pustelnik: 'I got used to Ken's unconventional way of playing and it was difficult to get used to Clive Brooks. In the old band I was like a hinge on the door between the other two. On stage somebody would instigate a speed change and the others would be into it instinctively. I think we lost a lot of spontaneity with Clive.'

As he went into 1973, Tony was already laying down the foundations for something else that would take him away from the band, albeit temporarily.

chapter 11

The Studio that Mac Built

'Out of all the artists I managed Mac was the most outstanding. He played better guitar than Clapton, Iommi and all the others.'
Wilf Pine

'I feel that I have something valid to say outside the framework of the Groundhogs and I want to get it out my system.'
Tony McPhee in 1973

During the recording of 'Hogwash' Tony had been very impressed with the overall sound of the album. When he told the engineer, Martin Rushent 'I'd love to get this sound at home,' Rushent's reply was 'Why don't you then?' That's when McPhee decided to buy the set-up at the old De Lane Lea studio, which was up for sale.

'It cost me five thousand pounds. I got a lot of equipment and some of it was historic. Included in the deal was the original machine that the Animals' 'House Of The Rising Sun' was recorded on.'

He had some recording facilities before this, but they were limited to Revox machines that could only deliver to demo standard. The deal for the eight-track equipment was done and, in January 1973, the roadies were ferrying parts of it to his house in Haverhill for installation in his garage. His ambition was never to record a Groundhogs album in London again!

St Francis, Haverhill. The magnificent asbestos edifice to the left is the famed TS Studios.
TS Personal Collection

Usually Tony was a mild-mannered, unassuming leader of a rock band. However, in January 1973 he gave a remarkable interview to Jerry Gilbert of *Sounds*, perhaps still smarting from the disappointing sales of 'Hogwash'.

When the name of Eric Clapton was mentioned he reacted uncharacteristically: 'I get the feeling I'm just a nuisance, that nobody wants to admit that I'm here. I know full well I can match any of those guys and that what I'm writing about is above it in a way because I'm trying to get across in the lyrics something a little more veering away from the normal and I'm just getting the feeling that not many people will accept it! I'm being dismissed on all counts because it's just down to trendy names.'

It was clear that Tony was frustrated by his lack of credit: 'When people said to me that they liked Groundhogs music I thought yes, Pete and Clive/Ken played on it but it's my music!' It was now a question of whether being in a band could satisfy Tony's ambitions.

In the February a tour on the college and smaller venue circuit saw their relationship with some sections of the press turn sour. Hitherto, Tony's main complaint about the press was being ignored, but the coverage they received had been almost overwhelmingly positive. However, it was around about this time they started to receive negative, even vindictive notices.

Melody Maker sent Geoff Brown to review the gig at the Stevenage Locarno. Although he was there to review the gig he even found time to criticise their back catalogue! Manager Wilf Pine was frustrated that his band was not getting a fair hearing when it came to the press.

In early April Tony appeared as a solo artist on *The Old Grey Whistle Test* when Finnish band Tasavallan Presidentti cancelled at short notice. He played two acoustic blues numbers, 'Me And The Devil' and 'Write Me A Short Few Lines', the latter written by an early influence, Fred McDowell.

Strangely, the Groundhogs had never appeared on the show. Shortly after, they embarked on a short tour of Denmark, France, Holland, Germany, Norway and Sweden. Clive Brooks hadn't been abroad all that much and, when they were in Norway, he was so excited by the huge amounts of snow he frolicked in it. But even Tony and Pete succumbed to the atmosphere as the band had a photo taken with snowballs in full *Gunfight At The OK Corral* pose.

The new rock management elite wasted no time in spending their new money and Patrick Meehan Junior and his ex-employer Don Arden were no exceptions. Tony remembers visiting

The only surviving record of the *Old Grey Whistle Test* appearance was taken from the TV by Clive Brooks.
TS Personal Collection

their houses – especially Meehan's in Coulsdon, just south of Croydon, where Tony's big night out was to play on the full-sized snooker table and slowly get pissed.

One night Tony was drinking Pernod and someone was spiking it with vodka, causing him to become uncharacteristically aggressive; he even offered John Fiddler of Medicine Head 'outside', although he can't remember why. It was at this time he first met Arden's young daughter, Sharon, who later married and managed wildman Ozzy Osbourne and went on to become a celebrity.

With touring completed at the end of April, Tony prepared to record his first solo album. He was very happy with the management situation: 'Being with Wilf was loads of fun; you felt impregnable with him. Nobody would mess you about while he was around. He was really sharp and he could suss situations very quickly. He wasn't popular with everybody, though. I remember we were playing a gig in Wales and I know Andrew Lauder was around, but he never came to see us. It was because he didn't like Wilf and he didn't like us going with him.'

For his part, Wilf Pine thought Tony was a tremendous talent and started to think of ideas to promote him. One of these was to form a supergroup, then next a solo album and tour. 'I told him he could do something with the blues and synthesisers. It was my idea to do something about the hunt, as Tony was passionate about it. I wrote a cheque to cover four ARP 2600 synthesisers.'

Though about to embark on this ambitious project, Tony remained ambivalent about synthesisers. In an interview with *Zig-Zag* just after 'Split' came out, he explained that: 'I'm not really a weird noise freak. I think it's much better and cleverer to get a strange sound out of an ordinary instrument, which is why I admired Hendrix so much. He could make Moog noises with a guitar.'

At that stage, few bands could see the potential of the synthesiser. In fact, Queen put 'No Synths Used' somewhere on the cover on all their early albums. It was only later they embraced them fully.

Tony's solo project more than troubled Pete Cruickshank, who was still reeling from all the changes initiated over the previous year: 'I thought the Groundhogs were being marginalised, it seemed to be going all one way as Wilf Pine seemed to concentrate on Tony. I wasn't too keen on Tony's project as the band would be off the road for a while.'

It was also clear that he saw Ken as a counterbalancing force in the band: 'It was good to have everything not going in the same way. It's a healthy alternative.' During the solo period Pete and Clive were put on a fixed wage, so had some money coming in.

Around this time Tony was offered a session with singer/songwriter Donovan at Morgan studios, London, for his 'Cosmic Wheels' album. While he was waiting in reception at the studio he heard a woman on the payphone say 'Rick

(Wakeman) can't get his synth working, can you come down?' Tony thought 'He's supposed to be a wizard! I should have told her I'll fix it for a hundred pounds.'

While Tony's knowledge of synthesiser music was limited, he knew that a lot more could be achieved with them and was keen to make his own mark.

When somebody asked him if his album was going to be like Mike Oldfield's 'Tubular Bells', he replied he'd never even heard of it! However, Tony was not only going to play all the instruments on his album, he was going to produce and engineer it in a studio he had built himself.

The benefits of owning a studio were many. Tony could get fully acquainted with the sound and even improve it before recording commenced. At home he could experiment to his heart's content. Tony was, last but not least, in complete control.

In the end the dream didn't happen because he didn't play the drums. When the Groundhogs had sound-tested the studio in early May, Clive Brooks had been keeping his drums there. During this time Tony tried to get to grips with them but gave up after only mastering the intro to Stevie Wonder's 'Superstition', so bought a Bentley Rhythm Ace drum machine instead.

The centrepiece of the album was a 20-minute, four-part concept called 'The Hunt'. The concept was that mankind has failed to shake off the barbarism that it needed to survive in its early years and, worse still, that hunting is executed as a ritual and portrayed as a 'sport'. It was animal cruelty amid pomp and the class system that Tony hated. While dabbling with the ARP he found the perfect way to start the piece, the sound of yelping hounds. An incredible atmosphere is created when the fanfare of the 'hunting horns' ushers in Tony's narration.

Wilf Pine tried very hard to rekindle interest in the band. TS Personal Collection

MUSIC IS THE MESSAGE

SOUNDS

SEPTEMBER 8, 1973   7p

McPHEE QUITS GROUNDHOGS

'There's something wrong with the basic sound'

Derek Block presents
TONY (TS) McPHEE IN CONCERT
THE ROUNDHOUSE
SUNDAY 16th SEPTEMBER
at 7.30pm TICKETS 70p
Tickets available from The Roundhouse
Box Office Telephone 267 2564
Open Monday - Saturday 10am - 8pm

The Roundhouse was the first 'explosive' gig on Tony's solo tour.
TS Personal Collection

Yelping hounds pack to form a Gorgon's head of gyrating tails ready to turn a stag's heart to stone at a single glance.
Each dog has a pedigree that would fill a ream of paper as have their masters boasting generations of good breeding.
Family trees with branches laden with the names of past landed gentry, their greatest contribution to the land being when they fall in their Autumn years, providing the earth with the same humus as their mongrel serfs.

When the spoken section ends, this triggers one of the most aggressive synth sounds ever, Tony singing the line 'No words could ever describe the hate I feel for these men'. At this stage the drum machine comes in and the tempo increases. Tony explains: 'With the drum machine I got a different rhythm by mixing a 3/4 and 4/4, and this triggered the synths to follow that rhythm because they were all linked up.' The first part concludes with a solo on the ARP.

The first part didn't come easily or very quickly, as Jerry Gilbert of *Sounds* outlines: 'Mac admitted that laying down the initial track was fairly boring as well as being the hardest part of the exercise since the musician was working blind.' But McPhee was a fast learner! 'Part Two' starts off in more laid-back style, a welter of cascading synths sounding rather mournful.

The penultimate part starts off with a most infectious riff and also contains one of the most interesting sections, as Tony explains: 'I used the synths to sound like bongos but by chaining the other synths it had them at a tone just higher and lower to increase the effect.'

The final part finds Tony really getting to grips with playing the ARPs as opposed to using them for effects. As he admitted to Jerry Gilbert: 'There was a lot of trial and error like deciding whether

TS with son Conan, Chris, schoolfriend Johnny Bryant, Cee Wetton and Jenny Bryant outside St Francis.
Pic courtesy Dave Wetton

to put the synthesiser through an amplifier. But the last track only took me about a day and by then I felt the sound was right on every part as opposed to the initial part of the track which took quite a while; so I ended up editing a bit on tape.'

The synths are cleverly used as Tony builds layer on layer. He put the National Anthem at the end because the Royal Family are part of the whole class problem. However, he decided, at the last minute, to cut it down to a snippet because he didn't want it to be in the listener's face. Wilf Pine wanted the longer version.

With 'The Hunt' in the can Tony set about recording the blues side of the album. During the early part of recording, Wilf phoned Tony and asked him for the titles of the songs. At that stage he only had 'The Hunt' as a title so he went into the garden and plucked the titles out of thin air there and then even though he hadn't written any of the songs at that stage! So he set about writing the music and lyrics around the titles he'd made up.

The first track is 'Three Times Seven', its theme that the path to adult life at twenty-one can be seen as three sections of seven. The first seven years is the child stage, years eight to fourteen adolescence and the final years end in adulthood. 'All My Money, Alimony' is another one of those interesting McPhee wordplays. The title didn't refer to Tony's marriage, but the line 'It didn't seem fair I should spend all my time working for you' seemed to foretell the future.

The third track is titled 'Dog Me Bitch', and features electric guitar. For some McPhee watchers it was more evidence that Tony didn't like women, thought this couldn't have been further from the truth. The final track is the curiously titled 'Take It Out'. This is the weakest out of the side and it's significant that Tony couldn't think of any words, so it remained an instrumental, albeit a fiery one. The outstanding track of the blues side is 'Morning's Eyes', with some great slide guitar, a love song to a deceased girl.

The synthesiser created hitherto unimagined possibilities and yet there was an element of uncertainty that Tony had never faced before in a studio, as he told Jerry Gilbert when it was all over: 'I tried to keep it melodic in essence and to give it form and shape because it's easy to use the

synthesiser purely to create an electronic sound.' The first few minutes of 'The Hunt' prove beyond doubt that Tony did exactly that. From start to finish the whole album had taken less than six weeks.

In retrospect, the album marshalled all of Tony's technical knowledge and ingenuity. He had always maintained he worked best under pressure. Gilbert brilliantly summed up the album as '1965 meets 1973'. But the album's title short-changed him somewhat for the sake of a bit of wordplay. The album should have been called 'The Many Sides Of Tony TS McPhee'!

Tony was happy with the music but wasn't so enamoured with the sleeve. The inner sleeve featured a photo of a mother and a baby clutching a pound note, which clearly alluded to 'All My Money, Alimony'. Many people thought it was Tony's wife and son but, in fact, they were unknown to him. One of the other ideas was the design by his eye. One side of the cover had 'tears' coming down his face, which was supposed to represent the blues side, while the computer printing on the other side represented new technology. He liked the cover apart from the picture of messy wiring on the inside which still irritates him.

While Tony had been recording his solo album, Wilf Pine came up with a couple of scams to excite press attention. The first concerned Tony going to the US to make a movie about a twentieth century wandering musician with two major established stars. One of them was rumoured (by Pine) to be Dustin Hoffman. The second scam created headlines in *Sounds* stating 'McPhee Quits Groundhogs' and quoting 'terrible disagreements' between Tony and the rest of the band.

When the paper came out Tony was in rehearsals for his solo tour. But, amazingly, the Groundhogs had performed their first gig since April at the recent Kendal Festival (26th August). They were rusty, and Irene Reed of *Melody Maker* picked up on it: 'Tony's voice didn't carry much at all and at times he and Pete Cruickshank seemed to be having difficulty in staying in the same key.' It's impossible to think why Tony would want to fit in a one-off date for the band while in the middle of hectic preparations for his solo tour. The album was released to coincide with the tour and *Melody Maker*'s Tony Stewart rated it 'something of a minor masterpiece'.

The solo tour was limited to 10 dates, opening at the Roundhouse, London, on 16th September. Tony would play on various guitars for an hour with the next hour showcasing his array of keyboards, which included the four ARPs and an RMI electric piano. The

centrepiece of the second half was 'The Hunt'. There wasn't much room for props but Clive Brooks loaned Tony a shop mannequin on a turntable with mirrors on it which was placed behind him. The opening night was not without incident, though. Just after Tony had finished the first number in the blues set there was a bomb scare and the place was evacuated; the police let the audience come back in after 15 minutes. Tony is pretty sure he knows who the culprit was and is still not amused...

Against all odds, the sheer intensity of 'The Hunt' came over well live. There was a touch plate on the drum machine which Tony used to trigger the synthesisers and, during the first part when he finished his narration, he hit the plate and the synths and drums came in like a ton of bricks. Tony recalls the effect it had on him: 'When that happened and I heard the synths I thought "Fucking hell!" Things went so well that there were times when I would have loved to have been in the audience myself!'

Ray Telford of *Sounds* was there and he corroborates the excitement generated: 'TS seems to utilise every aspect of his synthesiser and all the other boxes of tricks he plugs

Tony on the 'Two Sides' tour.
Pic courtesy Paul Brears

'The Two Sides of Tony TS McPhee.'
TS Personal Collection

***Sounds* poster featuring his famed Zemaitis guitar.**
TS Personal Collection

in and switches on. 'The Hunt', the longest piece performed in the set, drew possibly the most positive reaction and rightly so for it demonstrated McPhee's complete mastery and unbounded possibilities of the synthesiser. Neither was there a feeling that technology was being substituted for music. He can sound tender, soft and melodic one second and the next punching out heavy riffs.'

Melody Maker's Dave Lewis was also at the gig: 'After the unscheduled interruption by the demon bomb hoaxer, McPhee launched dramatically into his electronic wizardry, strutting like a mad professor from one control panel to the other.'

But there were some things he didn't like: 'There were some melodic moments, but some of it sounded like a jet plane passing low overhead and the glittering window-dresser's dummy with a spear revolving in the background was really very ham.'

It seemed as if reviewers were tripping over themselves to write a good review, *Record Mirror* writing: 'Those who had never seen him before were whispering what to expect. There was total respect. It was the sort of atmosphere normally reserved for legends of our times: a height that Tony is fast approaching. He is a really fine blues performer and the songs from his new album prove that he can compose good blues as well as perform them! Definitely one of the best acts I have heard for a long time.' Tony encored with a version of 'Crossroads' and everybody went home happy.

Things did not always go to plan. At one of the gigs, just before showtime, Tony was shaving but forgot to tighten the razor and ended up cutting himself several times. There was nothing else for it but to do the gig with plasters on his face! The final gig at St Albans was especially emotional and several fans told Tony later that it was very intense. Pete Cruickshank was at the gig: 'I was quite impressed with the show, it was very powerful. I didn't like the entire album but I liked the first part of "The Hunt" and it was well worked out. Looking back, I was surprised he never did another solo project.'

The tour was a complete success but many Groundhogs fans were biting their nails because of Wilf Pine's bogus headline about Tony going solo. They needn't have worried – he was itching to get back to the Groundhogs.

chapter 12

Groundhogs Blues

'I don't believe you have listened to the album.'
Tony McPhee's expunged line in a letter to Melody Maker

**'Some people thought Ken was crap because of his unique style.
I wasn't conscious of it at the time but we lost a lot of
identity after he left.'**
Pete Cruickshank in 2004

Solo tour completed, Tony started to think about getting the band back together. The follow-up to 'Hogwash' was the first Groundhogs album recorded at the McPhee studio though, as usual, the material was written at the last minute. He also had a new innovation for the album, the Synthi Hi Fli he had used on the 'Hogwash' tour. When Tony acquired a new piece of technology he exploited all its possibilities – as with 'Split', when he acquired a wah-wah pedal. His motto with new technology was 'If you've got it, use it'.

This was an important album, coming as it did on the back of Tony's well received solo work. He had to prove to some of the fans that the band had got a future. The album's opener is 'Light My Light' and is another of those wordplay games that just fits nicely.

The Synthi Hi Fli is in evidence right from the off but the music came from an old influence, as Tony recalls: 'I like progressions, that's the blues in me. There are certain progressions that go up and down; this one goes down. I also used some unusual chords again.' Tony's voice sounds earthy and led some to believe he was having problems but, in fact, it was a deliberate ploy to create a new aspect to the band's sound.

'Free From All Alarm' opens with a solo acoustic section showing that Tony McPhee is one of the few great electric guitarists who is comfortable with an acoustic. The structure goes from 7/4 to 6/4 and then 5/4. Those who perused the album sleeve while playing this would have been confused as it stated that Pete Cruickshank and Clive Brooks appear on the track. Just when you think it must be wrong Tony's elongated final 'alarm' is the signal for the rhythm section to kick in.

The third track and future live staple is 'Sins Of The Father', whose title mocks Chicory Tip's big hit 'Son Of My Father', the track Tony had considered to be one of the worst uses of a synthesiser. The next track 'Sad Go Round' provides one of his most inventive uses of wordplay. Science-fiction writer Ray Bradbury had written a story about a merry-go-round where the people got off the ride younger than when they got on.

Album cover for 'Solid'.

Tony liked that idea and developed it in the completely opposite direction. On the 'Sad Go Round', the consequences of taking a ride were negative. What makes the track even more interesting is the dreamy quality of the music which came to Tony while asleep. It's a pity it didn't get anywhere as a single because it's one of the band's finest moments.

The flip-side opener 'Corn Cob' showcases the Synthi Hi Fli, the lyrics betraying a growing estrangement. Pete and Clive aren't on the track. Tony laid down the guitar part late one night in the studio and then carried on with the bass. He also decided that the drum part would be minimal so he put a bass drum on it. 'Plea Sing, Plea Song' has a phased echo behind the guitar that sounds great.

By this stage of their career a Groundhogs album wouldn't be complete without a Mellotron classic and 'Snow Storm' provides it. He also plays the bass on this one and it's apparent immediately he has a different style to Pete. He plays a lot faster with a lot more top.

The reason he took Pete's place is because he knew what he wanted, so he reeled it off. But it did seem strange to fans when they perused the inner album sleeve. Tony had never done this before, though he was still writing the bass parts for Pete to play. The Synthi Hi Fli is used on his voice for extra effect.

The final track 'Jokers Grave' is a reference to TV show *Jokers Wild* and has a dark aspect to it, the 'Hello there' intro and manic synthesiser reflecting the spirit of the title. Clive uses bongo drums, an idea Tony got from the intro of 'Time' from Pink Floyd's 'Dark Side Of The Moon'.

He decided to call the album 'Solid' for no other reason that it sounded good. To many fans it was a most apt name, as it seemed to capture the spirit of the music. It was rumoured that the original title was 'Phart' and some stores had indicated they would refuse to stock the album. In fact, it was another Wilf Pine scam, a humorous way for the band to have one over on the press.

The band had delivered a good album but the sleeve was decidedly lame. In the past Tony spent a lot of time on the album art, but it was clear from 'Solid' that he had run out of ideas. Gered Mankowitz took the cover shot in his studio in London,

the band looking mean, moody and enigmatic. The back cover shot was even more puzzling as it showed the vacant chairs. Pete still thinks that the whole thing was unprofessional: 'We never actually saw the finished work, we only saw slides and you couldn't really get an idea of things.' Suffice to say the band were disappointed when they saw the sleeve. It's easily their worst cover.

Below the surface things were in bad shape, as Pete recalls: 'I thought "Solid" was a good album but to me it seemed more like a solo album. I liked "Light My Light" and "Sad Go Round" but on the whole it was another step away from the Groundhogs for me. When Tony played bass on two of the tracks I thought to myself "What's this?" I think anybody would have thought that. "Corn Cob" didn't seem right for us. "Jokers Grave" starts off well but it went on far too long and ends up a din. It seemed to me this new material gave a lot less scope for development live.

'Tony was experimenting a lot and was more into his own thing than before. In the studio he was becoming more insular. Everything was Tony and it seemed to me that it wasn't a healthy atmosphere. I didn't feel involved any more.'

Equipment list for the customs 'carnet' then necessary when working in Europe.
TS Personal Collection

GROUNDHOG's 26th MARCH. 74.

EQUIPMENT LIST

Item	Trade Description of Goods	No.	Value	Country of Origin
1	JBL High Frequency Horns PACE	#2	£680	USA
2	JBL Mid Range Horns	4	£800	USA
3	JBL Front loading Bass Horns	8	£1600	USA
4	Alice SM20 20-channel Mixer	1	£2000	UK
5	Alice 24volt Power Supply	1	£30	UK
6	Alice Belden Multicore Cable & Stagebox	1	£300	UK
7	Beyer Microphone Boom Stands	9	£100	Germany
8	Beyer Floor Microphone Stands	4	£24	Germany
9	Quad Amps. contained in 2 cases	10	£500	UK
10	Trunks containing Cannon to Cannon Leads	2	£150	UK
11	Shure Microphones	18	£750	USA
12	Hartman Bases & Rigging	3	£300	UK
13	3-phase Power Cable & Case	1	£200	UK
14	20-way Dimmer Pack & Control Board	1	£1100	UK
15	30 Hartman PAR 64 Lamps	30	£1200	UK
16	Cables for above lamps	30	£100	UK
17	Trunks containing Cells, Spares & Cables	2	£200	UK
18	Rank Strand CS1 Follow Spots & Cables	3	£1200	UK
19	Choke Boxes for CS1 Lamps	3	£80	UK
20	Magazines for CS1 Lamps	3	£80	UK
21	H/H 2x15 Cabinets	8	£2000	UK
22	H/H 1C100S Amplifiers	4	£500	UK
23	Mellotron & Volume Pedal	1	£600	UK
24	ARP 2600 Synthesisers	3	£3000	USA
25	ARP Keyboards	3	£600	USA
26	Schaller Wah Wah Pedal	1	£15	Germany
27	H/H TPA 100D Power Amplifiers	4	£200	UK
28	Dallas Arbiter Octave Splitter	1	£35	UK
29	Phaser	1	£400	UK
30	Synthi Hi Fli & Pedals	1	£300	UK
31	Swiss Echo & Pedal	1	£150	Switzerland
32	Shure Microphone Mixer	1	£80	USA
33	Footswitches	4	£20	UK
34	Gibson SG 6 String Guitar	1	£200	USA
35	Fender Stratocasters	2	£400	USA
36	Zemaitis 6 String Guitar	1	£250	UK
37	Fender Mustang 6 String Guitar	1	£100	USA
38	Harmony Regal Accoustic Guitar	1	£70	USA
39	Yamaha Accoustic Guitar	1	£50	Japan
40	Zemaitis Bass Guitar	1	£250	UK
41	Gibson EB3 Bass Guitar	1	£200	USA
42	Alice AD62 6-channel Mixers	2	£400	UK
43	Fender Musicmaster Amplifier	1	£80	USA
44	RMI Electric Piano	1	£600	USA
45	Crumor Electric Piano	1	£130	Italy
46	Davoli Guitar Amplifiers	2	£300	Italy
47	Drum Boards	2	£10	UK
48	Drum Risers	2	£20	UK
	Hayman Drum Kit:			
49	24" Bass Drum	1	£100	UK
50	16" Tom Tom	1	£60	UK
51	14" Tom Tom	1	£50	UK
52	13" Tom Tom	2	£50	UK
53	14" Snare Drum	1	£35	UK
54	14" Ludwig Snare Drum	1	£100	USA
55	Paiste Cymbals (14",16",18",20")	5	£200	Switzerland

In November 1973 the Hogs started an extensive UK tour supported by another of Wilf Pine's acts, Jonesy. It was disappointing that the band had only released the single 'Sad Go Round' at that point ('Plea Sing, Plea Song' was also later released as a single).

Tony was determined to use a new track for the flip-side; he had a basic riff which he worked on and also took the opportunity to lace it with plenty of synth. The track was completed very quickly and he called it 'Over Blue', it was later on the CD reissue, although it was never intended for inclusion. The single was released in time for the tour, but the album was delayed.

The tour comprised over 20 shows at medium to large venues. Tony decided it was the time to develop some theatrics, so they used dry ice, but it didn't always have the dramatic impact they hoped for. Tony's solo spot was suggested by Wilf, and the original idea was to do part of 'The Hunt'. A special rack was made to house the ARPs, but in the end Tony went off the idea as it was far too complicated to attempt live.

One of the things Tony was concerned with was the sound. In those days there were plenty of bands that played far too loud – Deep Purple proudly entered the *Guinness Book Of Records* as the loudest band. Tony explained in an interview: 'Recently we've been cutting down on the volume at gigs. When we do this, Anton has a chance to pull the vocals through. The louder you play, the more chance you have of losing the vocals somewhere along the line.'

Anton Matthews, the engineer on the solo tour, was a recording engineer from Olympic Studios in Barnes. He was in control of the equipment that the band used on stage at that time, which included 10 Quad 303 amps (five on each side) with 900 watts in total, controlled by an Alice mixer desk.

On the tour they premiered 'Light My Light' and 'Sins Of The Father' from the new album. All went well but Tony was quite perturbed by the behaviour of support band, Jonesy: 'We played the Sheffield City Hall and the dressing rooms were downstairs in one big room. All that separated the bands was a curtain. They never stopped arguing on that tour. I thought that's silly because if you do a bad gig so what?' His attitude was that mistakes are made and life's too short to dwell on them. In spite of the success of this tour, there were no foreign gigs – worrying for a band that had always gone down well in parts of Europe.

Pete felt the people who came to see them were now seeing a different band. 'Tony was using Mellotrons and synths more and more in the new material but the crowd were still shouting for "Cherry Red" and "Split Part One". Some people thought Ken was crap because of his unique style. I wasn't conscious of it at the time but we lost a lot of identity after he left.

The band then was more like some of the other bands.'

Ken remarked that what kept the Hogs glued together in the old days was constant working and, as a result, they were really tight. This was another problem in the Clive Brooks era; their workload was nowhere near what it was a few years earlier.

The early part of 1974 saw the Groundhogs play low-key gigs all over the country waiting for 'Solid' to be released in June. Under Roy Fisher they ended up being overworked but now they were moving in the opposite direction. Pete recalls those days with WWA: 'We seemed to spend a lot of time hanging around. I did feel they only took us on because it looked good on paper along with the rest of their other bands.' However, the Groundhogs had another album released before then. It was an LP that Tony McPhee didn't even know was coming out.

The simmering dissatisfaction towards the media, *Melody Maker* to be precise, that Wilf Pine felt came rising to the surface when United Artists released 'Groundhogs Best 1969-72' in April. Album reviewer Jeff Ward penned a negative critque for *Melody Maker* that aroused Tony's anger.

'When this bulky double album dropped on my desk, promising more than 80 minutes of Groundhog sound, my first reaction was "Oh my God! What I have I done to deserve this?" It concluded with: 'It's just an offensive noise and deadly dull. Sleeve notes indicate another "best" album in a couple of years. Save us!'

The middle section wasn't much better either: 'Although the tracks are not in sequence, certain stages of the band's, er, development can be witnessed.'

Written by Jeff Ward...not a fan, then.
TS Personal Collection

GROUNDHOGS: "Groundhogs Best 1969-72" (United Artists). When this bulky double album dropped on my desk, promising more than 80 minutes of Groundhog sound, my first reaction, to be quite truthful was: "Oh my God! What have I done to deserve this?" Even the title seemed a contradicition. I shuddered right down to my bootips — how could one of the most crass and insensitive bands in the world have a "best." Well anyway, the album selects tracks from five albums from "Blues Obituary" through to "Hogwasn." The numbers are not placed in chronological order, probably to disguise the fact the band never got any better. Tony McPhee has about as much musical sensibility as the bog roll he delights in singing about on side one. He just uses the blues form as a kind of punching bag for his guitar. Although the tracks are not in sequence, certain stages in the band's er, development can be witnessed; the dreadful "Express Man" from the rank blues period of '69; the Hendrix copy attempts, like "Eccentric Man," in '70; the morbid tries at sublimating the band during the "Mighty Groundhogs" period, all to no avail. It's just an offensive noise, and deadly dull. Sleeve notes indicate another "best" album in a couple of years. Save us! — J.W.

Tony, Clive and Pete at TS Studios.
Pic Mike Putland for *Sounds* feature.
TS Personal Collection

(1) Apart from being heavily involved in the UK music scene, Wilf had another less publicised life across the Atlantic. In a book based on his life, author John Pearson states he is one of only two Englishmen to be closely involved with the American Mafia! Thanks to a chance encounter with a leading figure in the Genovese family in New York, Wilf became accepted as a trusted friend and associate of influential godfather Joe Pagano. Joe was best man at Wilf's wedding and he also became involved with John Gotti, boss of the Gambino family.

After the Groundhogs, Wilf continued in management with Stray, Edgar Broughton Band and Jimmy Helms, the latter taking up more and more of his time. When Hemdale ceased to be quoted on the stock market, Wilf's interest in WWA also ended: 'This convinces me that the WWA bid had always been a ploy to get into Hemdale, since Hemdale had the prestige of being a publicly quoted company with a gambling licence for various bookmaking operations they conducted.' After giving advice to his acts where they could get new management he quit the music business in 1976. Before the end of 1977 he declared himself bankrupt.

Wilf got to know Charlie Kray back in England and, before long, was visiting his twin brothers (Reggie and Ronnie) in prison. He was also involved in the film made about them in the late 1980s starring the Kemp brothers from Spandau Ballet. Wilf was at Charlie's side when he died in prison. After several heart attacks Wilf is still going strong and is currently involved with another Kray film project staring Ray Winstone.

Wilf met up with Tony to talk about old times in 2004 at the Bournemouth gig of his tour with Alvin Lee and Edgar Winter (they have always kept in touch). The gold discs of Groundhogs, Black Sabbath and Stray still hang on the wall of Wilf's sitting room.

Incensed, Tony tried to phone Ward on numerous occasions at the office and at home but his mother always answered at home and said he was not in. One day Tony got Clive to phone and pretend to be Steve Lake (another *MM* reviewer), Ward came to the phone and Clive put the phone down, but when Tony called back immediately he got the same response from Ward's mother.

Things went from bad to worse when the aforementioned Steve Lake reviewed 'Solid' in *MM* a couple of months later under the headline 'Solid Boredom'! 'I don't for a minute believe that anybody in the band takes this kind of conveyor belt neo-sociological pop cum-heavy-metal seriously! Solid? It should be re-titled "Squalid". Better still, "Stale".'

This was the straw that broke the camel's back. Wilf Pine's initial reaction was to suggest they go down to the *Melody Maker* office in Fleet Street and throw the phones through the windows! Tony recalls that it was only his assistant, Clive Jenkins, who persuaded him that it would be a bad move.

Wilf's next course of action was to phone the paper's offices to speak to Steve Lake. But when Jeff Ward answered the phone, Wilf charmingly asked if he had ever seen the band live and why he didn't like them. Ward's main defence seemed to be that he wasn't the only one in the office who didn't like the band. Tony recalls the final piece of the conversation was that Ward would be best advised to look over his shoulder when leaving work because one day Wilf would be there to break his legs!

Wilf wasn't totally unaware of the implications of what he'd said as he contacted *Sounds* scribe Jerry Gilbert, who was doing some work for him: 'I got a phone call from Wilf. He told me he'd just made the mistake of threatening a journalist.' The next thing they knew, Wilf had a phone call from solicitors representing Ward, who stated that the telephone conversation had been taped (which was most unlikely). Wilf replied in his most charming manner, asking the solicitor's name and where he worked and then simply repeated the threat made to Ward.

By this time it was a full-blown feud between the two camps. However, it wasn't all bad news as *New Musical Express* weighed in with a great review: 'After a few listenings of this, I've come to the conclusion that the Groundhogs are well back in form! The production on this album is excellent and McPhee has obviously worked hard to achieve a sound that is tight and forceful but

with enough area to experiment in.'

Beverley Legge of *Disc* also came to the rescue: 'If ever a band suffered from prejudice it must be the Groundhogs. Hopefully this album will go a long way towards getting rid of that. It's packed with straightforward down-to-earth driving rock music with just a dash of blues.'

In 1964 Tony McPhee had penned an open letter to the press defending John Lee Hooker and Howlin' Wolf's musical integrity. Now he would be forced to defend his own.

In July, *Melody Maker* published his letter under the headline 'McPhee: I Believe In What I Write'. In the letter Tony set out his case against Messrs Ward and Lake. He starts off by stating that the animosity has had a recent history and notes that the nature of reporting has changed:

'Bad reviews are usually like kicks to the rump, they sting for a bit but don't really annoy. Now these two have aimed their kicks from the front straight to the groin and it hurts, the difference being whereas bad reviews are sometimes justified these two have just been plain vindictive and insulting and I feel I have to straighten them out on a few facts.'

Tony was upset that Lake had taken a line from 'Jokers Grave' as proof that the lyrics were garbage. 'I think you read the lyric sheet searching for fodder for your sarcasm.' The fact that Steve Lake 'declined to name the bass player' is proof that, as it wasn't on the sleeve, he didn't know it was Pete Cruickshank.

At face value it appears that it was a magnanimous gesture for the paper to print the letter. However, they left out one line which read 'I don't believe you have listened to the album'. Why leave that out if it wasn't true? Also, the paper was keen, if only as a sop to Wilf Pine, to show they were giving the other side a chance to air their views.

Their seriousness can be judged by the fact they put 'LP Winner' at the end of the letter (funnily enough Tony never did get his LP!).

Around about this time Tony started to develop the theatrical side more. His idea was to feature one of their greatest numbers, 'Soldier', as the set finale. At the end of the number the band went off stage and Clive Brooks changed into his soldier's uniform. What gave him time was a synthesised tape that engineer Anton Matthews played from Tony's ARP imitating bombers and explosions. Clive would then rush back on stage. At the tape's conclusion a spotlight would be trained on his face and with a starting pistol he would 'shoot' the light out.

MELODY MAKER, July 27, 1974—Page

McPhee: I believe in what I write

But, as Tony recalls, there were problems: 'We had a prop WW2 Sten gun but we weren't allowed to use a gun that fired blanks, so we used a starting pistol. The starting pistol was never really loud enough even when Clive pointed it at the microphone.' They persevered with this well into 1975 but, Tony recalls, at one gig Clive exclaimed 'this is getting boring'. Pete Cruickshank remembers this stunt very well: 'It didn't really work and we were losing our way. People came to hear the music and that was where our strength lay. We were never a visual band as we didn't have a frontman like Robert Plant.'

On the subject of stage work, fans were clamouring for a live album. By 1975 most of the big bands had released one, with the Groundhogs, Led Zeppelin and Black Sabbath the most notable exceptions. In an interview with *Progression* magazine the previous year Tony explained why:

'There were a couple of attempts at live recordings that were dire because we're sort of a problem in terms of giving a sufficient sound on tape. At the BBC, whenever we do the *In Concert* things it's very easy to blow those big tubes (on the transmitters) they've got, you know with an overload. So they have to try and limit it, get the whole sound compressed. But there are times when we go very soft and then I come in with a loud chord.'

It was a shame that the band didn't record a live album in this classic period.

Even though 'Solid' had made a welcome return to the album charts, the feud with *Melody Maker* left a sour taste in the mouth. As far as Tony was concerned there were too many things going wrong and there was more to come. He had felt down for quite a time and it's well documented that the lyrics on the album were depressing.

Due to all of their antics the show was extending to two hours, but at a gig in Cambridge Tony decided to curtail some of the theatrics, so the show was pruned down closer to an hour and a half. At the end of the show the promoter complained about being short-changed. It seemed to Tony that everybody was having a go at the Groundhogs. It seemed the change of management in 1972 didn't really reap dividends. For though WWA had plenty of ambition they didn't seem to have much vision. And when in late 1974 World Wide Artists was in dispute with Hemdale (their parent company), money stopped coming through to the band.

Wilf told Tony: 'Once you stop dealing in readies you don't know where you are.' All the other WWA artists were in a similar position. Wilf Pine advised the band to collect the gig money while, at the same time, the band joined Wilf's own company, Heat Music, still part of WWA. It was a situation that later led Tony to sum up the period as everything 'crumbling'. Wilf moved his office away from WWA's Dover Street headquarters.

Pete recalls this period of managerial chaos: 'We were at the offices and got talking to a couple of guys from Black Sabbath. They ended up by banging on the desk demanding to see some accounts. In the three years we were with WWA we had one set of accounts for one tour. At least with Roy Fisher we had a statement every month detailing the finances.

'I remember when I wanted to buy a house so I asked them for the money. They said they would deal with it but I wanted the mortgage in my name. If you asked for anything they would always say they would get it for you. I did get the house but I moved because I was frightened I would lose the house if anything went wrong. That's when I moved to Bury St Edmunds.'

In the end the band left WWA and immediately had an injunction slapped on them. (1)

Number of known gigs 1969-75.
Compiled by Joanna Deacon
TS Personal Collection

Year	Known Gigs*
1969	30
1970	100
1971	170
1972	41 (broken wrist)
1973	40
1974	60
1975	41

*Those confirmed with supporting evidence June 2005

Ferry to Scandinavia.
TS Personal Collection

109

Tony McPhee was completely down about the situation. In February 1975 he came up with a radical solution. He decided to disband the Groundhogs! He called Pete Cruickshank and Clive Brooks to his house in Haverhill and broke the news.

As Tony recalls: 'Pete took it badly, his chin was on the floor. He was very concerned about what he was going to do in the future. I felt bad about it but what could I do? Clive didn't say a lot at the meeting.' When the story broke in the press they were more forthcoming. In an interview with Pete Makowski of *Sounds*, Pete Cruickshank was down to earth: 'We knew it was going to happen but it still came as a surprise.'

Clive Brooks was more quixotic: 'The strange thing is that when we told Tony we were going to do interviews, he said okay but he was going to lay back and not say anything for a while.' Pete ruminated on the situation with Tony's silence: 'This makes the whole thing weird, we can only assume he's going to pursue a solo career or maybe start another Groundhogs with a different line-up, who knows?' The reason Tony didn't speak to the press was he didn't trust them.

With gigs to fulfil, the band headed to their final destination. Surprisingly the atmosphere at these gigs was quite good. On 4th April 1975 at the Kings Cross Cinema, London, the band bade farewell to their legion of fans. The only thing that Tony recalls about this gig is how cold the theatre was. Pete Cruickshank recalls the 'crappy' sound. The press were there to hound them into the grave. Allan Jones of *Melody Maker* made sure the band were not going to bow out with dignity – in print anyway! His novel approach to reviewing a gig could be summed up when he started to compare the state of the decaying theatre with the band. At least Tony ensured they would have to find another target for their bile.

The band members parted amicably but, just when the dust had finally settled, a tax demand for £10,000 landed on Tony's mat. When he pulled himself together he got an accountant to try and sort it out. In the early 1970s Tony, Pete and Ken had made the Groundhogs a partnership on Roy Fisher's advice to gain certain financial advantages. But in the end it backfired on them. Amazingly, the partnership had not been dissolved when Clive Brooks joined the band.

Top right:
Size matters!

Above right:
Clive, Pete & Tony waiting for the ferry home.

Right:
Traveling in the Bentley looked good and was comfortable but cold as the heater didn't work.
All pics, TS Personal Collection

The Inland Revenue thought that Tony was raking money in while, in fact, the band parted almost penniless. It was no consolation that the IR frequently used this tactic as a starting point for discussion to settle a claim (agreed later as £1,200). Two claims were made. The first was for 1971-72 when they changed management from Roy Fisher to WWA.

The second part of the claim was for the three years after 1972 (this meant WWA hadn't paid any tax for the band). In the end the tax losses were written off against Tony's name. But to do this his accountant had told the IR that Tony was the employer. This now meant Pete Cruickshank was classed as an employee liable to pay income tax and couldn't write any tax losses off as Tony had done that already!

It was then that the Inland Revenue came for Pete (they never approached Ken Pustelnik on this matter). He later phoned Tony and asked him why he had said he was the employer. Pete was also in dire financial straits and couldn't pay anything at that time either.

As he reflects: 'After many static pauses I put the phone down on him. I was still fighting the taxman well into the 1980s. In the end I managed to convince them I wasn't an employee but not before I paid a third of the tax for 1971-72, the final year with Ken.' Tony had to pay the remainder by selling equipment, Ken managing to avoid paying anything by disappearing.

Tony and Pete had been through a lot together and it was a sad way to end their relationship. They didn't speak to each other for 27 years.

That's snow business/snowballs at the OK Corral/don't bell-bottoms make you look bandy?
TS Personal Collection

Last Groundhogs gig...till next time!
Pic courtesy Tony Sherratt
TS Personal Collection

KING'S CROSS CINEMA
GRAND OPENING WEEKEND APRIL 4th + 5th
FRIDAY 4th: The final appearance of
THE GROUNDHOGS
IN THEIR PRESENT LINE-UP
with the amazing PETE BROWN'S FLYING TIGERS
and PERFORMANCE : D.J. JERRY FLOYD
SATURDAY 5th
JACK the LAD
and
5 HAND REEL
D.J. JERRY FLOYD
Information: 01-734 6801
FRIDAY Doors Open 7.30 until 1 a.m
Adm: £1.25, £1.00 + VAT
SATURDAY Doors Open 7.30 until 11.45
Adm: £1.75, £1.00 + VAT

chapter 13

Eleventh Hour

'McPhee is one of the original guitar heroes. The master of howling full-speed runs, clanging chords and high-pitched screaming.'

Melody Maker journalist, Chris Welch

Even though Tony McPhee was relieved the Groundhogs saga was finally over, it wasn't long before, like Pete Cruickshank, he started to concentrate on exactly how he was going to earn a living. In spite of his regular publishing money he realised he was going to have financial problems. For some time after April 1975 he focused on the idea of having a successful solo career like Rory Gallagher. His plan was to record a solo album and then go out with a new band. However, as the year frittered away, he was faced with a blank gig sheet.

UA promo: Martin Kent, Mick Cook, Dave Wellbelove and TS.
TS Personal Collection

GROUNDHOGS

It was around about this time that he received a call from Richard Cowley of Cowbell Agency (he formed the company with Kenny Bell). Cowley informed him that he was having enquiries about the possibility of Groundhogs gigs. At first Tony informed him of his solo plans but Cowley tersely told him 'you won't get any gigs'. Tony mulled it over and slowly came round to the idea of reforming the Groundhogs again. The question was who would be in the band?

Tony considered the Groundhogs his invention and this estranged Pete Cruickshank even more. After considering the Pink Fairies and Zzebra as potential backing musicians, Richard Cowley recommended ex-Home drummer Mick Cook, Martin Kent on bass and Dave Wellbelove on guitar.

At first Tony wondered how he was going to work with a second guitarist, but the funky rhythm section of Cook and Kent impressed him. As he related to *Beat Instrumental*'s Chris Simmonds: 'I had the chance of getting known musicians for the band, but I decided against it as I didn't see the need for people with preconceived ideas about music. This way I'll be able to mould together a really tight, cohesive band.'

Richard Cowley negotiated a record contract with United Artists when Tony was reunited with A&R man Andrew Lauder. He started to think about making an album with the new boys and decided he was going to instigate a new style of writing – more funky, but still with a healthy slice of blues. It was here that he realised Mick Cook could help:

'Mick was always going on about 'reverse beats' which I sort of understood, but I said I preferred them to be forward. At first it was off-putting but sometimes it would inspire me to come up with a more interesting lick.' By November 1975 they were ready to go into Tony's home studio to record the album that would be known as 'Crosscut Saw'.

In early November Tony got a call from Dave Wetton. The former bassist in the Seneschals was heavily involved with the fledgling Hunt Saboteurs and their movement was gaining not only more members but public sympathy. The BBC agreed to give them a 20-minute slot on BBC2's *Open Door* and Wetton came to the conclusion that 'The Hunt' would be appropriate music. Permission to use the track was willingly granted.

The programme consisted of a studio discussion (including Wetton) and documentary film of a real hunt, the first time that the public had ever seen such graphic illustration of the 'sport' and Tony's music/oratory provided a compelling companion to it. The programme was broadcast on 22nd November and provoked a massive increase in membership of the Hunt Saboteurs. (At the time of writing Tony still hasn't seen the programme).

Promo 2. TS, Martin, Mick and Dave taken in the garden at St Francis.
TS Personal Collection

Recorded in a few weeks, 'Crosscut Saw' is testament to the new direction Tony was looking for. This is evident in the first (and title) track, where Dave Wellbelove took the solo, showing that Tony wasn't frightened to delegate. 'Promiscuity' is next up and continues the laid-back style of the opening track, Mick Cook employing some of those reverse beats. Tony is pleading with girls not to sleep around on a song that turned out radically different from how he envisaged it, and is one of his favourites.

Third track 'Boogie Withus' sees Tony on more familiar territory, but this time with a two-pronged guitar attack. It's a rollicking journey and became the opening number of the show. Tony is back on form with his wordplay games. It's actually a play on the name of Googie Withers (a film heart-throb) but is not about her. Dave takes the solo again on this one. The first

Tony TS McPhee, Martin Kent, Mick Cook, Dave Wellbelove.
TS Personal Collection

Haverhill, Tony's cat, White Cat, was the centre of attention.

Tony had his new sound and looked forward to going out on the road with this band. A 30-date tour of the UK had been organised for February-March 1976 which kicked off at the Column in Nelson on the 20th. However, Tony confessed to Chris Simmonds there was a certain degree of the unknown about the situation: 'The whole idea of performing again is very strange because in the past we got used to touring solidly, with never a break of more than a couple of months.

'Now I've been off the road for almost a year, added to which I have a new band. It will be a completely different feeling. I just don't know how I'm going to take it.' Things appeared to be looking up as, just before the tour started, Penny Valentine of *Melody Maker* tipped 'Live A Little

side closes with the excellent 'Fulfilment' which includes some interesting acoustic work.

The second side opens with the joyous 'Live A Little Lady'. The lyrics are very important to Tony: 'The song is pleading with a young girl not to waste her life. It hurts me all these things about what my attitude to women is supposed to be. I've been a feminist for years, I've supported equality.' It's a catchy tune, laced with plenty of ARP synth, and was chosen as the single.

'Three Way Split' pieces three bits of music together, in echoes of the classic 'Split' album. 'Mean Mistreater' is the album's acoustic blues number and one of Tony's best. 'Crosscut Saw' closes with the autobiographical 'Eleventh Hour', so named as Tony is always leaving things to the last minute. The beginning is very atmospheric and it develops into a showcase for some of his best guitar work.

Tony was delighted with the album. He told Clive Wilson in an interview in early 1976: 'Luckily it sounded really solid and the whole thing came together within a month. It had to be spontaneous and it was.'

But he also had a startling admission: 'I think I'd been trying to a bit too hard with the effects trying to pull something out that wasn't there. So musically I've gone back to basics – there's a bit of synthesiser but it's mainly a guitar album because I think the thing to be is simply an exciting rock band.'

He was keen to have a different kind of sleeve for this album, described his idea to the artist, Mick Lye of the Blue Egg Studio, and left the rest to him. On the back cover picture, taken at

Lady' for the singles charts; in spite of this, it didn't make much of a dent.

Around the time of release *New Musical Express* contacted Tony for an interview. Tony Stewart was detailed to do the piece, but some time later Mac related to Newcastle University magazine that not much had changed with the music press:

'I've done a few things with Tony (Stewart) in the past and they have always been all right...but in effect he was saying "Who do you think you are coming back and making us listen to your stuff, what gives you the right?"

'I couldn't believe it. I thought "Oh no, don't start this again." In the end he wrote this little thing on the Thrills page which was really objectionable.' Part of the problem, apparent in Stewart's 'What are you still doing here?' attitude is that most of the journalists at this time were busy championing punk outfits and had little time for bands created in the 1960s.

Just before the tour started the band finally got on *The Old Grey Whistle Test*. Tony used a cordless guitar and had adapted a transmitter originally bought for his solo tour so that he could go from one keyboard to another. Only the guitarist out of Swedish band the Spotniks had ever used one before. The BBC crew had no faith it would work. Tony knew that it would, apart from the aerial soldered to the transmitter that was prone to coming off.

The band rehearsed in the back studio in the afternoon and recorded in the evening. They kicked off with the title track of the album 'Boogie Withus', highlighting the fact that Dave

takes the solo. At the end of the
number Bob Harris pointed out the
guitar transmitter system. Tony
remembers Harris chain-smoking and
having trouble with the autocue.

The tour went well and Tony ceded
a few solos to Dave Wellbelove, who
always played them the same way in
contrast to Tony who never played the
same solo twice. Andrew Lauder turned
up at the Derby gig and he witnessed a
great concert. Tony didn't realise the
show was being recorded and it stayed
on the reel for 28 years. When it was
finally released as 'The Groundhogs
Live 1976' by MLP, it showcased five
numbers from the new album; 'Boogie
Withus', 'Promiscuity', 'Eleventh Hour',
'Crosscut Saw' and 'Fulfillment' but
also included old favourites like 'Cherry
Red' and 'Split Part 2'.

The band played with a lot more discipline
than as a three-piece. However, the press were
still proving a problem, *Sounds* Chas De Whalley
was there for the Croydon gig and, though he
claimed to have liked 'Crosscut Saw', was still
firing off the clichés: 'He (Tony) picks the licks
like a Kray brother with a crowbar, puncturing
your skull in time with the bass and then
working the iron around until you think
that boredom alone might want to make
him stop.'

Lifelong fan Tony Sherratt witnessed a gig on
1st March 1976 at Quaintways, Chester. He
recalled that Tony had a novel way of
demonstrating the effectiveness of his transmitter:
'Having seen the Hogs in large venues, this was
the first for me at a nightclub. The set was a
tempest with Tony using radio pick-ups on his
guitar. At one point he disappeared off to the
toilet mid-song still playing a guitar break
without missing a note.'

The addition of a second guitar gave a totally
new dimension to Tony's songs especially some of
the older songs. Although Tony sometimes
bounced off the bass, in this concert he was able
to trade payoffs with a second guitar as well.
This meant less ad-libbing, but the playing was
inspirational as ever. Even to a smaller audience
Tony whipped up a frenzy of emotion and pulled
the fans and onlookers together. After an encore
of 'Cherry Red' the Hogs magic had worked its
spell and transformed the room into a pack of
Yelping Hounds.

This period was an unhappy time for Tony as
it had become apparent that he and wife
Christine had been drifting apart for quite a
while. The day after the Birmingham Barbarella's
gig (23rd March 1976) they had an album
signing for 'Crosscut Saw' at Virgin Records.
Tony was enamoured with one of the staff, Sue,
and pocketed her phone number when he left. It
was the start of a long relationship.

Tony had dropped the Mellotron but was still
using the ARP synthesiser. However, he had
another technological trick up his sleeve in using
a guitar interface unit which enabled him to play

Unidentified picture taken by a fan, showing the Synthi Hi Fli in its thin white box at the front of the stage.
TS Personal Collection

Mick Cook.
Pic from Kevin Wilkins and Tom Noble interview in *Out Now* magazine, 1976.
TS Personal Collection

the synth through his
guitar. This meant he
could play the synth
better than he could
before, as he wasn't really
a keyboard player.
However, on occasion he
had to have help.

In the summer of
1975 Tony had a visit
from Tony Gipp, a
celery farmer who was
also involved with a company called PACE
Electronics in Cambridge. Gipp had found out
that Tony lived locally and thought he was
loaded. He asked Tony if he was interested in
buying shares in the company. Tony was broke,
but visited workshops at Frenches Yard, and met
their electronics wizard Dick Parmee.

Dick showed Tony an enormous mixer which
included a number of startling innovations,
including LEDs instead of meters, but as a
prototype it was just too big.

A couple of years later they brought out the
MM (Mickey Mouse) mixers and amps that sold
in huge quantities as they were very good and
very cheap, so if he'd had the money to invest
Tony might have been a richer man.

PACE built the interface unit that converted
the guitar output into voltages required for the
synthesiser, the note obtained by using a metal
pick and the output of the guitar. The other was
wired into the frets of his guitar, the guitar
fretboard taking the place of the keyboard with
the result that only single notes could be played.
Around this time Tony was pictured in *Melody
Maker* with Gary Moore who was showing more
than a passing interest in this impressive piece
of technology.

When you are living in each other's pocket for
a long period, as you do in a band, there are
bound to be rough patches. Steve Rye's drinking
had hastened his departure, while Ken
Pusteilnik's problems had been drug-related. But
this time Tony was confronted by a problem he'd
never faced before – Dave Wellbelove's obsession
with cleanliness.

'I said it would be great if we hired a Winnebago rather than stay in hotels as this would give us a lot more freedom. Dave said "I couldn't do that, I have to have a shower every day". It wasn't exactly rock'n'roll either as he polished his guitar every day. I called it the immaculate conception.'

One day he turned up in jeans with turn-ups 'because they're in'. Everything he wore had to be pressed and he even used Oil of Ulay on his face and hands! Tony remembers they stayed in a bed and breakfast on the tour that had chamber pots under the bed. As a joke, Tony left a full one outside Dave's door. The owner of the B&B thought it was a complaint at the service provided!

Dave was shown the door and was soon on his way to join John Miles just after the tour ended – and Tony didn't have to look far for a replacement. Drummer Mick Cook recommended a guitarist he knew called Ric Adams who was much more to Tony's liking musically as he was much more aggressive in his playing and inventive in his solos. Ric wasn't totally unlike Wellbelove, however, and his guitar was also treated with more than a little TLC.

The band went straight into the studio to record the follow-up to 'Crosscut Saw' – which, due to the expense of studio time, was recorded at Tony's home studio. However, there were a few changes since the last time Tony recorded there, as the local planning office made him vacate the original studio due to the lack of planning permission. The result was some invention on the hoof by Tony.

He decided to move the equipment into the end room of the house and the band went into the garage, where he rigged up a remote to operate the recording equipment. They didn't have room for Mick Cook so they put him outside under the canopy from a 'Bettabake' van.

Unlike 'Crosscut Saw', the guitars went straight through the desk to ensure there would be no overspill from the drums. Tony was looking for a different sound on this album and it veered more towards country. New guitarist Ric Adams wasn't given as much scope as Dave Wellbelove and doesn't have any solos on the album.

The opener, 'Body Talk', sets the pattern for the rest of the album. It's a more accessible, almost commercial sound. The lyrical content is interesting as sex is seen as a purely physical act.

The track that follows this, the intriguingly titled 'Fantasy Partner', was inspired by Tony's idea that the ideal partner was only in your mind and unobtainable. The last line of the song, 'I wish she were alive,'

All in a day's work for Tony McTrousers...
Pic Paul Freestone
TS Personal Collection

sums it up. It's certainly an interesting couple of songs with which to open the album.

The next song, one of his favourites on the album, became a live staple. 'Live Right' has a teasing reference to Jesus: 'I was saying you don't have to follow anybody, why not be yourself as long as you don't hurt anybody else.' Tony was so proud of the production of this track he took the acetate to Andrew Lauder who was strangely unimpressed.

It was clear to him that Andrew didn't like the two albums he'd made for United Artists, especially 'Black Diamond': 'Andrew would always find something that was wrong, like too much bass and not enough of something else.'

The closer of side one is 'Country Blues' and starts off with a riff that sucks in the rest of

the band for a manic few seconds. While it's true that Tony hated living in the city he didn't like everything about the rural life. By this time he'd got pretty fed-up with farmers as they were always pleading poverty even though, to him, they all seemed to be doing pretty well.

The second side of the album has a lot of interesting moments. The opener, 'Your Love Keeps Me Alive', is notable as Tony readily admits to a Wishbone Ash harmony guitar influence, though he wasn't a fan of that style. The next track, 'Friendzy', was modified from Herbal Mixture's 'Please Leave My Mind' with a nice 6/4 riff to end.

'Pastoral Future' is one of the few instrumental tracks the Groundhogs recorded and it boasts a beautiful melody. 'I was in the studio late at night. I just had "Pastoral

Ric Adams.
Pic courtesy Ric Adams

Future" and a few other overdubs to finish and we had already booked the cut for the next day so I spent the night overdubbing and recording and, because I was so tired, it was all nice and laid back. Perhaps I should have done more instrumentals.' It was a brave decision to release it as a single (c/w 'Live Right'). The final track is 'Black Diamond' which, after a low-key opening, builds slowly to a crescendo.

The lyrics were inspired because the phrase was ambiguous, as Tony recalls: 'I loved the phrase and the whole idea that you didn't need material things. If you squeeze a lump of coal hard enough it becomes a diamond. It's a reminder that in the first place all we had was basics.' It's the best track on the album and a great one to end on. Looking back on the two albums he made for UA Tony is unable to choose his favourite. He prefers to pick out tracks like 'Eleventh Hour', 'Live A Little Lady' and 'Promiscuity' from 'Crosscut Saw' and 'Your Love Keeps Me Alive', 'Live Right' and the title track from 'Black Diamond'.

At 6am the next morning, with the album finished, Tony went to London to cut the album. He then met the rest of the band at Gered Mankowitz's photographic studio to shoot the picture that appeared on the back of the album. It was decided to shoot the band by a pyramid light, requiring Tony and Ric Adams to stand on a block so they would be taller than the light. Tony had been up then for over 29 hours and was virtually asleep as he stood by the warm studio light.

With the album in the can, the band went to Sweden for a short tour in September 1976, their first trip abroad as a four-piece. The show incorporated numbers from both of the UA albums; however, 'Cherry Red' was becoming their nemesis, as Tony explained to the Newcastle University magazine:

'We tried to get rid of that once but it didn't work! "Split", although it was great that it sold so well, it became the standard work and now it's very difficult to break away from it.' The band's reputation, to some people, went back a long way. The obligatory US tour was also discussed but again failed to come off, this time because Martin Kent had once been arrested for drug possession and couldn't get a visa.

On 13th September 1976 they played a gig in Stockholm that was also broadcast on the radio. The show went well, was quickly bootlegged – and is still selling! They had a problem with equipment on the tour. They were now using Orange equipment but unless it was turned right up you couldn't distort the guitar and this made it too loud. On stage Tony had a routine with Ric Adams where he would run his guitar down Ric's for effect. This went down well with the crowds, until one night the routine produced a scratch on Ric's guitar; that put paid to that routine as he was, like Wellbelove before him, very protective about his 'immaculate conception'.

The album was released in October to uninspired reviews. Not much had changed, as

Melody Maker demonstrated: 'The Groundhogs sound rather tired these days; perhaps it's due to the effort in touting endlessly repetitive riffs to audiences who've heard it all before and demand energy, at the very least, with their boogie. Tony McPhee is, at most, an average vocalist and the occasional synthesiser tricks are just damp squibs in the midst of sluggish mainstream action.'

It's a pity that the paper didn't acknowledge the change of musical direction that Tony had taken the band on. Furthermore, the reviewer acknowledges Tony's prowess with the guitar as that area is left untouched. More recently an internet site, *Allmusic*, made some interesting points, if a little flippantly:

'Riffs galore permeate this LP, McPhee displaying tons of creativity and there's no complaint with the music, which is first-rate. Perhaps if they found a dynamic lead singer this innovative version of the group may have reached the level of success Carlos Santana found in the early 1970s.

'The gruff vocal from Tony McPhee was still a bit beyond the reach of commercial radio at the time. In 'Live Right' he sounds like Mark Knopfler singing about Jesus, a solid track for FM radio but one that failed to catch on despite its flashes of inspiration.'

The band generally got on well although by this time Tony was getting fed up with Mick Cook, whom he referred to as a 'likeable fool'. Ric Adams lived above Mick and, when Tony visited him, he would sneak up to his flat. Usually Mick would get to know and Ric would tell Tony 'he knows you're here'. With a three-piece it was essential for everybody to get on because if two people get on well the other will be left out, but in a four-piece was less important.

The relationship between Martin Kent and Mick Cook was fraught, too. Kent was going out with Mick's sister and this was a bone of contention with the drummer They were always arguing about something. Tony recalls one particular night when they were on tour and staying in a bed and breakfast.

Just before they left for the gig Tony had 'apple-pied' the bed linen in Martin and Mick's room – they were sharing a double bed. Tony remembers hearing them arguing when they got back in their room and then, a few minutes later, there was laughter. Tony's trick had the desired effect, and for a while the ice was broken.

The Groundhogs toured the UK on and off into late 1976 but were facing a crisis. It was not as if they could have taken a break; the finances were always such that this was never an option. However, history was about to repeat itself as when, in the 1960s, the blues clubs started to go over to soul.

When the Hogs played Northampton Cricket Club, one of Tony's favourite gigs, he got talking to the manager who told him they had a great band playing the venue soon: the Sex Pistols. It was the first time Tony heard their name. By 1977 the club circuit had become a desert – punk rock had arrived. By the spring Tony knew the game was up and so the Groundhogs folded.

chapter 14
Epilogue

*'Tony McPhee made the blues his own and not just a homage.
He made it appealing to a young man turned off by every British bluesman,
but drawn to this man's passion to explore and
experiment with sound and structure in ways I had never heard
before, nor have since.'*
Karl Hyde, Underworld

*'Let's hear it for the Groundhogs, one of the most exciting bands the
UK has ever produced, who gave the blues their own
particular psychedelic treatment on a bunch of great albums.'*
Captain Sensible, the Damned

The end of the Groundhogs came as a surprise to fans, but the truth was that Tony had simply had enough of the band and the music. It would be seven long years before he got another Groundhogs together. Until that time, Tony steered well clear of Hogs material, forming new bands Terraplane, then Turbo (with Clive Brooks) and the Tony McPhee Blues Band in the early 1980s. However, from the time the latter had 'Blues' expunged from its name in 1982 Tony was moving towards the band he had spent so much time trying to escape from.

He had initially wanted a solo career like Rory Gallagher, but Gallagher launched his career before Taste had waned, whereas Tony embarked on his solo career after 'Black Diamond' when too many Groundhogs fans had seeped away. Had he started after 'Split' he would probably have had a much more successful time.

One of the anomalies of the band's career was the absence of a live album. In 1984, Tony got a call from a representative of Psycho Records. They wanted to issue a compilation of Groundhogs live recordings consisting of 'Live At Leeds', some BBC material and songs by the four-piece format from 1976 recorded in Stockholm. The album was called 'Hoggin' The Stage' and, much to

TS Personal Collection

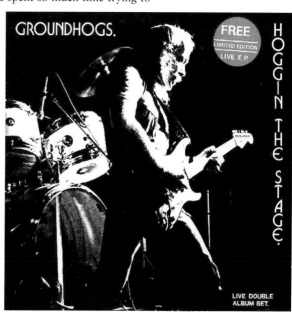

GROUNDHOGS.
FREE LIMITED EDITION LIVE E.P.
HOGGIN THE STAGE.
LIVE DOUBLE ALBUM SET.

(1) On a short tour of Scotland the Groundhogs played a gig in Irvine, just outside Glasgow, in October 1986. It was a nice gig, small and fully seated throughout. There was no PA when they arrived, but a call to the promoter solved the problem.

The van was parked in a compound that was fenced off as some bands had complained of stolen gear. They were in the bar till about 2am and Tony got talking to a couple of locals about his precious Gibson, which had taken a lot of wear and tear by then. 'I joked to them I should pension off my Gibson. I went back into the dressing room after the drink and saw the case open and the strap on the floor. The Gibson had gone. What happened was our roadie, Gonzo, had got bored and got it out of the van to play it.'

It seems that Gonzo had forgotten to put it back, and Tony is convinced the two guys he was talking to 'pensioned it off' for him. Even though the promoter made noises that he would investigate, nothing was ever heard of '54146'.

Tony's surprise, it made a dent in the independent charts. The time was right to bring back the Hogs.

The new line-up consisted of Mick Kirton on drums and Steve Towner on bass. The latter had been replaced by Alan Fish by the time the band entered Alaska Studios, near London's Waterloo Station, in September 1984 to record the first band album for eight years. The engineer was Gary Glitter's son, Paul Gadd, while the takes were fitted in to the timetable of a nearby railway line.

The album, called 'Razor's Edge', was a collection of hard-driving material and stands up well after all these years. In 1987 the band made another studio album; Mick Jones was on drums, replacing the briefly returning Ken Pustelnik, and former Hawkwind man Dave Anderson on bass. The recording venue was Anderson's Foel studios in Wales, while the record was released by the Demi Monde label, also owned by Anderson.

Tony had written the songs in a couple of months but some of the riffs had been purloined from his famous tape 'reservoir'. The album, a less heavy affair than 'Razor's Edge' and all the better for it, was given the defiant title of 'Back Against The Wall'. This was to be the last album of original material that Tony would ever record as the Groundhogs. One of the tracks was named '54146', the serial number of his stolen Gibson. (1)

In the early 1990s Tony started playing acoustic blues as a solo artist, while still keeping the Groundhogs going. In 1993 he recorded 'Foolish Pride', his first solo album in 20 years, following up with the excellent 'Slide

Eric Chipulina, Alan Fish, and
TS with Pete Correa
inset...drummers always
seem to be hiding behind
something!
Main Pic Paul Freestone
TS Personal Collection

TS Slide'. He also toured Europe, opening the show for Jefferson Starship.

Tony McPhee suffered a minor stroke in 1993 when playing at the Robin 1 at Brierley Hill. The band was just starting 'Split Part One' and the band thought Tony had broken a string: he knew differently. 'I couldn't play, I couldn't form the chords on the fretboard. I knew what had happened to me.' He somehow managed to get through the gig and even drove himself home. Happily there were no long-term side effects and, after recuperation, he carried on playing.

Meanwhile the Groundhogs had been through line-up changes, too numerous to mention here. In 1998 came one of their finest albums – 'Hogs In Wolf's Clothing', Tony's tribute to Howlin' Wolf, which he recorded with Eric Chipulina on bass and Pete Correa on drums.

TS Personal Collection

It came as a surprise that their next project proved a disaster. The Hogs were filmed at the Astoria, London, but Tony caught the flu a few days before and felt so bad during the gig that he disowned the performance.

The following year the same line-up recorded 'The Muddy Waters Songbook'. On 12th April 2003 the classic line-up of the Groundhogs reformed, their first gig a Punk Aid concert in Brixham, Devon. Fans were delighted to see Tony, Pete Cruickshank and Ken Pustelnik on the same stage together, and a gig in Shrewsbury later that year was filmed and later released as a DVD package alongside some historical material.

Having split the Hogs for the final time in 2004, Tony embarked on a major UK tour supporting Alvin Lee and Edgar Winter which ended at London's Royal Albert Hall. Acoustic blues now seemed closer to his heart, and next release 'Blues At Ten' was performed unplugged with his partner, singer Joanna Deacon.

Looking at the Groundhogs' musical legacy, it's no exaggeration to say that no rock CD collection should be without 'Thank Christ For The Bomb' or 'Split'. It's hard to understand why they never got the credit they deserved.

Then, as now, the Hogs were just not fashionable. But even the original line-up was never in vogue. Much has been written about John Lee Hooker and the British artists he worked with, but it's been conveniently forgotten that the only band to make an album with him was his favourite one – John Lee's Groundhogs!

The same could be said about Tony McPhee as a guitarist. His innovative slide blues style was a revelation and drew admiration from many quarters. From the late 1960s his finger-picking was one of the major factors in giving the Groundhogs their distinctive sound.

This is most apparent in the first few seconds of 'Strange Town' from 'Thank Christ For The Bomb', their most satisfying album. Tony was able to develop a style that nobody else got near and showed he was up there with the greats.

The next generation of musicians included individuals who loved the raunchy style of the band – notably the Damned's Captain Sensible, who introduced them on stage at their first reunion gig in 2003, Karl Hyde of Underworld, Peter Hook of New Order, Stephen Malkmus, Mark E Smith of the Fall, Julian Cope and guitarist Tony Doggen of Spiritualized.

This affinity with punk is not exaggerated or retrospective: for evidence, when Terraplane were mistakenly booked as Terror Plane in 1977, the crowd of punks who turned up were won over by McPhee's rasping guitar licks. Furthermore, bands like the Fall, the Datsuns and Queens of the Stone Age have played Groundhogs material on record or stage.

Tony McPhee has had a great career, and there is still history to be written. Of course, all of this could have been different if he had accepted the offer from Chris Barber in 1964!

Tony and Joanna.
TS Personal Collection

A short reunion in 2003 pleased many and produced a DVD performance at Shrewsbury's Buttermarket.
Pic Joanna Deacon
TS Personal Collection

Appendix 1
SELECTED DISCOGRAPHY

GROUNDHOGS

Tony McPhee, John Cruickshank, Pete Cruickshank, Dave Boorman, Tom Parker

1964
John Lee's Groundhogs – Shake It / Rock Me Baby –
Interphon I-7715 – USA only

1965
John Lee Hooker and John Lee's Groundhogs – **And Seven Nights** – Verve Folkway 3003 – USA. Released in UK in 1971 on XTRA 1114
Mai Lee, I'm Losing You, Little Girl Go Back To School, Little Dreamer, Don't Go Messin' With My Bread, Bad Luck And Trouble, Waterfront, No One Pleases Me But You, It's Rainin' Here, It's A Crazy Mixed Up World, Seven Days And Seven Nights

Tony McPhee, John Cruickshank, Pete Cruickshank, Terry Slade, David Ware, Fred

1966
John Lee's Groundhogs – I'll Never Fall In Love Again / Over You Baby – Planet 104

Tony McPhee, Pete Cruickshank, Ken Pustelnik, Steve Rye

1968
The Groundhogs – **Scratching The Surface** – Liberty 83199
Rocking Chair, Early In The Morning, Walking Blues, Married Men, No More Doggin', Man Trouble, Come Back Baby, You Don't Love Me, Still A Fool

The Groundhogs – You Don't Love Me / Still A Fool – Liberty LBF15174

Tony McPhee, Pete Cruickshank, Ken Pustelnik

1969
The Groundhogs – **Blues Obituary** – Liberty 83253
BDD, Daze Of The Week, Times, Mistreated, Express Man, Natchez Burning, Light Was The Day

The Groundhogs – BDD / Gasoline – Liberty LBF 15263

1970
The Groundhogs – **Thank Christ For The Bomb** – Liberty 83295
Strange Town, Darkness Is No Friend, Soldier, Thank Christ For The Bomb, Ship On The Ocean, Garden, Status People, Rich Man Poor Man, Eccentric Man

The Groundhogs – Eccentric Man / Status People Liberty 15346

1971
The Groundhogs – **Split** – Liberty 83401
Split Part One, Split Part Two, Split Part Three, Split Part Four, Cherry Red, A Year In The Life, Junkman, Groundhog

The Groundhogs – **Live At Leeds** – Promo
Cherry Red, Garden, Split Part One, Groundhog, Eccentric Man

1972
The Groundhogs – **Who Will Save The World** –
United Artists 29347
Earth Is Not Room Enough, Wages Of Peace, Body In Mind, Music Is The Food Of Thought, Bog Roll Blues, Death Of The Sun, Amazing Grace, The Grey Maze

Tony McPhee, Pete Cruickshank, Clive Brooks

The Groundhogs – **Hogwash** – United Artists 29419
I Love Miss Ogyny, You Had A Lesson, The Ringmaster, 3744 James Road, Sad Is The Hunter, S'one Song, Earth Shanty, Mr Hooker, Sir John

1973
The Groundhogs – Plea Sing, Plea Song / Over Blue – United Artists 006

Tony McPhee, Pete Cruickshank, Ken Pustelnik, Clive Brooks

1974
The Groundhogs – **Best 1969-1972**
United Artists UDF31
Groundhog, Strange Town, Bog Roll Blues, You Had A Lesson, Eccentric Man, Earth Is Not Room Enough, BDD, Split Part One, Cherry Red, Mistreated, 3744 James Road, Soldier, Sad Is The Hunter, Garden, Split Part Four

Tony McPhee, Pete Cruickshank, Clive Brooks

The Groundhogs – **Solid** – World Wide Artists 004
Light My Light, Free From All Alarm, Sins Of The Father, Sad Go Round, Corn Cob, Plea Sing Plea Song, Snow Storm, Jokers Grave

Tony McPhee, Dave Wellbelove, Martin Kent, Mick Cook

1976
The Groundhogs – **Crosscut Saw** – United Artists 29917
Crosscut Saw, Promiscuity, Boogie Withus, Fulfillment, Live A Little Lady, Three Way Split, Mean Mistreater, Eleventh Hour

The Groundhogs – Live A Little Lady / Boogie Withus – United Artists 36095

Tony McPhee, Ric Adams, Martin Kent, Mick Cook

The Groundhogs – **Black Diamond** – United Artists 29994
Body Talk, Fantasy Partner, Live Right, Country Blues, Your Love Keeps Me Alive, Friendzy, Pastoral Future, Black Diamond

The Groundhogs – Pastoral Future / Live Right –
United Artists 36177
Tony McPhee and various line ups

1984

The Groundhogs – **Hoggin' The Stage** – Psycho 024

Tony McPhee, Alan Fish, Mick Kirton

1985

The Groundhogs – **Razor's Edge** – Landslide LP 102
Razor's Edge, I Confess, Born To Be With You, Once
More Chance, The Protector, Superceded, Moving Fast
Standing Still, I Want You To Love Me

When Alan Fish joined the band Tony sent him a
cassette of some of the new material with his lead
parts on to devise a bass part to go along with it, like
putting a jigsaw together. Tony hadn't written enough
material, so he included Muddy Waters' 'I Want You To
Love Me'.

Mick Kirton recalls this track: 'We never actually
played it before we recorded it. It was recorded on the
first take. To me, that song is so vibrant and Tony
played so well on it.' There's a lot of energy, with
Kirton's drums coming across as really powerful. He
was using double bass drums and they really thundered.

The band really kicked live too, Alan Fish recalls:
'We played at Gillies, Manchester. It was one of those
great nights and we played for three hours. Afterwards
we had people come up to us and say they had never
heard a band play like that before.'

Tony McPhee, Dave Anderson, Mick Jones

1987

The Groundhogs – **Back Against The Wall**
– Demi Monde DMLP 1014
Back Against The Wall, No To Submission, Blue Boar
Blues, Waiting In The Shadows, Ain't No Slaver, Stick
To Your Guns, In The Meantime, 54146

'Blue Boar Blues' was based on the famous motorway
service station at the Watford Gap where bands used to
meet up and exchange stories of their adventures on the
road. Tony remembers gazing in awestruck fashion at
Gene Vincent sipping his cup of tea there.

Tony McPhee, Dave Anderson, Mick Jones

1988

The Groundhogs – **Hogs On The Road** – Demi Monde
DMLP 1016
Express Man, Strange Town, Eccentric Man, 3744
James Road, I Want You To Love Me, Split Part Four,
Soldier, Back Against The Wall, Garden, Split Part One,
Waiting In The Shadows, Light My Light, Me And
The Devil, Mistreated, Groundhog, Split Part Two,
Cherry Red

The band is in blistering form as they run through a
well-balanced selection of material. The album was
supposed to have been recorded in Germany but all
they used from the tapes was the applause! It was
actually recorded live in the studio at the Old Smithy,
Worcester. To make things more convincing Tony
apologised during 'Soldier' for using the term
'dirty hun'.

Tony McPhee, Alan Fish, Mick Kirton

1989

The Groundhogs – **No Surrender** (Razor's Edge Tour
1985) – HTD LP02
Razor's Edge, 3744 James Road, Superceded, Light My
Light, One More Chance, Garden, Split Part Two,
Eccentric Man, Strange Town, Cherry Red

Tony McPhee, Alan Fish, Mick Jones

1993

The Groundhogs – **Groundhog Night** – HTD CD12
Shake For Me, No More Doggin', Eccentric Man, 3744
James Road, I Want You To Love Me, Garden, Split
Part One, Split Part Two, Still A Fool, I Love You Miss
Ogyny, Thank Christ For The Bomb, Soldier,
Mistreated, Me And The Devil, Cherry Red,
Groundhog, Been There Done That, Down In
The Bottom

The gig attracted few fans because it wasn't advertised
properly. It cost £1,100 to hire the BBC mobile but
Tony was happy with the result.

*Tony McPhee, Pete Cruickshank, Ken Pustelnik,
Clive Brooks*

1994

The Groundhogs – **BBC Radio One Live In Concert** –
Windsong WINCD054
Split Part One, Cherry Red, Split Part Two,
Groundhog, Still A Fool, Ship On The Ocean, Free
From All Alarm, Dog Me Bitch, Light My Light, Sins
Of The Father
Tracks 1-4 24/2/72 – Tracks 5-11 23/5/74

*Tony McPhee, Pete Cruickshank, Ken Pustelnik,
Steve Rye*

1996

Four Groundhogs Originals – EMI CDHOGS1
Scratching The Surface, Blues Obituary, Thank Christ
For The Bomb, Split

Tony McPhee, Eric Chipulina, Pete Correa

1998

The Groundhogs – **Hogs In Wolf's Clothing** –
HTD CD81
Smokestack Lightnin', Baby, How Long, Commit A
Crime, Forty Four, No Place To Go, Ain't Superstitious,
Evil, So Glad, My Life, Sittin On Top Of The World,
Shake For Me, Wang Dang Doodle, How Many More
Years, Nature, Down In The Bottom

Tony McPhee, Alan Fish, Mick Kirton
The Groundhogs – **No Surrender** (Razor's Edge Tour
1985 Part Two) – HTD CD 86
Razor's Edge, Baby, What Have I Done Wrong, I Want
You To Love Me, Light My Light, Split Part Two,
Superceded, Garden, Split Part One, Groundhog,
Cherry Red

*Tony McPhee, Pete Cruickshank, Ken Pustelnik,
Clive Brooks*
The Groundhogs – **On Air 1970-72** (BBC) –
Strange Fruit SFRSCD053
Garden, Eccentric Man, Split Part One, Split Part Two,
Mistreated, I Love You Miss Oygny, You Had A
Lesson, Earth Shanty, 3744 James Road, Sad Is The
Hunter, Split Part Four, Cherry Red

Tony McPhee, Eric Chipulina, Pete Correa

1999

The Groundhogs – **The Muddy Waters Songbook** –
HTD CD91
Stuff You Gotta Watch, She's Alright, I've Got A Rich
Man's Woman, Can't Call Her Sugar, Forty Days And
Forty Nights, Mean Ole Frisco, I'm Ready, Young
Fashioned Ways, Hoochie Coochie Man, I Feel So
Good, Mean Red Spider, Tiger In Your Tank, Mannish
Boy, Got My Mojo Workin', Country Blues

Tony McPhee and various line ups

2000

The Groundhogs – **HTD Years (Compilation)** –
HTD CD115
Baby How Long, Dry Land (demo), Soldier, Country
Blues, Shake For Me, Down In The Bottom, Over

Pressure (demo), Garden, Evil, Never Again (demo), One More Chance, 3744 James Road, Groundhog, Cherry Red

Tony McPhee and various line ups

2001
The Groundhogs – **3744 James Road** (Compilation) – Castle CMDDD 277
Tracks taken from Hogs In Wolf's Clothing, Muddy Waters Songbook, No Surrender, Groundhog Night (Double CD)

Tony McPhee, Eric Chipulina, Pete Correa

The Groundhogs – **Live At The Astoria** – Talking Elephant TECD 026
Shake For Me, Eccentric Man, 3744 James Road, I Want You To Love Me, Split Part One, Split Part Two, Mistreated, Still A Fool, Cherry Red, Groundhog, Down In The Bottom

Tony McPhee, Jon Camp, Mick Jones

The Groundhogs – **The Lost Tapes Volume One** – Blue Flame BFBL 004 (Italy)
Live In London 1989

Tony McPhee and various line ups

The Groundhogs – **The Lost Tapes Volume Two** – Blue Flame BFBL 005 (Italy)
Live In Milan June 1994 & Live In Stockholm (Cherry Red only) 1976

Tony McPhee, Pete Cruickshank, Ken Pustelnik

2002
The Groundhogs – **The Radio One Sessions** (1970-71) – Strange Fruit SFRSCD106
Garden, Still A Fool, Cherry Red, Eccentric Man, Split Part One, Split Part Two, Mistreated

Tony McPhee, Pete Cruickshank, Clive Brooks

The Groundhogs – **BBC Live In Concert** (1972-74) – Strange Fruit SFRSCD112
Cherry Red, Split Part One, You Had A Lesson, 3744 James Road, Sad Is The Hunter, Split Part Two, Split Part Four, Ship On The Ocean, Soldier

Tony McPhee, Dave Wellbelove, Martin Kent, Mick Cook

2004
The Groundhogs – **UK Tour 1976** – MLP05CD
Boogie Withus, Promiscuity, Corn Cob, Eleventh Hour, Crosscut Saw, Fulfillment, Light My Light, Split Part Two, Cherry Red

TONY McPHEE

1966
Ain't Gonna Cry No More / Someone To Love Me – Purdah

When You Got A Good Friend / You Don't Love Me

Herbal Mixture – Tailor Made / A Love That's Died – Columbia DB8027

Herbal Mixture – Machines / Please Leave My Mind – Columbia DB8083

Champion Jack Dupree – **From New Orleans To Chicago** – Decca LK/SKL4747
Tony appears on two tracks – Third Degree and Shim, Sham, Shimmy

1967
Eddie Boyd – **Eddie Boyd And His Blues Band** – Decca LK/SKL4872
Tony appears on two tracks, Dust My Broom and Save Her Doctor

1968
Hapshash And The Coloured Coat – **Western Flier** – Liberty LBF83233
Tony plays guitar on all tracks

1969
John Dummer Blues Band – **Cabal** – Mercury. SMCL 20136
Tony plays guitar on all tracks

John Dummer Blues Band – Travelling Man / 40 Days – Mercury MF1040

John Dummer Blues Band – Try Me One More Time / Riding At Midnight – Mercury MF1119

Big Joe Williams – **Hand Me Down My Old Walking Stick** – Liberty 83207
Tony was producer

Andy Fernbach – **If You Miss Your Connexion** – Liberty
Tony was producer only

1973
The Two Sides Of Tony TS McPhee – World Wide Artists – WWA 001
Three Times Seven, All My Money, Alimony, Mornings

Eyes, Dog Me Bitch, Take It Out, The Hunt Part One, The Hunt Part Two, The Hunt Part Three, The Hunt Part Four

1977
Terraplane (Tony McPhee, Wilgar Campbell, Alan Fish) – Down In The Bottom / Shake For Me – Not released

Tony was now working in his own house producing new bands on his 16-track Ampex. It was here that he met Alan Fish who was these with his band called Wedgewood and it occurred to him that he might the bass player to fit in with Campbell. Tony asked him to put some bass on two tracks, Willie Dixon's 'Down In The Bottom' and Howlin' Wolf's 'Shake For Me', chosen because they knew them well.

1979
Billy Boy Arnold backed by Terraplane (Tony McPhee, Wilgar Campbell, Alan Fish) – **Checkin' It Out** – Red Lightnin' RL 0029

Billy Boy Arnold backed by Terraplane – **Superharps** (EP) Red Lightnin' 0027

A friend of Alan Fish had a record label called Red Lightnin', based in East Anglia, and was looking for a band to back bluesman Billy Boy Arnold on an album. In early October 1977 Terraplane went into Pathway Studios, London, to record 'Checkin it Out'.
The first day was for rehearsal and the next they recorded the album and an EP. Tony thought Arnold was underrated and a good harp player, and this is one of the classiest albums he ever appeared on outside the Groundhogs with a lot of strong material. Unfortunately the album was delayed and when it was eventually released Tony didn't even know about it.

Mike Batt – **Tarot Suite** – Epic EPC 86099
Tony plays guitar on one track

Mike Batt, who had produced the Groundhogs' first album, had tried to contact Tony via Rory Gallagher without success. The session was already booked so within a few days Tony went down to London to play on a track called 'Tarota'. It was the only thing he recorded in 1979.

1983

Tony McPhee Band (Tony McPhee, Steve Towner, Mick Kirton) – Time Of Action / Born To Be With You – TS001

These self-penned tracks by Tony were recorded on 29th March 1983 at Wood Cray Manor Farm in Berkshire. Mick Kirton recommended the studio as he had recorded an album there with his band Roadworks (Steve Towner was the guitarist). Towner, who was a talented artist, illustrated the sleeve with Tony's signature. One thousand were pressed and sold at gigs.

1993

Tony McPhee – **Foolish Pride** -HTD CD10
Foolish Pride, Every Minute, Devil You Know, Masqueradin', Time After Time, On The Run, Took Me By Surprise, Whatever It Takes, Been There Done That, I'm Gonna Win

1994

Tony McPhee – **Slide TS Slide** – HTD CD26
Reformed Man, Mean Disposition, Slide To Slide, From A Pawn To A King, Tell Me Baby, Hooker & The Hogs, Someday Baby, Driving Duck, No Place To Go, Me And The Devil, Death Letter, Can't Be Satisfied, Still A Fool, Write Me A Few Short Lines, Down In The Bottom
Tracks 1-6 recorded at Tony's home studio in 1994, Tracks 7-15 recorded on the Jefferson Starship European Tour of 1993

1997

Bleaching The Blues – HTD CD72
When You're Down, All Your Women, There's A Light, Went In Like A Lamb, When Your Man Has Gone, Many Times, All Last Night, When You're Walking Down The Street, Meeting Of The Minds, Bleaching The Blues, If I Had Possession, Love In Vain, Floatin' Bridge, Terraplane Blues, Little Red Rooster

SELECTED COMPILATIONS

1968

Blues Anytime Volume 1 – Immediate IMLP 014
Someone To Love Me, Ain't Gonna Cry No more

Blues Anytime Volume 2 – Immediate IMLP 015
When You Got A Good Friend, You Don't Love Me

Me And The Devil – Liberty 83190
Tony appears on four tracks – Me And The Devil, No More Doggin', Death Letter and Rollin' And Tumblin'. The latter is a duet with Jo Ann Kelly

1969

I Asked For Water She Gave Me Gasoline – Compilation – Liberty 83254
Tony appears on four tracks – Oh Death (with Jo Ann Kelly), Gasoline, Rock Me (Groundhogs with Jo Ann Kelly), Don't Pass The Hat Round

Gutbucket – Liberty LBX 3
Me And The Devil, Still A Fool (Groundhogs)

Son Of Gutbucket – Liberty LBX 4
Oh Death, Mistreated (Groundhogs)

1971

Same Thing On Their Mind – Sunset SLS 50209
Me And The Devil, Gasoline (with Jo Ann Kelly)

All Good Clean Fun – United Artists UDX 201/2
Cherry Red (Groundhogs)

1972

Paradiso – United Artists (Holland) 5C 062 93 544
Still A Fool (Groundhogs)

1986

Blues On Two – BBC REN610
Express Man (Groundhogs) radio session with Ken Pustelnik

Moving Fast, Standing Still – Raw Power RAW LP 021
Razor's Edge and Two Sides Of Tony TS McPhee plus the Purdah 1966 tracks

1994

The Best Of AOG – HTD CD20
Includes the two Terraplane tracks and two tracks from Groundhog Night

1995

Alexis Korner Memorial Concert Vol 3 – Indigo IGOCD 2025
I Can't Be Satisifed

2002

Tribute To Fleetwood Mac – Blue Flame BFCD002
Stop Messin' Around, I've Lost My Baby, One Sunny Day

2004

Blues At Ten – Blues Matters BMRCCD20042 – with Joanna Deacon

Blues At Ten, Messin' My Mind, I Won't Take Love, Strange Place, Young At Heart, Oh Death, Blues Is A Man, Devilled, PMT Blues, Better Off With The Blues, Lost Boys, Don't You Feel My Leg, Single Lives And Family Ties, Graveyard Blues, Christmas Tree

GIG LIST

THE SENESCHALS

10 December 1961	Tooting, Elephant & Castle - possible first gig
28 April 1962	Nunhead, St Thomas Hall first Nunhead gig
29 June 1962	Wimbledon, Wimbledon Park - instrumental gig
7 July 1962	Nunhead, St Thomas Hall - got new outfits
14 July 1962	Ensham Girls School - 'fabulous'
30 July 1962	Tooting, Conservative Club - 'too loud'
25 August 1962	Kemsing - Dollarbills also on the bill
2 September 1962	Audition for gig at Castle - failed
29 September 1962	Nunhead, St Thomas Hall - Ray singing at first gig, after three rehearsals
24 October 1962	Tolworth
3 November 1962	Bermondsey - 'very hip indeed'
11 November 1962	Tooting, Elephant & Castle - audition for gig at Castle was a success
22 November 1962	Tooting, Castle
24 November 1962	Nunhead, St Thomas Hall - 'exceptionally hip, man'
29 November 1962	Tooting, Elephant & Castle
8 December 1962	Bruce Hall - 'hip'
18 December 1962	Bishop's Grant School
19 January 1963	Nunhead, St Thomas Hall - bad winter of '63 blizzard

11 February 1963	Balham, Bedford Hotel - 'rush gig'
14 February 1963	Companies House, City Road
15 February 1963	West Norwood, Thurlow Arms
16 February 1963	Nunhead, St Thomas Hall
23 February 1963	Streatham, St Andrews Hall
30 March 1963	Nunhead, St Thomas Hall - 'pretty hip'
6 April 1963	Bruce Hall - probably Tony's last gig with Seneschals

THE DOLLARBILLS

10 May 1963	Chelsea, Café Des Artistes - probably Tony's debut
31 August 1963	Cardiff, Sophia Gardens - Vince Hill also on the bill
4 October 1963	Nunhead, St Thomas Hall,
19 October 1963	London, Kingston Jazz Cellar
14 December 1963	London, South London Motors
20 December 1963	Finsbury Park, Crawdaddy

JOHN LEE'S GROUNDHOGS

28 January 1964	London, Jazz Club - supporting the Animals
2 February 1964	Bromley, Blue Opera Club, Royal Bell
6 February 1964	London, Jazz Club - supporting Alex Harvey Soul Band
20 February 1964	London, Jazz Club
27 February 1964	London, Jazz Club
10 March 1964	London, 100 Club - changed name from Jazz Club - supporting the Animals
17 March 1964	London, 100 Club - supporting the Animals and the Pretty Things
31 March 1964	London, 100 Club - supporting the Animals and the Pretty Things
16 April 1964	London, 100 Club - supporting Graham Bond Organisation
23 April 1964	London, 100 Club - supporting Graham Bond Organisation
7 May 1964	London, 100 Club - with Champion Jack Dupree
14 May 1964	London, 100 Club - supporting Alex Harvey Soul Band
28 May 1964	London, 100 Club - supporting Graham Bond Organisation
6 June 1964	London, White Hart Hotel
23 June 1964	London, 100 Club
6 July 1964	Manchester, Twisted Wheel - backing John Lee Hooker, to 12th July
8 July 1964	Blackpool, Cleveleys
12 July 1964	London, Beat City - end of John Lee Hooker tour
23 September 1964	London, 100 Club
1 October 1964	London, Flamingo - backing John Lee Hooker, two shows each gig - plus John Mayall
7 October 1964	Nottingham, Dungeon Club
10 October 1964	Manchester, Twisted Wheel
15 October 1964	Double D Club
18 October 1964	London, Flamingo - plus John Mayall
23 October 1964	London, Flamingo
24 October 1964	Windsor, Ricky Tick - 7:30 pm

24 October 1964	Guildford, Ricky Tick - 9:30pm to 1:00am
31 October 1964	London, Flamingo
4 November 1964	Manchester, Twisted Wheel - final gig backing Hooker
7 November 1964	London, Flamingo - backing Jimmy Reed - plus Chris Farlowe
9 November 1964	*Beat Room* BBC 2 - backing Hooker
13 November 1964	Richmond, Crawdaddy - backing Jimmy Reed
14 September 1964	Windsor, Ricky Tick - 7:30 pm - backing Jimmy Reed
14 September 1964	Guildford, Ricky Tick - 9:30 to 1:00 - backing Jimmy Reed
15 November 1964	Windsor, Ricky Tick 6:00pm backing Jimmy Reed
15 November 1964	Reading, Ricky Tick - backing Jimmy Reed
18 November 1964	London, Flamingo - backing Jimmy Reed
21 November 1964	Manchester, Twisted Wheel - backing Jimmy Reed
23 November 1964	Harrow - backing Jimmy Reed
27 November 1964	London, Flamingo - backing Jimmy Reed
4 December 1964	London, Manor House
12 December 1964	R&B Club Romany Dance, Mitcham
18 February 1965	London, Marquee - with Rod Stewart and Soul Agents
12 March 1965	Manor House, London
14 July 1965	London, Refectory, Golder's Green
21 July 1965	London, Refectory, Golder's Green
31 July 1965	London, Pontiac, Putney
13 August 1965	London, Marquee
27 August 1965	Refectory, Golder's Green, London
30 August 1965	London, Marquee
1 October 1965	Bromley Hill, Bromel Club
25 October 1965	London, Marquee
29 October 1965	London, Refectory, Golder's Green
4 November 1965	London, Marquee - with Graham Bond Organisation
26 November 1965	London, Refectory, Golder's Green

THE GROUNDHOGS

9 November 1968	Boston, Glyderdome and London, Roundhouse with Led Zeppelin
9 November 1968	London, Roundhouse - backing JLH
8 December 1968	London, Studio 51
7 February 1969	London, Marquee
8 February 1969	Blues Scene '69, Festival Hall - Tour supporting John Lee Hooker - also on the bill Champion Jack Dupree, Aynsley Dunbar Retaliation, Jo Ann Kelly
9 February 1969	Bristol, Colston Hall - Blues Scene '69
11 February 1969	Birmingham, Town Hall - Blues Scene '69
12 February 1969	Portsmouth, Guild Hall - Blues Scene '69

127

13 February 1969	Croydon, Fairfield Hall - Blues Scene '69
14 February 1969	Pontypool - backing JLH
15 February 1969	Manchester, Free Trade Hall - Blues Scene '69
17 February 1969	Bath - JLH tour continues to 10th March
18 February 1969	Blackpool
19 February 1969	Grimsby
20 February 1969	Leytonstone
21 February 1969	Leicester
22 February 1969	Colchester
23 February 1969	London, Crystal Palace Hotel
24 February 1969	Newcastle
25 February 1969	London, Klook's Kleek
26 February 1969	Portsmouth, South Parade Pier
27 February 1969	Southampton
28 February 1969	London, Philippa's, Streatham
1 March 1969	Bournemouth
2 March 1969	Nottingham
3 March 1969	Bishops Stortford
4 March 1969	Brighton
5 March 1969	Tolworth
6 March 1969	Welsh College Of Technolgy
7 March 1969	Plymouth
8 March 1969	London School Of Economics
9 March 1969	Tunstall
10 March 1969	London, Royal Albert Hall - end of John Lee Hooker tour
17 March 1969	London, Resurection
4 May 1969	London, Marquee
13 June 1969	London, Marquee
27 June 1969	London, Marquee
4 July 1969	London, Marquee
22 July 1969	London, Marquee
9 August 1969	Plumpton Festival
19 August 1969	London, Marquee
25 August 1969	Croydon, Star Hotel
2 September 1969	London, Marquee
16 September 1969	London, Marquee
30 September 1969	London, Marquee
24 October 1969	London, Marquee
6 November 1969	London, Marquee
18 December 1969	London, Marquee
26 December 1969	Birmingham, Mothers
10 January 1970	Cardiff
16 January 1970	Derby
23 January 1970	Leicester
26 January 1970	London, Speakeasy
29 January 1970	London, Marquee
30 January 1970	Salford
6 February 1970	Kent
14 February 1970	Southampton University
16 February 1970	Sunderland
20 February 1970	Reading University
22 February 1970	London, Roundhouse
23 February 1970	Wolverhampton, Catacombe Club
26 February 1970	Blackpool
27 February 1970	Leicester
1 March 1970	Birmingham, Mothers
2 March 1970	Richmond Athletic Ground
4 March 1970	Hampstead
5 March 1970	London, Revolution
6 March 1970	University Of Essex Blues Club
7 March 1970	Bangor
13 March 1970	London, Marquee
14 March 1970	Lancaster
18 March 1970	Chelmsford, Eyes Club
19 March 1970	Maidstone College
20 March 1970	Windsor College
22 March 1970	Bletchley Youth Club
24 March 1970	Bournemouth Poly
28 March 1970	Hamburg, Germany
29 March 1970	Hamburg, Germany
30 March 1970	Hamburg, Germany
1 April 1970	Birmingham, Mothers
2 April 1970	Epping
3 April 1970	Burnley, Municipal College
4 April 1970	Bolton, Octagon Theatre
7 April 1970	Carlisle
8 April 1970	Derby, New Penny Club
9 April 1970	Blackpool Technical College
10 April 1970	Glasgow, Club Maryland
12 April 1970	Peterborough, Cloud Nine
16 April 1970	Bristol, Old Granary
17 April 1970	Sunderland, Fillmore North
28 April 1970	Wallaston
30 April 1970	Penzance, Winter Gardens
1 May 1970	Worcester
2 May 1970	Plymouth, Van Dyke
6 May 1970	Birmingham, Mothers
7 May 1970	Brighton, Big Apple - Ken hit in the face with chair
8 May 1970	Coventry, University Of Warwick
10 May 1970	Southall, Northcote Arms
13 May 1970	Canterbury
15 May 1970	Derby Art & Technical College
16 May 1970	Pershore Horticultural College
20 May 1970	Kings Lynn, Corn Exchange
21 May 1970	London, Marquee
22 May 1970	Leicester, Rondo
23 May 1970	Swansea Festival
24 May 1970	Manchester, Electric Circus
28 May 1970	Preston, Amethyst Club
29 May 1970	Maidstone, Technical College
30 May 1970	Northampton, Blissworth
1 June 1970	Wolverhampton, Catacombe Club
3 June 1970	Richmond, Castle Hotel
5 June 1970	Sunderland, Fillmore North
7 June 1970	Birmingham, Mother's
8 June 1970	Aylesbury, Friars Club
14 June 1970	Shaftesbury Theatre
17 June 1970	Camberwell, Fox On The Hill
18 June 1970	Guildford
19 June 1970	Maryland Club, Glasgow
20 June 1970	Malvern, Winter Gardens
21 June 1970	Croydon, Greyhound
24 June 1970	Southampton, Floral Hall
25 June 1970	London, Marquee
26 June 1970	Walthamstow, Chez Club
27 June 1970	St Helens Technical College
28 June 1970	Letchworth, Keys Club
1 July 1970	German Tour - ends on 20th July
24 July 1970	London, Marquee - supported by Supertramp
25 July 1970	Twickenham, Eel Pie Island
26 July 1970	Doncaster
30 July 1970	Worthing, Assembly Room
2 August 1970	Southhall, Farx
5 August 1970	Barnet, Resurection
6 August 1970	Birmingham, Mothers
8 August 1970	Plumpton Festival
15 August 1970	Halifax, Krumlin Festival
28 August 1970	Isle of Wight Festival
6 September 1970	Croydon, Greyhound
13 September 1970	Manchester, Free Trade Hall - supporting Canned Heat
22 September 1970	Birmingham, Town Hall - supporting Canned Heat
29 September 1970	London, Marquee
2 October 1970	Southall, Farx

5 October 1970	Salisbury, Resurection
9 October 1970	Epping, Wake Arms
17 October 1970	London, Polytechnic of Central London - supporting If
18 October 1970	Southall, Farx
19 October 1970	Romford, Kings Head
21 October 1970	Tooting, Castle
22 October 1970	Blackpool, Locarno Ballroom
31 October 1970	London, Lyceum - supporting Free, the Strawbs and Curved Air
1 November 1970	Birmingham, Mother's
5 November 1970	Southall, Farx
20 December 1970	Birmingham, Mother's
22 December 1970	London, Marquee
30 December 1970	Bradford
31 December 1970	Brighton, Big Apple - supported by David Bowie
1 January 1971	Newcastle
5 January 1971	Windsor
8 January 1971	Swansea
9 January 1971	Bristol
10 January 1971	Bromley, Bromley Theatre
11 January 1971	Dunstable, Civic Hall
12 January 1971	Salisbury, Resurection
15 January 1971	Swansea
16 January 1971	Narbeth
17 January 1971	Southall
19 January 1971	Barry
20 January 1971	Tooting
22 January 1971	Lancaster
24 January 1971	Redcar
26 January 1971	Crawley
27 January 1971	Liverpool
28 January 1971	Derby
30 January 1971	Isleworth
31 January 1971	Bexley
2 February 1971	Hartlepool
3 February 1971	Poole
5 February 1971	Wollaston
6 February 1971	Dagenham
9 February 1971	Southend
10 February 1971	Repton
12 February 1971	Preston
13 February 1971	Colchester
19 February 1971	Beckenham
20 February 1971	Bristol
21 February 1971	London, Roundhouse (Mick Jagger attends; Stones support slot follows)
23 February 1971	Leeds
24 February 1971	Portsmouth
25 February 1971	Glasgow
26 February 1971	Edinburgh
27 February 1971	East Kilbride and Glasgow
28 February 1971	Dunfermline
1 March 1971	Newcastle
3 March 1971	Sidmouth
4 March 1971	Newcastle, City Hall - tour supporting Rolling Stones (all dates two shows)
5 March 1971	Manchester, Free Trade Hall
6 March 1971	Coventry Theatre
8 March 1971	Glasgow, Green's Playhouse (one show)
9 March 1971	Bristol, Colston Hall
10 March 1971	Brighton, Big Apple (one show)
12 March 1971	Liverpool, Empire Theatre
13 March 1971	Leeds University (one show)
14 March 1971	London, Roundhouse - Rolling Stones tour ends
19 March 1971	Blackpool
20 March 1971	Folkestone
22 March 1971	Cleethorpes
26 March 1971	Huddersfield
27 March 1971	Halifax
28 March 1971	London, Lyceum - with Gypsy & Egg
30 March 1971	Wood Green
31 March 1971	Weston-Super-Mare
1 April 1971	Derby
2 April 1971	Rickmansworth
3 April 1971	Plymouth
4 April 1971	Kenilworth
6 April 1971	Crawley
9 April 1971	Abbey Wood, Harrow Inn
10 April 1971	Nelson
11 April 1971	Croydon, Greyhound
13 April 1971	Birmingham
15 April 1971	BBC Top Of The Pops album slot
16 April 1971	Leytonstone, Red Lion
17 April 1971	Aylesbury, Assembly Hall
18 April 1971	Bexley
19 April 1971	Nottingham
22 April 1971	Swansea
24 April 1971	Bournemouth
25 April 1971	Taunton
26 April 1971	Chelmsford, Civic Theatre
30 April 1971	Hilversum, Holland
05 May 1971	Twickenham, Winning Post - supported by Thin Lizzy
7 May 1971	Brighton, Sussex Sports Centre
8 May 1971	Lincoln Arts Festival of Music (at Racecourse) - Funkadelic, Arthur Brown's Kingdom Come
9 May 1971	Guildford, Civic Hall - with Wild Turkey
11 May 1971	Newcastle, City Hall
12 May 1971	Oxford, Town Hall - with Wild Turkey
13 May 1971	Chatham, Central Hall - with Wild Turkey
14 May 1971	Hampstead Country Club
15 May 1971	Norwich
21 May 1971	York
27 May 1971	London, Elephant & Castle
5 June 1971	Felixstowe, Pavilion
7 June 1971	Malvern, Winter Gardens - Wild Turkey
8 June 1971	Bristol, Colston Hall
11 June 1971	Sunderland, Bay Hotel
12 June 1971	London School of Economics
14 June 1971	Llanelli, Glen Ballroom
15 June 1971	Manchester, Free Trade Hall
17 June 1971	Town Hall, Watford - special guests Osibisa
18 June 1971	Southampton, Guildhall - with Gentle Giant
19 June 1971	Plymouth, Guildhall - with Gentle Giant
21 June 1971	Sheffield, City Hall
23 June 1971	Bristol, Colston Hall
25 June 1971	Hull University
26 June 1971	Harrogate, Opera House
27 June 1971	Croydon, Greyhound
4 July 1971	Kenilworth, Kinetic Cellar
7 July 1971	Twickenham, Winning Post - plus Home
9 July 1971	Newcastle, Mayfair
10 July 1971	Kilmarnock, Grand Hall
11 July 1971	Jazz Club, Redcar
16 July 1971	Birmingham, Kinetic Circus
17 July 1971	Dagenham, Roundhouse
18 July 1971	Wolverhampton, Civic Hall
21 July 1971	Torquay, Town Hall

22 July 1971	Penzance, Winter Gardens
23 July 1971	Barnstaple, Queens Hall
24 July 1971	Dunstable, Civic Hall - plus Egg
29 July 1971	Boscombe, Royal Ballroom
30 July 1971	Devizes, Town Hall
31 July 1971	High Wycombe, Town Hall - supported by Man
4 August 1971	Paradiso, Amsterdam, Holland
13 August 1971	Swansea
14 August 1971	Reading, Town Hall
20 August 1971	Southport, Floral Hall
22 August 1971	Public Hall, Preston
27 August 1971	Harrogate, Royal Hall
28 August 1971	Weeley Festival - plus Faces, Colosseum, Rory Gallagher
29 August 1971	Corby, Festival Hall
4 September 1971	British Rock Meeting Festival, Speyer, Germany - with Black Sabbath Rod Stewart and the Faces, Family, Fleetwood Mac
5 September 1971	Rock Festival, Vienna, Austria - bill same as Speyer
10 September 1971	Buxton Sound 71 Festival - headlined plus Edgar Broughton, Juicy Lucy Gentle Giant and East of Eden
11 September 1971	London, Queen Elizabeth Hall - plus Gentle Giant
12 September 1971	Munster, Germany - supporting John Mayall
13 September 1971	Kiel, Germany
14 September 1971	Stadthalle, Karlsruhe, Germany
15 September 1971	Frankfurt, Germany
16 September 1971	Nurnberg, Germany
17 September 1971	Berlin, Germany
18 September 1971	Zofingen, Germany - end of Mayall tour
20 September 1971	Munich, Germany
2 October 1971	Sutton Coldfield
7 October 1971	Copenhagen, Denmark
8 October 1971	Odense, Denmark
9 October 1971	Aarhus, Denmark
10 October 1971	Stockholm, Sweden
15 October 1971	Stockport
16 October 1971	Bracknell, Sports Centre
22 October 1971	Neath, Gwyn Hall
23 October 1971	London School of Economics - plus Gentle Giant
31 October 1971	Gravesend, Civic Hall - plus Egg
6 November 1971	Barking, North East Polytechnic - plus Egg
7 November 1971	Hemel Hempstead, Pavilion - plus Egg and Quicksand
8 November 1971	Bristol, Colston Hall - plus Egg and Quicksand
10 November 1971	Enfield, Middlesex Polytechnic
11 November 1971	Hanley, Victoria Hall - plus Egg and Quicksand
12 November 1971	Liverpool, St George's Hall - plus Egg and Quicksand
13 November 1971	Weston Super Mare, Winter Gardens - plus Egg and Quicksand
15 November 1971	Oxford, Town Hall - plus Egg and Quicksand
17 November 1971	Manchester, Free Trade Hall - plus Egg and Quicksand
19 November 1971	Plymouth, Van Dyke Club -
	plus Egg and Quicksand
21 November 1971	Westcliff On Sea, Palace Theatre - plus Egg and Quicksand
22 November 1971	Southampton, Guildhall - plus Egg and Quicksand
25 November 1971	Guildford, Civic Hall - plus Egg and Quicksand
27 November 1971	Birmingham, Town Hall - plus Egg and Quicksand
28 November 1971	Redcar Jazz Club, Coatham Hotel - plus Egg and Quicksand
29 November 1971	Sheffield, City Hall - plus Egg and Quicksand
30 November 1971	Bradford, St George's Hall - plus Egg and Quicksand
1 December 1971	Newcastle, City Hall - plus Egg and Quicksand
3 December 1971	Norwich, St Andrews Hall
4 December 1971	Leeds University - plus Egg and Quicksand
5 December 1971	Wolverhampton, Civic Hall - plus Egg and Quicksand
8 December 1971	Aberdeen, Music Hall - plus Egg and Quicksand
9 December 1971	Dundee, Caird Hall - plus Egg and Quicksand
10 December 1971	Glasgow, Greens Playhouse - plus Egg and Quicksand
11 December 1971	Edinburgh, Empire Theatre - End of tour
13 December 1971	Reading
1 January 1972	Dagenham, Roundhouse
8 January 1972	Leicester
10 January 1972	Chatham - with Jo Ann Kelly
13 January 1972	Cheltenham, Town Hall
14 January 1972	Sunderland
21 January 1972	Salford
22 January 1972	Walthamstow
31 January 1972	Tunbridge Wells, Assembly Hall
25 February 1972	Lancaster University - plus Alexis Korner and Johnny Johnson and the Bandwagon
8 March 1972	Italy
25 March 1972	Boston, Starlight Rooms
27 March 1972	Birmingham, Town Hall
8 June 1972	WMC Studios Memphis, Memphis, Tenn - US tour
9 June 1972	Overton Park Bandshell, Memphis, Tenn - with Edgar Winter
10 June 1972	Warehouse, New Orleans - with Edgar Winter
11 June 1972	Sports Arena, Atlanta, Go
14 June 1972	Curtis Hixon Hall, Tampa, Fl
15 June 1972	Auditorium, West Palm Beach, Fl
16 June 1972	Vets Memorial Coliseum, Jacksonville, Fl - with Edgar Winter and Black Oak Arkan's
17 June 1972	Sportatorium, Hollywood, Fl - with Edgar Winter
20 June 1972	Civic Center, Savannah, Ga - with Edgar Winter
22 June 1972	Rockford Armory, Rockford, Ill
26 June 1972	Maple Leaf Gardens, Toronto, Canada - with Humble Pie
27 June 1972	Forum, Montreal, Canada - with Humble Pie
9 July 1972	Mt Pocono, Pocono Music

	Festival - with Black Sabbath, Humble Pie and Edgar Winter
11 November 1972	Farnborough, Technical College - supported by Badger
17 November 1972	Birmingham, Town Hall - supported by Gentle Giant and Stray
18 November 1972	Edinburgh, Empire Theatre - supported by Gentle Giant and Stray
19 November 1972	Dundee, Caird Hall - supported by Gentle Giant and Stray
20 November 1972	Glasgow, Greens Playhouse - supported by Gentle Giant and Stray
23 November 1972	Oxford , New Theatre - supported by Gentle Giant and Stray
24 November 1972	Margate, Dreamland - supported by Badger
25 November 1972	Cambridge, Corn Exchange - supported by Badger
26 November 1972	Newcastle, City Hall - supported by Gentle Giant and Stray
29 November 1972	Aberystwyth University - supported by Badger
30 November 1972	Hanley, Victoria Hall - supported by Gentle Giant and Stray
1 December 1972	Manchester, Free Trade Hall - supported by Gentle Giant and Stray
2 December 1972	Northampton, Cricket Ground - supported by Badger
3 December 1972	Bristol, Colston Hall - supported by Gentle Giant and Stray
5 December 1972	Bradford, St George's Hall - supported by Gentle Giant and Stray
6 December 1972	Barry, Memorial Hall - supported by Badger
8 December 1972	Bournemouth, Winter Gardens - supported by Gentle Giant and Stray
12 December 1972	Hull, City Hall - supported by Gentle Giant and Stray
13 December 1972	Slough, Community Centre - supported by Badger
14 December 1972	Chatham, Central Hall
15 December 1972	Sheffield, City Hall - supported by Gentle Giant and Stray
16 December 1972	Liverpool, Stadium - supported by Gentle Giant and Stray
22 December 1972	London, Rainbow Theatre - supported by Gentle Giant and Stray
27 January 1973	Canterbury, University of Kent
10 February 1973	Southend, Kursaal Ballroom
17 February 1973	Malvern, Winter Gardens
2 March 1973	London, Sundown Edmonton
19 May 1973	London, Imperial College
31 May 1973	Croydon, Fairfield Hall
11 June 1973	Summer Rock Festival, Frankfurt, Germany
02 August 1973	London, Alexandra Palace Festival - supporting Black Sabbath
26 August 1973	Kendall Pop Festival - also Greenslade and Gallagher and Lyle
16 September 1973	London, Roundhouse - Tony McPhee Solo Tour
17 September 1973	Leeds, Town Hall
18 September 1973	Birmingham, Town Hall
19 September 1973	Folkestone, Leas Clift Hall
20 September 1973	Chatham, Central Hall
22 September 1973	Barnsley, Civic Hall
25 September 1973	Harrogate, Royal Hall
26 September 1973	Southport, Floral Hall
27 September 1973	Buxton, Playhouse Theatre
29 September 1973	St Albans, Civic Hall - End Of Solo Tour
5 November 1973	Portsmouth, Guildhall - supported by Jonesy
7 November 1973	Bournemouth, Winter Gardens - supported by Jonesy
13 November 1973	Glasgow, Apollo Theatre - supported by Jonesy
14 November 1973	Aberdeen, Music Hall - supported by Jonesy
18 November 1973	Oxford, New Theatre - supported by Jonesy
20 November 1973	Guildford, Civic Hall - supported by Jonesy
21 November 1973	Birmingham, Town Hall - supported by Jonesy
22 November 1973	Barrow-In-Furness, Civic Hall - supported by Jonesy
23 November 1973	Newcastle, City Hall - supported by Jonesy
24 November 1973	St Albans, Civic Hall - supported by Jonesy
25 November 1973	Liverpool, Royal Court Theatre - supported by Jonesy
26 November 1973	Brighton, Dome - supported by Jonesy
27 November 1973	Leeds, Town Hall - supported by Jonesy
29 November 1973	Preston, Guildhall - supported by Jonesy
30 November 1973	Sheffield, City Hall - supported by Jonesy
1 December 1973	Bristol, Colston Hall - supported by Jonesy
2 December 1973	Gravesend, Woodville Hall - supported by Jonesy
3 December 1973	Manchester, Free Trade Hall - end Of tour with Jonesy
22 December 1973	London, Rainbow Theatre
16 March 1974	Bradford University Bradford - warm-up for Solid Tour
17 March 1974	Guildford, Civic Hall
19 March 1974	Birmingham, Barbarellas
14 April 1974	Croydon, Greyhound
26 April 1974	Ipswich, Manor Ballroom - Solid Tour
30 April 1974	Hull, City Hall
3 May 1974	North London Polytechnic
11 May 1974	Cambridge, Technical College
12 May 1974	London, Marquee
17 May 1974	Southampton University
24 May 1974	Newcastle, Mayfair Ballroom
27 May 1974	Spennymoor, Top Hat Club
28 May 1974	Leeds, City Hall
29 May 1974	Bradford, King Georges Hall
30 May 1974	Cleethorpes, Winter Gardens
31 May 1974	Sheffield, City Hall
5 June 1974	Manchester, Stoneground
6 June 1974	Liverpool, Stadium
7 June 1974	Newcastle, Mayfair Ballroom
14 June 1974	Hatfield Polytechnic
15 June 1974	Reading University
16 June 1974	Plymouth, Guildhall

20 June 1974	Penzance, Winter Gardens
25 June 1974	Oxford, New Theatre
27 June 1974	Stafford, Top Of The World
28 June 1974	St Albans, Civic Hall
29 June 1974	Harlow, Spurriers Park
30 June 1974	Croydon, Fairfield Hall
4 July 1974	Portsmouth, Guildhall
5 July 1974	Swindon College - end of Solid Tour
4 October 1974	Coventry
8 October 1974	Bristol
11 October 1974	Wolverhampton
16 October 1974	Greenwich
21 October 1974	Manchester, Free Trade Hall
24 October 1974	Blackburn
26 October 1974	Northampton, County Ground
27 October 1974	Twickenham, Winning Post
2 November 1974	Aylesbury, Friars Club
3 November 1974	Newark, Palace
9 November 1974	Swansea, Patti Pavilion
10 November 1974	Croydon, Greyhound
12 November 1974	Birmingham, Barbarellas
15 November 1974	Nottingham, Trent Polytechnic
17 November 1974	Chelmsford, Chancellor Hall
23 November 1974	Sheffield University
26 November 1974	London, Marquee
5 December 1974	Southport, Floral Hall
6 December 1974	Bath University
7 December 1974	Dagenham, Roundhouse
10 December 1974	Hanley, Steam Machine
12 December 1974	Great Yarmouth, Tiffany's
13 December 1974	Glasgow University
17 December 1974	Tunbridge Wells, Assembly Hall
19 December 1974	Maidstone Polytechnic
20 December 1974	Slough Community Centre
21 December 1974	Liverpool, Stadium
28 December 1974	Folkestone, Leas Cliff Hall
5 January 1975	London, Roundhouse
10 January 1975	Derby College Of Arts
11 January 1975	Leicester
20 January 1975	Salisbury, City Hall
25 January 1975	Cambridge, Corn Exchange
27 January 1975	Huddersfield Polytechnic
31 January 1975	London, Regent Street Polytechnic
1 February 1975	St Albans, Civic Hall
2 February 1975	Westcliff-on-Sea, Queens
7 February 1975	Uxbridge, Brunel University
8 February 1975	Oldham Technical College
13 February 1975	Metz, France
14 February 1975	Paris, France
15 February 1975	Uzes, France
16 February 1975	Marseille, France
21 February 1975	Hereford
22 February 1975	Folkstone, Leas Cliff Hall
28 February 1975	Swansea, Patti Pavilion
1 March 1975	Hastings
8 March 1975	Ewell, Technical College
12 March 1975	London, Marquee
13 March 1975	Guildford
14 March 1975	London, South Bank Polytechnic
15 March 1975	Dagenham, Roundhouse
17 March 1975	Solihull, Civic Hall
21 March 1975	Newcastle, Mayfair
22 March 1975	Peterborough, Technical College

25 March 1975	Luxumbourg
26 March 1975	Trier, Germany
27 March 1975	Saarbrucken, Germany
29 March 1975	Frankenthal, Germany
30 March 1975	Ludwigshafen, Germany
31 March 1975	Kaiserslautern, Germany
04 April 1975	London, King's Cross Astoria - Final Gig with Pete Cruickshank

GROUNDHOGS AS FOUR PIECE

28 July 1975	Sheffield
4 August 1975	Manchester
10 August 1975	Lewes
18 August 1975	Derby
25 August 1975	Chorley
21 September 1975	Stockport
17 February 1976	*Old Grey Whistle Test* BBC
28 February 1976	Bristol, Roundhouse
29 February 1976	Croydon, Greyhound
1 March 1976	Chester, Quaintways
2 March 1976	Huddersfield, Ivanhoe's
4 March 1976	Chatham, Central Hall
5 March 1976	Brighton, Sussex University
6 March 1976	Manchester, UMIST
7 March 1976	London, Roundhouse
9 March 1976	Cardiff, Top Rank
12 March 1976	Ipswich, The Manor
13 March 1976	Maidenhead, Fox
14 March 1976	Twickenham, Winning Post
16 March 1976	Stoke, North Staffs Polytechnic
17 March 1976	Plymouth, Fiesta
19 March 1976	Brunel University
20 March 1976	Aylesbury Friars
21 March 1976	Middlesborough, Town Hall
23 March 1976	Birmingham, Barbarella's
24 March 1976	Derby, Kings Hall
26 March 1976	Lincoln Technical College
27 March 1976	Northampton County Ground
28 March 1976	Bournemouth, Winter Gardens
30 March 1976	Salisbury, City Hall
31 March 1976	Bradford, Guildhall
1 April 1976	Crewe, Civic Hall
2 April 1976	Newcastle, Mayfair
10 September 1976	Radio Concert Stockholm, Sweden
8 October 1976	Liverpool Stadium
9 October 1976	Newcastle University
10 October 1976	Redcar, Coatham Hotel
11 October 1976	Chester
13 October 1976	Sheffield
14 October 1976	Stoke
15 October 1976	London, Woolwich
16 October 1976	Maidenhead
19 October 1976	Birmingham, Barbarella's
20 October 1976	Derby
21 October 1976	Sunderland
22 October 1976	Edinburgh
23 October 1976	Glasgow
25 October 1976	Doncaster
28 October 1976	Glamorgan
30 October 1976	St Albans
31 October 1976	Croydon, Greyhound - Final Groundhogs gig of 1970s

Appendix 2
BIBLIOGRAPHY

Books
Sex, Drugs & Rock'n'Roll, Edited by Jim Driver, Constable Publishing, 2001
Blues: The British Connection, Bob Brunning, Blandford Press, 1986
London Live, Tony Bacon, Balafon, 1999
Rolling With The Stones, Bill Wyman, Dorling Kindersley, 2002
Blues Rock Explosion, Edited by Summer McStravick & John Roos, Old Goat Publishing, 2001
One Of The Family - The Englishman And The Mafia, John Pearson, Century, 2003
Boogie Man: The Adventures Of John Lee Hooker, Charles Shaar Murray, Penguin,
50 Years Of Rock Music, Chambers Encyclopaedia Guide, W & R Chambers, 1982
The Great Rock Discography, MC Strong, Canongate Books, 1996
The Complete Rock Family Trees, Pete Frame, Omnibus Books, 1993
Mothers 68-71: The Home Of Good Sounds, Keith Duffy, Birmingham Council, 1997
Virgin Encyclopaedia Of Rock, Virgin Books, Colin Larkin
Tony TS McPhee - A Biography and Discography, Paul Freestone, Self Published, 1981

Fanzines and Music Papers
The two Groundhogs fanzines, *Hogs Feedback* and *Yelping Hounds*, were used extensively. Mick Stones and Paul Freestone ran these but, alas, both are now defunct. I found these publications helpful. Tony Sherratt's website, *Squealing Pups*, was also a mine of information. As well as the net, I referred to numerous music-related publications, mainly *Melody Maker, New Musical Express, Sounds, Disc, Beat Instrumental, Blues Unlimited, Record Mirror* and *Rolling Stone*.

The Tony McPhee Archive
An extensive array of articles, pictures, contracts and other interesting memorabilia of the music business that reflects Tony's forty-year-plus career.

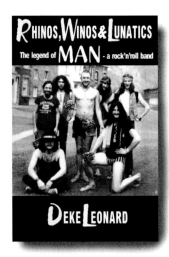

RHINOS, WINOS & LUNATICS
The Legend of Man
a rock'n'roll band
By Deke Leonard

- ■ Extent: 176pp, 15.4 X 23.3 cm
- ■ ISBN: 1-900711-09-1
- ■ Price: £11.99

First issued in 1996, *Rhinos, Winos & Lunatics* has gained a reputation as one of the legendary on the road rock'n'roll travelogues. It tells the story of eight years in the life of a rock band – Man, Wales' most durable musical exports.

Man have made 18 albums and undergone as many line-up changes, involving four drummers, four keyboard players, four guitarists and five bass players. Guitarist Deke Leonard 'has attempted to escape on numerous occasions but has always been recaptured'.

He writes with wit, verve and panache of the 1968-76 period, the post-'Sgt Pepper' years when rock music expanded its frontiers as never before. The result is a book that tells the story of an era, not just a band.

Deke Leonard's 'prequel', *Maybe I Should've Stayed In Bed*, was published in 2000 to rave reviews. Its success has stimulated interest in *Rhinos*, which has been out of print for several years. This 'remixed' edition includes a new cover and double the number of photos of the original.

What they said about '*Rhinos, Winos & Lunatics*':

'I picked this book and simply tore through its pages in an evening and an afternoon. The reason? '*Rhinos, Winos & Lunatics*' is the funniest book of the rock genre I've yet to read. A must for all of you, Manfans or not. *Facelift*

'Deke Leonard's '*Rhinos, Winos & Lunatics*' is wonderful. The definitive insider's account, its also written delightfully, with a stoned cynical lyricism that makes turning the page an absolute pleasure. Top Stuff'. *Making Music*

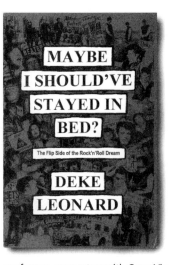

MAYBE I SHOULD'VE STAYED IN BED
The Flip Side Of The Rock'n'Roll Dream
By Deke Leonard

- ■ Extent: 240pgs
- ■ ISBN: 1-900711-09-5
- ■ Price: £12.99

The 1960s music scene with wit...and a distinctively Welsh slant.

Illustrated with high quality eight-page archive photo sections. *Maybe I Should've Stayed In Bed?* charts the early years of guitarist Roger 'Deke' Leonard, a founder member of legendary Welsh rock band Man in 1968. Initially a reluctant performer, encounters with Gene Vincent and Johnny Kidd awoke his ambitions to become a rock'n'roll star, though an early band was banned from Welsh venues for being 'too sexy'. The provincial press held Deke's troupe 'responsible for the moral decay so evident in 1960s society', while the *Daily Mirror* called them 'the biggest freak-out to hit South Wales!'

The rock'n'roll dream seemed there for the taking, so they broke up, scattering to the four corners of Swansea before re-grouping more successfully as Man. But that's another story, as told in Leonard's first book *Rhinos, Winos & Lunatics!*

Written with a humour rarely seen in rock biographies, it is a fascinating social commentary on Wales in the 1960s as the seeds of today's success – Manic Street Preachers, Catatonia etc – were sown.

DOWN BY THE JETTY - THE DR FEELGOOD STORY
by Tony Moon

- ■ Extent: 128 pgs, illustrated throughout
- ■ ISBN: 1 900711 15 X
- ■ Price: £11.95

The focus of Dr Feelgood's act was a contrasting pair of frontmen: gravel-voiced vocalist Lee Brilleaux and manic, staring guitarist Wilko Johnson. When Johnson quit in 1977 the critics claimed the Feelgood story was over, but they not only survived but thrived to produce over 20 LPs and play 200 gigs a year to reinforce their reputation as the hardest-working outfit around.

In April 1994, the Feelgoods took a body blow with Lee Brilleaux's death from cancer at the age of 40. It seemed the party was over – but two years down the line manager Chris Fenwick, in harness since 1972, decided to pick up the pieces and to preserve the Feelgood trademark as had been Brilleaux's wish. It's a trademark which, like all the classics – Aston Martin, Dr Martens, Purdey and Norton – cannot be simply bought off the shelf, and Dr Feelgood remains today the definitive face of British rhythm and blues.

Authorised by the band and extensively illustrated from their archives, Down By The Jetty (named after their first album) celebrates Dr Feelgood's 30th anniversary. Revised and updated since its 1997 appearance, it features a superb new cover illustration from cult artist Vince Ray which will make it stand out in any company.

What they said about the first edition:

"Brimful with idealism and tons of carefully collected details."
Hartbeat

"This work is indispensable..."
Good Times

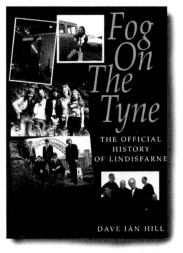

FOG ON THE TYNE - THE OFFICIAL HISTORY OF LINDISFARNE
by Dave Ian Hill

- ■ Extent: 160 pgs, including over 120 pictures
- ■ ISBN: 1900711 07 9
- ■ Price: £14.95

'They gave me the idea that this "music stuff" was something to have a go at.' Chris Rea
'To use an Irish expression, their blood's worth bottling!'
Jake Burns (Stiff Little Fingers)
So how do *you* remember Lindisfarne? Topping the charts in 1972 with their album 'Fog On The Tyne', or letting Gazza loose on the title track in 1990? Touring colleges with a then-unknown Genesis? Or maybe one of their spinoff projects like Radiator, Jack The Lad or songwriter Alan Hull, who produced many memorable solo moments.

Whatever the answer, you'll get something out of Fog On The Tyne – The Official History of Lindisfarne, which puts to bed 30 years of bawdy, booze-fuelled history while opening a new chapter kicked off by an excellent new album, 'Here Comes The Neighbourhood'. Putting the sad death of Alan Hull behind them.

Author Dave Ian Hill has interviewed producers, DJs, fans and fellow musicians as well as group members past and present to get the true flavour of a unique band. Also, Lindisfarne have opened their photographic archives to allow publication of many previously unseen pictures guaranteed to entertain and amuse.

Among the facts revealed is that Phil Collins was offered the drummer's job and, when he turned it down, was told he was making 'a big, big mistake'...that Alan Hull had to pay the estate of painter René Magritte £4000 to use his painting on the cover of 'Pipedream' (the bar bill during recording ran to four figures too, and this was in 1972)...Chris Rea's abiding debt to the band, whom he supported on a national tour...and the truth behind a cross-Australia flight with Slade and Status Quo that led to banner headlines of popstar excess.

To order, contact enquiries@northdown.demon.co.uk or see our website, www.northdown.demon.co.uk